S0-BKN-412

ABYDOS: HOLY CITY OF ANCIENT EGYPT

OMM SETY AND HANNY EL ZEINI

Copyright 1981

by

L L Company

ISBN 0-937892-07-6

Library of Congress Number: 81-81128

L L Company
2066 Westwood Blvd.
Los Angeles, California 90025
United States of America

OMM SETI

Ancient Egypt affinity

T.G.H.J. writes:

Miss Dorothy Eady, who died at Abydos in Upper Egypt last week, was better known as Omm Seti to the many thousands of tourists who have in the past 25 years visited the famous temple of Seti I at Abydos.

Dressed incongruously in woollens or a twin-set, with head scarf and shawl, hung about with ancient Egyptian beads, and bare footed, she greeted visitors to the temple which she regarded as home, showing off the splendours of its painted reliefs with the proprietorial air and familiar knowledge of a stately home owner.

Born in Blackheath on January 16, 1904, Dorothy Louise Eady from her earliest years, according to her own recollections, experienced a close affinity to the ancient Egyptians, and in particular to the person of King Seti I of the Nineteenth Dynasty. The Egyptian Department in the British Museum became her school and university where she received encouragement, and, she claimed, some instruction in hieroglyphics from Sir Ernest Budge.

Employment in the office of a magazine devoted to the cause of Egyptian independence introduced her to her future husband Imam Abdelmiguid. In 1933 she travelled to Egypt to marry, and she never returned to England.

THE LEGENDARY

OMM SETY

(1904 - 1981)

Last Photograph

Coauthor

of

ABYDOS: Holy City
of
Ancient Egypt

When a son was born, she gave it the name Seti, and in due time became generally known as Omm Seti ("Mother of Seti"); her married name was, more properly, Bulbul Abd el-Megid. When her husband left Egypt to work abroad, Dorothy Eady was employed by Professor Selim Hassan who was at that time excavating at Giza. For twenty years she assisted Selim Hassan and, subsequently, Professor Ahmed Fakhry, in their exploration of the pyramid fields of the great Memphite Necropolis, contributing editorial and other specialist skills in the preparation of field records and of the final published reports.

Visits to Abydos in 1952 and 1954 convinced her of the certainty of what she believed to have been her previous life in the great temple there, and in 1956 she was transferred to Abydos by the Egyptian Antiquities Service, by whom she was officially employed. In Abydos she remained for the rest of her life, with only occasional short vists to Luxor and other not-too-distant places.

Her home became a simple mud-brick peasant house, her companions a succession of cats, a goose, her donkey, and an occasional snake. Abydos and Seti's temple were her domain; in the sanctuaries of the temple she resumed the rituals of antiquity, as she interpreted them. She was in her devotion matter-of-fact, and quite free from occult irrationalism.

At Abydos she planned her tomb and her burial rite, so that she after death might travel to the beautiful West, to join Osiris, Seti and all those with whom she felt she belonged.

(The TIMES (London)
Apr. 29, 1981.)

"OMM SETI AND HER EGYPT" is a story of an old English lady who has lived in the shadow of the famous Temple of Seti the First at Abydos. Omm Seti means mother of Seti. Her original name was Dorothy Eady and she came from London. When a small child she fell down stairs, was knocked unconscious but taken to be dead, and ever since her revival believed that she came from the Egyptian entourage of the 19th Dynasty (c1300 BC) of the Pharaoh Seti. She believed that she knew the temple that he had built with its beautiful coloured reliefs. She determined to go to Egypt, married an Egyptian, worked for the Antiquities Department in Cairo and was eventually transferred to her dream place Abydos where she has lived ever since.

Omm Seti has now become one of the most famous characters in Egypt and many tourists go to Abydos not just to see the monuments but to see Omm Seti herself. She has a great knowledge of the temple and the scenes inside and it is information which would otherwise not be available to travellers. She has built her tomb in her garden, says that she believes in the ancient Egyptian religion and is looking forward to returning to the place from which she came.

The film is also about the area of Abydos which includes First Dynasty tombs (c3000 BC), important Middle Kingdom excavations (c2000 BC) and, of course, the Temple of Seti the First. Dr. Rosalie David who wrote her thesis on the temple's religious ritual scenes which are amongst the most beautiful reliefs in Egypt, talks about their significance, Harry James, Keeper of the Department of Egyptian Antiquities at the British Museum tells of the significance of Abydos as a religious area and we show the history of excavations there including those of Sir Flinders Petrie.

OMM SETI AND HER EGYPT - the third of eight Chronicle programmes - is to be transmitted on Wednesday 6th May on BBC-2 at 8.10. The narrator is Erik de Mauny and the film has been produced by Julia Cave. The duration is 50'.

(From announcement of BBC Documentary May 1981.)

An incredulous smile froze on my lips as I watched the Chronicle film OMM SETI AND HER EGYPT (BBC 2, 8.10). Could I be absolutely positive it was all a lot of eyewash? Of course I couldn't. And neither will you be able to. In any case, it makes marvellous television. The facts, briefly, are these: Dorothy Eady, a Londoner, then three, fell downstairs, was concussed, given up for dead, woke up, started crying because she wanted to go home (she was at home) and started dreaming about an Egyptian temple. Subsequently, sitting among the glass-encased mummies at the British Museum, she felt these were her people. Years later, she visited her ancient Egyptian temple, at Abydos, and recognized the figures in the bas reliefs as if they had been so many photographs in her family album.

To the end of her life--Dorothy Eady died last month--she believed a priestess's spirit had entered her body during her childhood coma, and she spent her last years within a stone's throw of her beloved temple, a frail but resilient old lady surrounded by cats and homage-payers. An example of her irreverent sense of fun: Isis and Osiris, two of the figures on the temple walls, were brother and sister as well as husband and wife. "Good system", says Omm Seti (the name she eventually acquired). "It did away with the mother-in-law".

(From Peter DAVALLE, The Times (London) May 6, 1981.)

OMM SETY
(1904 - 1981)

I first met Mrs. Bulbul Abdelmiguid (nee Dorothy Eady), affectionately known as Omm Sety among her friends, in December 1956. It was still the aftermath of the Suez War and the invading soldiers of Britain, France and Israel were preparing for a reluctant withdrawal from Sinai and the Canal Zone. I was showing some friends from Cairo around the magnificent Sety's Temple in Abydos when the inspector of the Antiquities Department accompanying our group left us suddenly to chat with a lady, evidently a foreigner, who was, to my great astonishment, walking bare-footed. Later we were introduced to each other through our mutual friend the inspector.

I was told she was working in the Antiquities Department as a "draftsman" and that she had asked for a transfer from Giza to El Aroba El Madfouna (Abydos) which is almost three hundred miles south of Cairo. Omm Sety was then in her early fifties, a strong robust woman with a very disarming smile and a fantastic sense of humor. We chatted for a few minutes about the war and I was quite taken aback by her wrath and unchecked fury about the whole affair. In her anger she qualified the invaders as "Ibu El Kelb," sons of dogs. It was quite evident that the streak of Irish blood in her was strong indeed. Her genuine anger was very "Egyptian," unassumed and quite sincere.

Then I could not restrain myself from asking her why she was walking about bare-footed inside the temple. Her answer was prompt and sternly firm: "This is a holy shrine built for our Lord, Osiris. Nobody should be allowed to walk here with his shoes on. If I were given the authority to do so I would not allow anybody to visit this holy place with his shoes on but I am just a poor insignificant employee of the Antiquities Department." From the beginning I was aware that this was no ordinary woman just in love with the place but a very unusual person with firm convictions that I learned to respect as the years went by.

At the time I was working as director-general of the biggest sugar factory in Africa and the second largest in the world. Of course I had visited the Sety temple several times before meeting Omm Sety and many were the moments I spent in wonder and admiration in front of the magnificent reliefs inside and outside the temple. The nature of my work gave me very little time to spare for regular visits to Abydos, which lies twenty miles north of our sugar factory in Nag-Hammadi, but I managed somehow to find a few hours every now and then to visit the temple with my wife and be shown around by Omm Sety. Those visits with Omm Sety were not only instructive, entertaining and extremely interesting but also they became, in the long run, very absorbing.

She adhered very faithfully to the Ancient Egyptian calendar, kept strict observance of all the feasts, fasting days and, above all, the Feast of Osiris when she would really get quite absorbed in devout prayers. We carefully refrained from visiting her on those specially sacred days of Pharaonic Egypt. Of course it took us very little time to realize that Omm Sety was an impossible mixture of the psychic, the mystic, and the clairvoyant qualities. But above all, she was a fanatic follower of OSIRIS whom she believed is buried inside the "island" of the Osirion. In her hours of distress, difficulties or even sickness she would to to the Osirion, wash her face in that pool of stagnant, forbidding water always found inside this enigmatic shrine and come out a radiant, fresh and happy woman. This, among other things, was something I really never quite understood about Omm Sety. But her faith was infallible and unwavering in everything connected with Osiris.

Of course, Omm Sety, once we became close friends, talked to me about her "Previous Life," "visits," "appearances" of a spiritual nature and she wrote me a diary of the occasional presence of King Sety I in a "materialized" form and their long conversations. Being a woman of very transparent honesty and unquestionable integrity I believed every word she wrote down. I really never believed before in incarnation or "astral body" perhaps because I never had witnessed any supernatural or spiritual phenomena or experiment. But after a long visit to Nepal and India in 1978 and meeting with Buddhist and Brahman mystics I now realize how very little we know about the realm of the spirit. Experiences very much like those witnessed by Omm Sety were related to me by Buddhist monks and sages high in their Himalayan sanctuaries. Not that I doubted anything she ever told or wrote down to me, but being of a pragmatic upbringing and education, the world of metaphysics was unknown to me. A lot of what Omm Sety wrote down to me in her diaries became less enigmatic and made more sense to my practical frame of mind after I came back from Nepal three years ago.

We were friends for a quarter of a century and both my wife and myself learned to love and trust her and believe everything she said. She was ill for a very long time. Her first heart attack happened less than ten years ago and she had been suffering from a broken thigh bone for over a year, yet her death on the 21st of April this year came as an awful shock to us.

Although she was crippled by this unfortunate accident and was unable to move all by herself, even with the help of crutches, yet somehow I felt she would outlive this misfortune and could be able to walk again. In her last letter to me she was so happy to be able to go to the temple on two occasions in the company of the British Broadcasting Company group and with the National Geographic Magazine team. The effort and the pain of her broken bone must have been quite agonizing but morally she should have felt extremely happy to be able to visit the temple after an absence of almost one year.

Abydos in general and the Sety Temple in particular were really all her life and everything she really cared for. We and all her innumerable friends feel that Abydos will never be the same without Omm Sety. Archaeologists, Egyptologists, Rosicrutians, tourists . . . etc., etc. who always sought to meet her and ask for her advice or just drop for a chat with her will certainly feel her absence very acutely. On the rare occasions we talked about death she never pronounced the word. She would very cheerfully say something like this "When I go to Amenti (West), His Majesty "King Sety I" will be at the head of the reception committee. Just fancy me having a royal reception in Amenti. But if you happen to be around you must do the "Hetep Di Nisout" prayer for me. I will write it down to you." She never did write this prayer but her last desire to be buried as close as possible to the temple has to be met.

A few days before her death and feeling perhaps that the end was near, she flatly refused to receive a Christian priest or to have a Muslim burial. "I belong to neither, I want to be buried among my own people." Her "own people" as I have always known were the people of the 19th dynasty in Sety and Ramsses II times, people who worshiped Osiris, Isis and Horus and kept the Ancient Egyptian calendar and fasted during the Osirian Feast. "Her People" were the inheritors of the first empire in history extending from the shores of the Nile to the land where rivers ran "upside down" as the Egyptian soldiers put it when they saw the Euphrates and Tigris running down from North to South and not vice versa like their own Nile.

There were moments when I felt that Omm Sety, who very frequently became absentminded, was the prisoner of place, surroundings and time. Of course by living in Abydos she has fulfilled the cherished dream of her life and the first fifteen years must have been the happiest, the most fascinating and the most exalted of her life but she kept telling me how she longed to join "His Majesty," meaning the only person she ever loved or cared for. Once, she told me, during one of Sety's "appearances," Omm Sety expressed the wish to take her own life to join him in Amenti. His warning against her committing suicide was both stern, firm and royally final. She never thought of it again in her later days because it would anger the "Lord," Sety told her.

In this part of the world the word "Friendship" assumes very special proportions and a profound meaning. By losing Omm Sety I did not lose just a very good friend and co-author of the five books we wrote together, but above all a real "Pal" full of good nature and an unfailing sense of humor. Somehow I feel she must be happy now among "her people" and making fun of all around her in Amenti . . . at least I hope so.

Hanny El Zeini
Cairo, Egypt
June, 1981

● الانجليزية التى وهبت حياتها لرعاية اثار الفراعنة ●

أُم سيتى عاشقة أمجاد الاجداد

※ كتب ـ سمير غنيم :

على بعد ٥٥ كيلو مترا من مدينة سوهاج جنوب وادى النيل وبالتحديد فى المنطقة المعروفة باسم « عرابة ابيدوس » او كما يسميها اهل الصعيد « العرابة المدفونة » يطل فى شموخ على الحاضر معبد متكامل من أعظم المعابد الفرعونية على الاطلاق وقام على بنائه الملك سيتى الاول وابنه رمسيس الثانى .

استقبلتنا على باب المعبد « ام سيتى » وهى سيدة تعدت التسعين تضع على راسها قبعة كبيرة تحمى راسها الصغير من حرارة الشمس . ابتسمت وهى تستقبلنا وترحب بنا ..

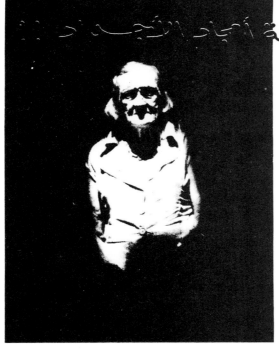

ابن « اوزوريس » هنا فى هذا الهيكل كانت تتم مراسم دينية لها قداستها .. كان كاهن المعبد يدخل الهيكل حيث تمثال « حورس » الذهبى فيخلع عنه ملابسه وجواهره ، ثم ينكب فى خشوع بالغ على غسله بالعطور والزيوت العطرية ثم يلبسه ثيابا جديدة ويضع عليه مجوهراته وزينته ثم يخرج من الهيكل بظهره وهو يمحو اثر اقدامه عن ارض الهيكل بمكنسة طويلة .

كانت تتكلم وكانها عاشت ذلك العصر السحيق او انها مصرية قديمة عادت اليها الروح !

زهرة اللوتس ، كما ان النقوش على الجدران بارزة بعكس نقوش ابنه رمسيس الذى كان يعتمد على الحفر .

كانت الكتابات الهيروغليفية تزين حوائط البهو .. اشرت الى بعض الرسوم وطلبت منها ان تقرا ما كتبه الاجداد .. قالت وهى تقرا صفحة من صفحات التاريخ العظيم : الملك القوى .. ملك الوجهين القبلى والبحرى ، محبوب من سيدتين ، له العمر المديد ، ذو باس فى الحرب : « سيتى ابن الشمس » .

كنا قد وصلنا الى هيكل ضخم .. انه هيكل « حورس »

قلت « لدورثى ايدى » وهو اسمها الانجليزى الذى غيرته الى : « بليل عبد المجيد » : اراك تخلعين حذاءك وانت تدخلين المعبد الفرعونى .

قالت ـ « ام سيتى » ـ وهو اسم الشهرة بلكنتها العربية البسيطة : « على فكرة كان دخول المعبد محظورا الا على الملك والامراء وكبار رجال البلاط ، ثم انه كانت هناك تقاليد ينبغى مراعاتها قبل دخول المعبد ، منها عدم تناول البصل او الثوم او السمك والفول .

توقفت « ام سيتى » وهى تشير الى نهاية البهو : ـ هنا ينتهى بهو رمسيس الثانى (الولد الشقى) . قالته وهى تبتسم وكانها احدى مربياته التى عرفت كل صغيرة من تصرفاته .

ودلفنا الى بهو الملك سيتى الاول (الاب) وهو يضم ٣٦ عمودا هاماتها على شكل

تمسك بحذائها وتضعه تحت ابطها وتدخل من باب المعبد وسالتها :

ـ لماذا تخلعين الحذاء ؟

قالت بلكنة عربية وهى تنظر الى قدمى وكانها تعتب على : دا مكان مكدس ..

وطبعا لم تكن تقصد ان المعبد مكدس بالبشر او بالتماثيل او غير ذلك ولكنها قصدت انه مكان مقدس بالقاف وليست بالكاف .

قلت لها : منذ متى وانت هنا ؟ ..

ـ الاف السنين ! !

كنا قد وصلنا الى البهو الذى بناه « رمسيس الثانى » وبه ٢٤ عمودا من الحجر الجيرى تتوج كل عمود زهرة البردى ، وعلى حوائط البهو لوحات تصور « الملك رمسيس الثانى » وهو يركب عجلته الحربية ممسكا بالاسرى .

HANNY M. EL ZEINI

Hanny M. El Zeini was born in 1918, graduated in 1941 as a chemist from the Cairo University and joined the Egyptian Sugar & Distillery Company whose eight big factories are dispersed in different regions of Upper Egypt and adjacent to all the important archaeological sites of ancient Egypt.

He developed an early passion for Egyptology as a very absorbing hobby and consequently has witnessed and followed very closely all the important excavations in the different areas. Later and by the help of his co-author and friend Omm Sety, he learned hieroglyphs and acted as part-time consultant for some excavators for both Egyptian and foreign missions. Dr. El Zeini is a well-known desert traveller and has been actively recording rock drawings and inscriptions all over both eastern and western deserts of Egypt for the past 25 years. His collected data will be published; and it may shed new light on the origins of Egyptian civilization.

During his numerous travels in the desert, he discovered some unrecorded Neolithic sites, a few old and abandoned Coptic monasteries and some unknown hideaways of Anchorites in almost inaccessible valleys and ravines; all of which will be published later. He is in close association with the U.N.E.S.C.O. Group for the study of Nag-Hammadi Gnostic Papyri.

Dr. El Zeini introduced the Egyptian sugar industry to the world in 1961 when he invented a new patented process known all over the world as "The Egyptian Cane Diffusion." Besides being a member of several archaeological societies, he works as a United Nations Industrial Development Organization consultant for the sugar industry.

Dr. El Zeini's beautiful photography compliments Omm Sety's account of the history, temples and locale of Abydos in Upper Egypt. Together they have performed a great service to the world. Dr. El Zeini has said that the world deserves a translation of every bit of the hieroglyphs recorded on stone.

Significance

Were the ancient Egyptians dedicated to excellence in the fine arts? Are we to believe that some common conclusions about the temple are the most important which can be made? It is admitted that the art work is beautiful and that those who made it intended for it to last forever (especially that under the supervision of Sety I). I cannot be convinced that a pharaoh **could be** motivated to devote such a huge share of the national treasury to the construction of such a shrine for it to be only as a legacy to the world of fine art or even to establish the fact that the maker (Sety I) adored the gods. We must look beyond beauty to grasp the real significance of the Temple of Sety I and of all the temples of ancient Egypt.

The ancient Egyptians had a religious priesthood tradition which bears strong similarities to other ancient traditions and our hypothesis is that they all had a common origin. Pre-Christian-era knowledge of the eventual coming of Jesus Christ long preceding his birth seems to be part of the Egyptian religious lore. The son Horus seems almost the same name as the son Jesus. The pronunciation was probably even closer. And how much Egyptian interchange is there between the concepts of the "sun" and the "Son"?

A temple has always been the house of god (or the gods). That literally is the case in ancient Egypt for the temples housed a statue of the specific god for whom the temple was dedicated or statues of many different gods. In ancient Israel the house of the Lord was a place on earth in which the great Jehovah could come and speak with the prophets. The ancient Egyptians obviously used much symbolism and their god statues most likely were symbolic of real living gods who supposedly communicated with High Priests and Pharaohs.

One reason why the ancient Egyptian temples are of such extreme interest is that they embody so many of the world's great religious ideas. Examples follow.

1. Man is created in the image of God, both male and female (Genesis 1:26). The Egyptian gods and goddesses are human. Even Horus, with the falcon head, is human with the symbolic bird head. The symbolism seems to be related to the spirit (falcon) of god which overshadowed Isis when she conceived Horus. In the Biblical parallel, the Holy Ghost overshadowed Mary when Jesus was conceived and the Holy Ghost was often spoken of as being in the form of a dove (a bird). Hence, a reason for a bird head. The idea of a mother among the gods or goddesses is of interest.

2. There is more than one eternal-- and eternal opposition as well as an eternal good. The struggle between Osiris and his wicked brother Set illustrates the concept of the presence of both good and evil in the world. See the evil serpent on page 13. And the "pig" which devours the damned on the day of judgment has a close Biblical parallel. The evil spirits driven from two possessed persons entered into the bodies of swine (Matthew 8:32).

3. Man is a child of God. Each of the pharaohs considered himself as a son of God, so somehow, all people are. And man has a spirit or soul. The Bible considers God to be the father of spirits (Hebrews 12:9). Ka was the equivalent of spirit in ancient Egypt and was separated from the body at death but could reenter it (page 91). Bird-headed gods are symbols of the Ka of the gods and are considered to be spirits and not as a person literally with a bird head (The Holy Ghost of the Bible is a spirit often appearing in the form of a dove or a bird).

4. The resurrection is a reality. The message of the empty tomb of Jesus to the world was a literal resurrection for all, but Osiris many centuries earlier was the same symbol to the ancient Egyptians. Osiris was murdered and subsequently resurrected.

5. A man may become a god. This idea is found in various forms throughout the world but perhaps the most dominant form of it is found in the Egyptian temples where the rituals undertaken are actually supposed to transform the initiate into a god. Someone penned that the "universe is a great machine for the making of gods."[1] The Old Testament implies the same, "Ye are gods" (Psalms 82:6), at least gods in embryo. The New Testament injunction to "Be ye therefore perfect even as your father which is in Heaven is perfect" (Matthew 5:48), implies that a man certainly may become like God. Mormons say, "As man is God once was, as God is man may become."

....

[1]Quoted by T. Madsen in The Instructor 1963, 98:205.

ix

Ancient Egyptian godhood was reserved for the pharaohs and their wives (or a select one of their wives). The great message of the Abu Simbel temples to the world is that a man--a pharaoh--Ramesses II, the so called braggert, and his favorite wife Nefertari, can, through temple ritual, be transformed into the presence of the gods as gods themselves. The candidates might have been unworthy and the temple procedure apostate in the eyes of modern church members, but underneath it all loudly comes the great idea that the ultimate destiny of a man is to eventually become a god. But I doubt that the Supreme God of the universe intended for anyone to make it as fast as Ramesses II did or supposed that he did. Kingly abuses of the idea are obviously legion and the problems of "Divine Right of Kings" evidently started right here in Egypt.

Mormons are modern temple builders. In the Mormon concept, the temple points the way, is available to all the faithful, and perfection comes through a lifetime of obeying and keeping covenants made in temples. And the progression continues after death. The idea that the destiny of a man is to became a god was had by Ramesses II and other pharaohs, but a world of difference exists in the concepts of Ramesses and of Mormons and other Christians.

6. The family is eternal. The ancient Egyptians had no embarassing hang-ups about fatherhood and motherhood. The Holy Trinity in the Osiris temple was a father-mother-son, all gods-all eternal. Other holy triads exist among Egyptian gods and all represent the family eternal. Ramesses II chose to have his wife Nefertari also elected to godhood, each in separate temples, to preserve his marriage into the eternities. Their children are preserved in identity by sculpture in the temples in eternal-like gesture. The family was thus united for eternity.

7. The dead can be saved through ritual work. Ancient Christians practiced baptism for the dead (I Corinthians 15:29). Ancient Egyptians developed whole temple rituals for deceased pharaohs whose proxy work was believed necessary for the eternal life (and godhood) of the deceased initiate. In the Temple of Sety I, one finds a list of some 60 pharaoh ancestors for whom temple work was supposedly done (also see page 154 concerning the List of Kings). Some pharaohs built temples for fathers and grandfathers who had not built their own.

8. There is a great final judgment day, and there is a graded salvation. In the Egyptian version the heart of the dead is weighed on the balance under the supervision of Horus (the Bible says that Jesus is the Judge). The position of Pharaoh in the hereafter was to be higher than that of his subjects.

The main purpose of a temple was to ritually prepare an initiate (a pharaoh was the candidate) for eternal life. Since the temple was to last forever and since the pharaoh had to justify his claim to godhood, the temple walls and ceilings and pylons were often covered with scenes of the pharaoh's deeds--victories, exploits, etc. His importance was to be known and remembered through all eternity. That was part of the first room of the temple.

How can temple rituals prepare one to be a god or at least to have eternal life? There is no easy answer for such a question, but the idea does explain the motivation for building so many many temples throughout the land. Parts, at least, of the eternal life rituals were repeated in the tomb rooms of the pharaohs probably to "guarantee" that all was well and also as a map to show the way.

Literal translations are probably without meaning for some of the steps in the temple ritual. It has to be assumed that when the pharaoh is offering food and drink to the gods, some deep symbolism is involved. It means much more than a courteous hospitable gesture. Actually it seems to be part of a covenant (contract or agreement) being made. Many covenants--many presentations! Out of it all the pharaoh expected an endowment of eternal life. He therefore goes through standardized (the same basics in each temple) procedures through which he receives the "Key of Life" from the god of the temple and then penetrates the veil of the temple to be in the presence of the gods (see page 222). And does not the basic patterns of temple structure place the room of the gods (or god) at the head (end) of the temple--the last place to enter on a journey to be in the presence of God? The long-axis structure of temples allowed the initiate to progress step-by-step to the final goal.

The real meaning of the Egyptian temples is mind-exploding. Yet it will be unnoticed by the overwhelming majority of those who come to see. They will come, look, be thrilled, and still go away not knowing what they have seen. Most will be, as so well put by Omm Sety, "worshipers at the Shrine of Beauty." To a few, however, another dimension will be seen. Much excitement awaits the few who have "eyes to see and ears to hear."

The purpose of a temple was to make a man into a god. A higher concept is presented in a poem by Lorenzo Snow:

"Hast thou not been unwisely bold,
Man's destiny to thus unfold?
To raise, promote such high desire,
Such vast ambition thus inspire?

"Still, 'tis no phantom that we trace
Man's ultimatum in life's race;
This royal path has long been trod
By righteous men, each now a God:

"As Abra'm, Isaac, Jacob, too,
First babes, then men-to gods they grew.
As man now is, our God once was;
As now God is, so man may be,-
Which doth unfold man's destiny.

"The boy, like to his father grown,
Has but attained unto his own;
To grow to sire from state of son,
Is not 'gainst Nature's course to run.

"A son of God, like God to be,
Would not be robbing Deity;
And he who has this hope within,
Will purify himself from sin.

You're right, St. John, supremely right:
Whoe'er essays to climb this height,
Will cleanse himself of sin entire--
Or else 'twere needless to aspire.[2]

The great annual New Year Festival deserves some comment (pages 56, 166). When Ramesses II stood in the temple courtyard to address his people, he performed a rite repeated many times at many places. The local place was always considered to be the center of the universe, the site of creation, the most holy and sacred. Ramesses' promise of continued "prosperity" was the essential important ingredient for which he could expect continued gratitude and subservience of his people. The annual New Year Rite has been studied by Nibley (1957)[3] who said that every ancient king must provide prosperity and victory to insure his continued stay in office. Ramesses II did just that.

According to Nibley, other features of the New Year Festival included proclamations, census, sacrifice offerings, exhortations to the common people, declarations that the king was a god on earth, bringing of gifts and passing out of gifts, ritual rebirth of the king, choirs and heavenly choirs, a divination of the future (forecast of never-ending happiness), king's judgment of the people, bowing or kneeling of the population in acceptance of the speech and the bestowal of a new name as part of a vow or covenant to support the king. Ramesses II did most of these.

A Book of Mormon king in about 200 B.C. presided over a great "transfer of kingship" festival in which the same procedures mentioned here were carried out.[4] King Benjamin promised "prosperity" too but only if the people kept the commandments of God. Originally this must have been the idea of the ancient festivals.

Arthur Wallace
Editor

[2] "Improvement Era," June 1919, pp. 66-61.
[3] An Approach to the Book of Mormon. 1957, p. 263.
[4] Mosiah 2-5.

TABLE OF CONTENTS

Modern historians divide Egyptian history into periods and dynasties. But this is an artificial system as the Egyptians themselves did not follow it. Neither (with but one known[1] exception) did they date events from a fixed era but from the regnal years of the reigning king.

The dynasties numbered I to XXX and were first used by Manetho, an Egyptian priest, who, in the reign of Ptolemy III, wrote a history of Egypt in Greek. He ended a dynasty whenever there was a break in the male line. But as in ancient Egyptian law, succession was through the female line, there was no break, and any man marrying the Royal Heiress was considered to be a legitimate king so long as his wife was alive.

However, the division into dynasties is a convenient one, and so it has been retained.

The fact that there was no fixed era for dating events causes some difficulties in the chronology, and we have to rely for the length of a reign on the last dated monument of a particular king.

This only gives the minimum of years. Some few dates can be fixed with certainty. This is when mention is made of the rising of the star Sirius with the sun taking place in a certain year of a king's reign. This date can then be fixed astronomically. From this we can be certain that the XIIth dynasty began in 2000 B.C. and the XVIIIth dynasty in 1580 B.C. But for earlier periods we are groping in the dark.

For example, Professor Flinders Petrie put the accession of Mena, the founder of the Ist dynasty, at 4777 B.C.,[2] but Breasted gives it as 3400 B.C.[3] The difference occurs because earlier historians mistook the length of the First Intermediate Period (VII-Xth dynasties) and the Hyksos Period. Petrie gives the former as 3290-3100 B.C. and the latter 2098-1587 B.C. Later discoveries have proved that both these periods were actually much shorter, and as perhaps the most reasonable dating is that of Breasted, we will abide by him.

THE ARCHAIC PERIOD	I-IInd DYNASTIES	3400-2980 B.C.
THE OLD KINGDOM	III-VIth DYNASTIES	2980-2475 B.C.
THE FIRST INTERMEDIATE PERIOD	VII-Xth DYNASTIES	2475-2160 B.C.
THE MIDDLE KINGDOM	XI-XIIth DYNASTIES	2160-1788 B.C.
THE HYKSOS PERIOD	XIII-XVIIth DYNASTIES	1788-1580 B.C.
THE NEW KINGDOM	XVIII-XXth DYNASTIES	1580-1150 B.C.
THE DECADENCE	XXI-XXVth DYNASTIES	1150-663 B.C.
THE SAITIC PERIOD	XXVIth DYNASTY	663-525 B.C.
THE LATE PERIOD	XXVII-XXXth DYNASTIES	525-332 B.C.
THE PTOLEMAIC PERIOD		332-30 B.C.
CONQUEST BY ROME		30 B.C.

[1] The Four Hundred Years "Stela of Ramesses II"
[2] Petrie, "A History of Egypt", Vol. 1 p.10.
[3] Breasted, "A History of Egypt", p.21.

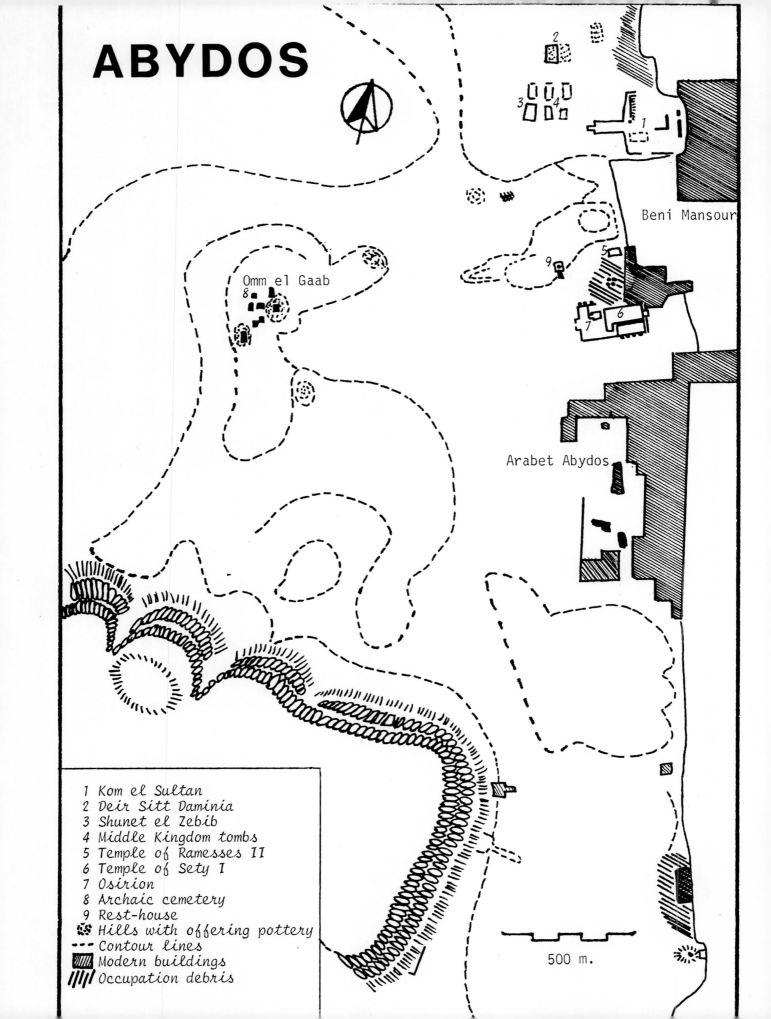

ABYDOS

Beni Mansour

Omm el Gaab

Arabet Abydos

1 Kom el Sultan
2 Deir Sitt Daminia
3 Shunet el Zebib
4 Middle Kingdom tombs
5 Temple of Ramesses II
6 Temple of Sety I
7 Osirion
8 Archaic cemetery
9 Rest-house
Hills with offering pottery
Contour lines
Modern buildings
Occupation debris

500 m.

Fig. 1. *The general area of Abydos. The villages are near the hills. In the middle distance, the hill known as the "Lord of Offerings" can be observed.*

HOLY CITY OF ANCIENT EGYPT

Introduction.

Strung out along the edge of the desert in the Sohag province of Egypt are three small villages, Ghabat, Arabet Abydos and Beni Mansour (see map).[1] To the east, the green fertile plain stretches away to the distant Nile; to the west is the desert and the limestone mountain. This mountain with its curious, horizontal strata projects eastward to the south and north taking the form of a crescent, so that the villages seem to lie in its protective embrace (Fig. 1).

These projections were in ancient times considered as either spiritual entities or the homes of such beings, and they were called "Lord of Offerings" (Fig. 2) and "Lady of Life" (Fig. 3). Strewn all over the desert between them are innumerable high mounds covering the graves of those who chose this place as their last abode.

This then is the site of ancient Abydos, the Holy City of ancient Egypt

....

[1]The last two village names are recent changes. Until a few years ago, Arabet Abydos was known as Araba el Madfouna, and Beni Mansour was called El Kherba. The names Araba el Madfouna and El Kherba will be found on all of the older maps.

the earth, from lands of which Sety never dreamed, if not to pray to Osiris, at least to admire and marvel at the exquisite workmanship of the sculpture, and praise the skill and patience of those unnamed men whose hands left us this legacy. Shall we call these modern people tourists or worshipers at the Shrine of Beauty? Or is there something even more important beyond all the beauty and wonder?

Fig. 2. The site of Abydos (looking south). In the distance (left), the projection of the mountain called "Lord of Offerings."

and the oldest known place of pilgrimage. In a way, Abydos was the focus of the oldest civilization, and a place to which many a heart yearned. We shall not be far from the truth when we say that this was the Jerusalem of the Ancient World.

One can imagine the hustle and bustle of thousands of people from all parts of Egypt coming on foot, by boat, in countless caravans to pay a short visit to this holy place. It may be a very modest point on the map now, but in the following pages we will try to tell the story of Abydos, the place that was once the divine center of a very ancient civilization. And we shall see how the great pharaohs vied with each other in building monuments here in honor of the beloved God Osiris.

Yet, of all their

efforts so far discovered, none can equal the glorious gift which Pharaoh Sety I made to Abydos and its God -- his magnificent temple (see sketches). In the great days of the XIXth dynasty, pilgrims from all over the Egyptian Empire flocked to pray in the courts of this wonderful building.

Today, people come from the farthest ends of

Fig. 3. The site of Abydos (looking north) showing the Temple of Sety I and (right) the projection in the mountain called "Lady of Life."

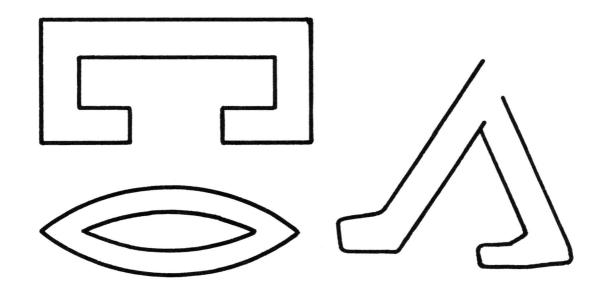

PERI

RISE

PART I

PERY = THE RISE

CHAPTER ONE

AS IT WAS IN THE BEGINNING

Bird's-eye View of Abydos.

The story of Abydos began far back in the mists of prehistory when semi-nomadic hunters and cattle-breeders wandered along the desert's edge. It was not until the rise of the Ist dynasty that the mists began to clear away. The kings of that time, Mena-Narmer and his successors, were living in the city of Thinis (now El Birbeh, a little to the north of Girga),[1] but for some un-

....
[1]The modern name of the town Girga, on the western bank of the Nile, comes from the ancient name Girget which means "settlement" or "suburb." Actually, Girget was once the suburb and river-port of Thinis.

known reason, they decided to build their tombs at a place later to be known as Abydos. Why they should have chosen this place is something of a mystery as it lies about 35 kilometers (22 miles) to the south of Thinis.

It is known that in ancient Egypt, royal tombs were never built on virgin ground but always near some older cemetery, so one may think that the presence of some nearby pre-dynastic graves governed their choice. But there are also plenty of pre-dynastic burials much nearer to Thinis-- at Salmani for example. And so the mystery of the choice remains unsolved. However, the answer to the question may lie in the curious gap in the mountain later to be known as Pega-the-Gap. The ancient Egyptians believed that this gap led directly to the Kingdom of the Dead; this belief may have been held from or even before the Ist dynasty.

Fig. 1-2. General view looking to the west. In the distance (upper center) may be seen the cleft in the mountain once known as Pega-the-Gap.

As the royal tombs are close to this gap (Fig. 1-1), its presence may have inspired the kings to build their "Houses of Eternity" on the very threshold of the Hereafter (Fig. 1-2).

Fig. 1-1. Pega-the-Gap is in the background. The street leads to the Temple of Sety I.

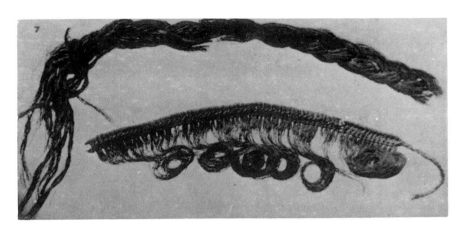

Fig. 1-3. A *plait* and *false-fringe* of human *hair* from the Archaic tomb of King Djer.

The Wrong God.

The tombs themselves were rectangular structures of the type known to archeologists as mastabas. Some of them had rough stone floors, wooden roofs and paneling in the burial chamber and many were surrounded by the graves of attendants, women, dwarfs (always great favorites in royal and noble households) and pet dogs. One of these tombs, that of King Djer (Ist dynasty), was later regarded as that of Osiris, and every year thousands of worshipers came to it bringing with them food and drink offerings in earthenware jars. Finally, the whole of the surroundings of the tombs became literally buried under these crocks, and to this day, the site is known in Arabic as, Omm el Gaab ("Mother of Potsherds").

The tombs were ransacked at an early date, probably during the first Intermediate Period, when the internal security of the country left much to be desired; in fact, it was practically nonexistent. They fared little better in modern times when the French Expedition under Amelineau "excavated" them with dynamite. Professor Petrie, working on behalf of the Egyptian Exploration Society, came along at the beginning of the twentieth century and painstakingly cleared up a little of the mess. He was rewarded by some wonderful finds.

In the Tomb of King Djer (Ist dynasty), Petrie's men found a human forearm adorned with four bracelets of gold, turquoise, lapis lazuli, and amethyst; the work of the goldsmith and lapidary, who made these bracelets in the early dawn of history, has never been surpassed. They and the forearm were found wrapped in some linen rags and thrust into a hole in the brickwork of the tomb.[2]

2............................
[2]These bracelets are now

Evidently they had been looted by some ancient thief who hid them from his comrades-in-crime and was never able to come back to collect them (he was probably killed in some brawl).

In the same tomb Petrie found a plait and false-fringe of "Kiss-curls" made of human hair (Fig. 1-3). In the case of the fringes, the hairs were knotted into a narrow woven band of thread exactly like the best modern hair-work and are perfectly preserved.

Other finds were some gaming pieces in the form of beautifully carved lions and hounds; the lions are of rock crystal and the hounds of ivory, and one wonders how they were worked with copper tools.[3]

The kings of the IInd dynasty also built their tombs at Omm el Gaab, and some of their courtiers followed suit. As all these tombs needed a number of priests for their care there is no doubt that a small hamlet sprang up on the edge of the cultivation to house these men and their families. There was also a modest little temple lying a little over one kilometer (0.6 mile) to the north of the royal tombs. It was later called the Temple of Osiris, but may have originally been for Wepwawat,

....
in the Cairo Museum, in the "Jewel Room" Nos. 4000-4003.

[3]Cairo Museum, No. 3052.

5

Fig. 1-4. Shunet el Zebib. The eastern face showing the double walls.

Fig. 1-5. Shunet el Zebib. Part of the western face showing the original crenellations and the double wall.

the jackal-headed guardian of the necropolis. This meant more priests and more houses and so the little hamlet became a village.

Shuna Pa Hib becomes Shunet el Zebib ("Mummy Hilton").

To the IInd dynasty belongs the mysterious building now known as Shunet el Zebib; no one seems to know what its original purpose was. It has been called a tomb, a "funerary palace," a fortress and even a depository, or temporary resting place for mummies of persons who in later times made their final pilgrimage to Abydos after their death and used the Shunet el Zebib as a kind of "Mummy Hilton."

We do know for certain that during the Late Period it was used as a cemetery for the sacred ibis. Thousands of these birds were found there mummified and buried in pottery jars. This seems to have been the origin of the modern name which in Arabic means "the Storehouse of Raisins" The word "shuna" (storehouse) is the same in the ancient Egyptian language; probably the name was "Shuna Pa Hib," the "Storehouse of the Ibis."

The building still stands to a height of 11 meters (36 feet) and has double walls, the inner one being crenellated. It measures 137 meters (450 feet) from north to south and 91 meters (300 feet) from east to west. The inner walls are 7.5 meters (25 feet) thick (Figs. 1-4, 1-5, 1-6).

There are at least three other similar buildings in the vicinity. One is almost totally destroyed, but another is well preserved and encloses the Coptic Church of Sitt Daminia built in the VIIth century A.D. (Fig. 1-7).

From Abydos to Memphis.

The kings of the IIIrd dynasty deserted Abydos as a cemetery and built their tombs near Memphis in Lower Egypt. But Djoser owner of the Step Pyramid at Sakkara, also built an enormous traditional mastaba tomb of mud-bricks at Beit Khallaf about 50 kilometers (30 miles) to the north of Abydos.

Here we may mention that many of the kings of the Ist and IInd dynasties, who have tombs at Abydos, also have tombs at Sakkara. Sakkara was the necropolis of Memphis, the capital founded by Mena-Narmer after he had united Upper and Lower Egypt into a single kingdom. One of the fascinating mysteries of Egyptian history is the fact that it is not known for certain in which of these tombs the kings were actually buried. But as Abydos was the necropolis of their hometown Thinis, and as the tombs there were surrounded by the graves of the royal favorites and pets, while those at Sakkara were not, it would seem more probable that Abydos was the actual burial place, and the Sakkara mastabas, which were large and fine, were cenotaphs built to impress the people of the newly conquered Lower Egypt.

Although no longer the traditional royal burial place, Abydos continued to flourish nevertheless, and this was because of the spread of the religion of Osiris. This cult seems to have been the faith of the common people while the royal and state religion was the Solar Cult. For this reason, we hear practically nothing of Osiris until the late IVth dynasty. Until that time, the only inscribed monuments were royal or were tombs or stelae given as a royal gift to favored nobles. The common folk, with their uninscribed graves, were the "silent majority."

Abydos During the Old Kingdom.

By the time of the IVth dynasty, people were making yearly pilgrimages to Abydos in order to visit the Tomb of Osiris. The little three-roomed

Temple of Wepwawat was enlarged; in its vicinity, we find comtemporary objects bearing the name of Khenty-Amentiu. This name means, "First (or President) of the Westerners" i.e. the dead, and at an early date was given to Osiris. But some scholars think that Khenty-Amentiu was a separate god, or may have been an epithet of Wepwawat. However, the very close links between Osiris and Abydos suggests that he had always been worshiped there.

We now find the name of Abydos in writing. Actually it was called Ab-du (of which Abydos is the Greek form), and seems to mean, "the Great Breeze" and "Nedit." So these names may have referred to special quarters, for the village had now become a thriving town. The last two names were also given to the canal which at that time linked Abydos with the Nile. Traces of this once great canal still exist and pass in front of the Temple of Sety I. The name of the nome or

administrative district was Ta-wer, "The Great Land", and was written with the sign of the sacred standard of Abydos thought by some to be a post supporting a basket containing the severed head of Osiris (Fig. 1-8). One of the scenes in the Temple of Sety I seems to support this theory, but as the story of the dismemberment of Osiris does not occur in the earlier versions of his history (in the Pyramid Texts), this could hardly be the original explanation of the meaning of the emblem.

Although the kings of the IVth dynasty continued to be buried near Memphis in Lower Egypt, they had by no means forsaken Abydos. That mysterious building now known as the Osirion seems by its style and method of construction to date from this time.

Fig. 1-6. The walls of Shunet el Zebib (southern end) showing the original eastern entrance (center) and the double walls (right).

Fig. 1-7. Deir (convent) of Sitt Daminia, built in a IInd dynasty enclosure similar and near to the Shunet el Zebib.

Fig. 1-8. Temple of Sety I. Main Entrance. North side. The standard of Abydos.

ABYDOS TEMPLES

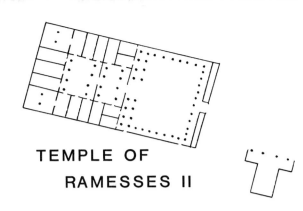

TEMPLE OF
RAMESSES II

TEMPLE OF RAMESSES I

TEMPLE OF SETY I

OSIRION

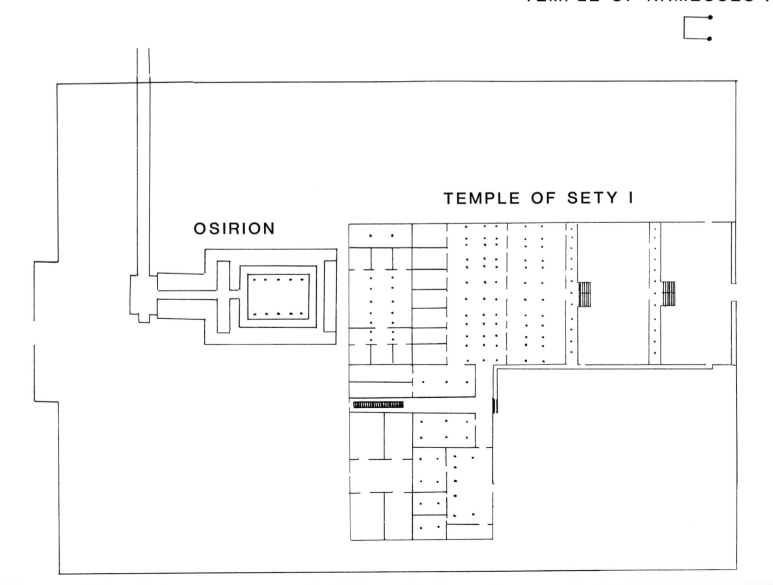

CHAPTER TWO

THE OSIRION AND RELATED ANNEXES

The Osirion.

This imposing subterranean building is one of the great puzzles of Egyptian Archeology. No one really knows who built it or for what purpose, and so far as is known, there is not another one like it in the whole of Egypt. Curiously enough, certain elements of its architecture closely resemble the "Gates of the Sun" in Peru, high up in the Andes Mountains. This imposing, fascinating, mysterious building of bewildering charm deserves from us some detailed description.

The entrance to the Osirion was discovered in 1909 by Miss (later Professor) Margaret Murray, who was then working under Professor Flinders Petrie for the Egyptian Exploration Society. But it was not until the early 1920's that the whole building was excavated and an account was published by Professor Henri Frankfort.[1] Because he found the name of Sety I in the decoration of the ceiling of one of the rooms, he attributed the building to him and called it the Cenotaph of Sety I. This king's name was also found on a black granite dove-tailed cramp inserted between two blocks

of a red granite architrave.[2] The latter were apparently springing apart, and the cramp was inserted to hold them together. This is only one of the many restorations to ancient monuments carried out by Sety. But it is no proof of his contribution to the construction of the building.

The Osirion has also been attributed to the Middle Kingdom, but judging by its style, the method of building, the material used, and its original stark simplicity, it seems much more likely to be a product of the early IVth dynasty although the level at which it lies might tempt one to think of a much earlier date. That it was not built by Sety I may be deduced from the following facts:

a. When any king built a monument, he always put an inscription saying, "He made it as his monument for his father, Osiris (or whatever was the name of the god to whom it was dedicated) This formula, which is repeated over and over again in temples, is not found anywhere here.

b. The entrance to the building lies outside the northern Temenos Wall of the temple (see sketch).

....
[1]H. Frankfort, "The Cenotaph of Sety I at Abydos".

[2]The red granite is typical of that of Asswan, and is found only in that region, some 500 kilometers (310 miles) south of Abydos.

If Sety had built it, we should expect to find it inside the Temenos.

c. It is obvious, as we shall see, that it was the presence of this building which forced the architects to change the plan of Sety's temple (see sketch). A certain amount of "holiness" seemed to be attached to the building since part of Sety's temple is actually constructed over the ruins of an older temple, but the architect found it imperative to avoid building in any way over the Osirion itself.

d. The inner corners of the walls of the halls and chambers are cut in one block of stone (Fig. 2-1) thus avoiding a vertical joint. This is a characteristic of IVth dynasty architecture and may also be seen in the Valley Temple of Khafra beside the Great Sphinx of Giza.

e. The massive granite pillars are all monolithic (Fig. 2-2), another Old Kingdom characteristic, whereas the pillars and columns of the temple are all built up in sections. Also, no granite was used in the temple.

f. The Entrance Passage
    and two of the chambers
    have saddle roofs,
    another Old Kingdom
    characteristic. All
    the roofs in the temple
    are flat or vaulted.

g. There is no connection
    at all between this
    building and the temple.

h. Frankfort made sondage
    pits down the outside
    walls of the main hall.
    At the bottom he found
    pottery of the Archaic

*Fig. 2-1. (Below) Great
Hall of the Osirion. One
of the small cells (north-
east). Note the corner
cut in one stone (second
course) typical of the
buildings of the IVth
dynasty.*

*Fig. 2-2. (Right) View
looking east showing the
forced entrance to the
east Transverse Hall
(center left), and the
entrance to the west
Transverse Hall (lower
right). The Osirion.*

Fig. 2-3. (Above) View of Osirion looking northwest showing how it was covered with sand.

Fig. 2-4. (Above) Entrance Passage. West wall. King Mer-en-Ptah. Scenes and inscriptions anticipate the King's death and refer to him as "the Osiris Ba-en-Ra Horep-her-Maat, the True of Voice (i.e. the Justified).

Period and early Old Kingdom. There was no more pottery until very near the present ground level when pots of the XXXth dynasty were found.

These suggest that in the period between these dates, the monument was buried in the sand and was inaccessible (Fig. 2-3). Perhaps the structure was built during the early IVth dynasty (maybe by Khufu himself), became neglected and buried under the sand after the downfall of the Old Kingdom and was redis-covered when Sety's men were digging the foundations for his temple, and so forced them to change the plan of the latter as we shall see later.

It is certain however, that Sety made some repairs to the Osirion. He certain-ly had the ceiling of one of the chambers sculptured; again we must stress that he made no claim whatsoever to having built the monument.

The Entrance Passage.

As we have said, the original entrance lies some distance outside the northern Temenos Wall of the Temple of Sety I. It leads to a long passage which slopes gently down-wards. This passage is cut in a strata of sandy clay and lined, paved and originally roofed with blocks of limestone. The

Fig. 2-5. (Left) Entrance Passage. West wall. "Book of Gates." The Night Solar Boat (details). The Osirion.

northern end of the passage must have been partly destroyed in very ancient times as Sety had it restored by lining its walls with the same huge mud-bricks used in the construction of the Temenos Wall, and where the latter wall passes over the passage, a massive vaulted roof was built of the same material. South of this restoration, the saddle roof of the passage was of limestone. Apparently the walls were originally undecorated, but Mer-en-Ptah, the grandson of Sety I (Fig. 2-4), had them crudely painted in color with copies of two funerary works that were popular in the royal tombs of the New Kingdom. On the western wall is the "Book of Gates" (Fig. 2-5). On the eastern wall, "The Book of What is the Underworld." Both are believed by modern scholars to be a kind of "guide book" to the underworld, and to describe the nightly passage of the Sun God through these regions. In the "Book of Gates" the twelve hours of the night are represented by twelve sections of the underworld divided from each other by gates guarded by fire-spitting cobras. Through these sections, the Sun God, in the form of a ram-headed man, is towed in his boat by various gods and spirits and the dead King sails with him as a passenger.

Many are the obstacles in the way, but these are overcome. The evil

Fig. 2-6. Entrance Passage. West wall. ("Book of Gates"). The Night Solar Boat. In the prow stands Sia (Intelligence). King Mer-en-Ptah kneels before the cabin. In the cabin is the Night Sun God Ra-iwt. The serpent Apep coils around the cabin. Behind the cabin is Heka (Magic). The Osirion.

serpent Apep seeks to bar the passage of the Solar Boat but is prevented (Fig. 2-6). In another place he is bound by chains pegged into the ground, from which he struggles vainly to escape.

At midnight the boat reaches the section in which is the dreaded Court of Osiris where the God is seated in judgement upon all who had died during the day. The heart of the deceased, as being the seat of the conscience, is weighed in a balance

Fig. 2-7. Entrance Passage. West wall. ("Book of Gates"). The evil serpent Apep chained down and menaced by jackal-headed gods. The Osirion.

against an ostrich feather symbolizing absolute Truth and Justice. In this scene, the upright post of the balance is replaced by a mummiform being whose shoulders support the cross-beam. Some gods ascend the stairs leading to the throne of Osiris, and above, a pig, the Devourer of the Damned, is driven away in a boat by a spirit in the form of an ape (Fig. 2-8).

A very curious scene shows a number of gods carrying a long serpent from whose back protrude human heads (Fig. 2-9). The accompanying inscription says that these heads only appear when the Sun God enters this section of the underworld. As he passes by, the heads all sing a hymn of praise, but when he has vanished

Fig. 2-8. (Right) Entrance Passage. West wall ("Book of Gates"). The Judgement Hall of Osiris. Osiris, apparently wearing the Double Crown, is seated at the top of a flight of stairs. Before him is the balance (top of stairs) in which the heart (conscience) of the deceased is weighed against the Feather of Truth. A curious feature is that the support of the balance, in the form of a mummy-Amit, the Devourer, who eats the heart of evil-doers, is here shown in the form of a wild pig standing in a boat and threatened by an ape (over the stairs). At the top left-hand corner is Anubis (scene is partly obliterated).

Fig. 2-9. *Entrance Passage. Eastern wall. ("Book of Gates") The serpent with the singing heads (upper row). The Osirion.*

from their sight, the heads are reabsorbed into the serpent's back! School-boy naughtiness!

After the highly ethical idea underlying the scene of the Judgment Hall of Osiris, this scene of the serpent and its singing heads seems to be childish nonsense, and it is hard to understand intelligent and objective men like the pharaohs of the XIXth dynasty taking it seriously. Moreover, there are certain scenes which have no bearing at all on their accompanying inscriptions. These things make one wonder if there is a hidden meaning to the "Book of Gates" for which we do not hold the key. This is mere conjecture, for which we have no proof. But we are inclined to believe that the scene of the multi-headed serpent must have some worthy and basically serious interpretation.

The last majestic scene at the southern end of the passage is an impos-ing composition and is supposed to represent "The Dawn" (Fig. 2-10). A huge figure of the God Nun triumphantly raises the Solar Boat out of the Primeval Ocean. The ram-headed night form of the Sun God is now replaced by the scarab, Kheperi, God of the Morning Sun. With his serrated forelegs, the great scarab lifts up the solar disk towards the Sky Goddess Nut who stretches out her arms to receive it. She stands on the head of a male human figure bent round in a circle so that his toes touch the back of his head. He is inscribed, "Osiris

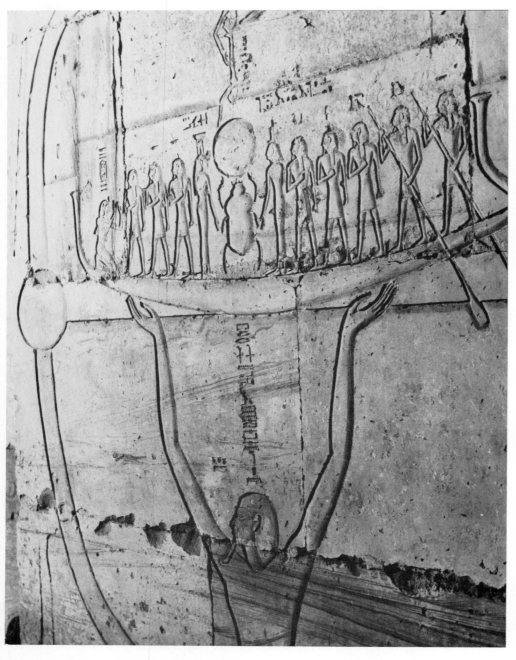

Fig. 2-10. Entrance Passage. West wall. Scene of the Dawn, from the "Book of Gates." Nun, God of the Primeval Ocean, raises up the Solar Boat at the end of its journey. Kheperi, God of the Morning Sun, in the form of a scarab, raises up the solar disk which is received by the Sky Goddess Nut. The Goddess stands on a male figure which is bent backwards, its feet touching the back of its head. It is inscribed "Osiris who Encircles the Dwat" (the Underworld). To the right of Kheperi stands the Goddess Isis followed by Geb, Shu and Heka. Hu and Sia work the steering oars. To the left stands Nepthys, and King Mer-en-Ptah kneels in the bows. The Osirion.

who encirlces the underworld

Dante's "Inferno," B.C.!

"The Book of What is the Underworld," which is inscribed on the eastern wall of the passage, is an ancient version of "Dante's Inferno" and gives much space to the sufferings of the dead who in their lifetime were displeasing to the gods. Some are beheaded (Fig. 2-11) and burned black. Others are turned upside down and have their hearts cut out (Fig. 2-12), while the shadows and spirits of others are immersed in great cauldrons of boiling water (Fig. 2-13).

The Antechamber.

At the southern end of the passage is a rectangular antechamber on the western wall of which is a finely incised and colored scene showing King Mer-en-Ptah presenting offerings to Osiris, before who stands Horus (Fig. 2-14). Some of the offerings are placed in colored baskets which are identical with those made in Asswan at the present day (Fig. 2-15). Between the King and Osiris is a version of chapter CXLI of the "Book of the Dead" enumerating all the names or epithets of Osiris.

A small side-chamber leading out of the southern end of the antechamber is also decorated with scenes and inscriptions from the "Book of the Dead".

Fig. 2-11. Entrance Passage. East wall. Men in Hell. The three to the right are supposed to be beheaded and burned. The Osirion.

Fig. 2-12. Entrance Passage. East wall. Evil persons turned upside-down in the Other World and having their hearts cut out. Note the master draughtsman's corrections to the figures. The Osirion.

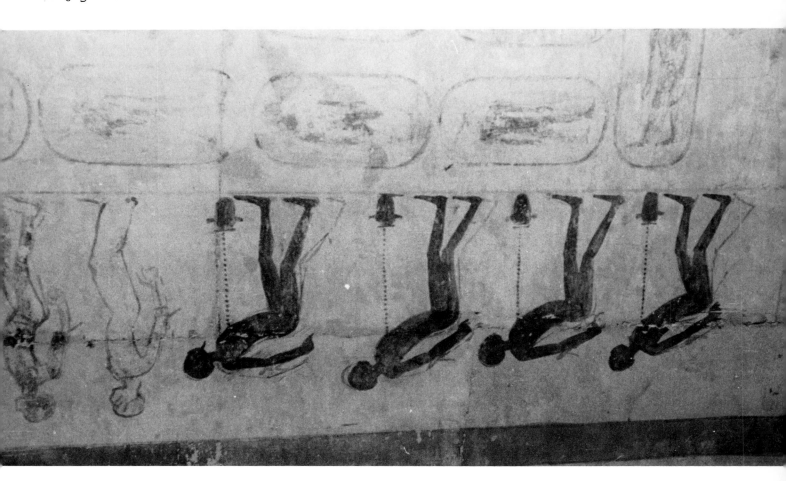

Fig. 2-14. Antechamber. West wall. Mer-en-Ptah burning incense, offerings presented by him and part of the list of the epithets of Osiris, from the "Book of the Dead." The Osirion.

Fig. 2-13. *Entrance Passage. East wall. The shadows (top row) and spirits of evil-doers upside-down in a pool of boiling water. The Osirion.*

From the eastern wall of the antechamber, a passage leads to a long, narrow Transverse Hall, the granite saddle roof of which has now fallen in. From here, a short passage leads eastward into the grand, imposing Central Hall.

The Central Hall.

Walls of huge blocks of dark red sandstone surround a rectangular island of even greater blocks of red granite on which stand ten monolithic pillars of the same material. These pillars measure 3.90 meters high, 2.37 meters wide and 2.13 meters thick (12.8 feet X 7.8 feet X 7.0 feet) and have an average weight of about fifty tons each!

Between the island and the walls of the hall is a channel of water about two meters (6.6 feet) wide and nine meters (30 feet) deep. Originally

there was no permanent access to the island from any other part of the building. Neither was there access to the side walls of the hall in which are seven small, square cells opening onto a narrow ledge (about 60 centimeters --2 feet--wide) and on the same level as the surface of the island. These cells, which were originally closed by wooden doors, are six in each of the northern and southern walls, two in the western wall, and three in the eastern wall. The ledge onto which the cells open is interrupted on its western and eastern sides by two pilasters, or engaged pillars. At the eastern and western ends of the island, is a small and narrow flight of thirteen steps which descends part of the way into the channel.

The water in the channel was originally

Fig. 2-15. *Antechamber. Details of the colored offering baskets. The Osirion.*

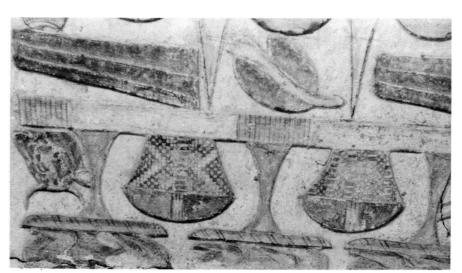

introduced through a long underground passage, roofed, walled and paved with limestone that led eastward to the ancient Nif-wer Canal.[3] The Roman writer Strabo, mentions this passage and says that it was constructed of stone and was without joints!

Most of the granite roof of the hall is missing but from what remains, it is clear that the form was most unusual. At the northern and southern sides, the roof sloped upwards but the central part was flat. In fact, it resembled the undersides of the lids of some Old Kingdom sarcophagi.

How the hall was lit and ventilated we do not know, but Strabo mentioned that the roof was covered externally by a great mound, surrounded by a grove of trees. There are still some circular, stone-lined pits at the southern and northern sides of the building, and when excavated, they contained earth and the roots of large trees.

Even in its roofless state, the Great Hall is an inspiring sight in its massive simplicity (Figs. 2-16, 2-17, 2-18). Like

....

[3]In modern times, the bed of the Nile has risen, and consequently the level of the subsoil water. Therefore, this wonderful monument is now permantly flooded, and only the Entrance Passage, the antechamber and small side-rooms are still high and dry.

Fig. 2-16. View of the Great Hall showing the forced entrance to the east Transverse Hall (center). Above, the west wall of the Temple of Sety I. Lower left is the entrance to the west Transverse Hall.

the valley Temple of Khafra at Giza, it was originally undecorated, but Mer-en-Ptah had the eastern wall sculptured with scenes of himself offering to various gods. He also commenced but did not finish the decoration of some of the architraves.

The Eastern Transverse Hall.

Lying behind the eastern wall of the Great Hall is another Transverse Hall. It is exactly the same as the one on the western side except that this hall had no connection originally with the rest of the building. Its present entrance is through a hole in the back wall of the central square cell of the eastern wall of the hall, and this hole was forced through in modern times. Yet,

during the reign of Sety I, this Transverse Hall must have been accessible as he had decorated its saddle roof with a wonderful scene of the Sky Goddess Nut stretched out over the world (Fig. 2-19). The accompanying texts, in the form of a dramatic script, tell how Nut complained to the Great God that her husband Geb had insulted her by calling her "Sow that Eats her Young"! Called to order about this, Geb defends himself by saying that every evening Nut gives birth to her children the stars, but in the morning she eats them, therefore he is justified in the name that he called her. After some more domestic mud-slinging on both sides, the Great God pronounces his decision by saying that Nut may eat her children every morning,

Fig. 2-17. The Great Hall. Note the remaining blocks from the roof (upper center), and below, the forced entrance to the eastern Transverse Hall.

of steel and concrete were sunk in the ground to below water level between the western wall of the temple and the eastern wall of the Transverse Hall. But during this operation no connecting passage or stairway linking the two buildings was discovered, so we still do not know how Sety's men got in to decorate the roof.

The Purpose of the Osirion.

What was the purpose of this mysterious building? The fact that Mer-en-Ptah decorated the Entrance Passage with scenes and texts normally found in royal tombs suggests that in his day the building was apparently

but she shall not fail to give birth to them again at night, and added sternly, "And she shall not be called, 'Sow that Eats her Young.' So that is that!"

About twenty years ago from the time of writing, the western part of the Temple of Sety I was in danger of collapsing, so fourteen great piers

Fig. 2-18. Architrave of the Great Hall decorated by Mer-en-Ptah.

Fig. 2-19. (Left) Temple of Sety I. The Osirion. The eastern side of the "Sarcophagus Chamber." The Goddess Nut. Note that her body is spangled with stars. Nut here represents the night sky about to swallow the sun. Below her (right), "The Gods of the East. The Gods of the West. The Gods of the North. The Gods of the South." Setepri ("The Chosen"), Her-set-ef ("He who is Upon His Seat"), Kesi-wr ("The Great Bower"), Khefert ("Food"), Menemy, Sary (Ascender"), Meb-Seshed ("Lord of a Fillet"), Imen-mu ("Secret Waters"). Below: The Solar Boat towed by the Ikhemw-wrdj ("The Untiring Stars"). The inscription surrounding and behind the boat had been re-cut in incised signs.

regarded as a tomb. The Great Hall itself suggests a stone sarcophagus, and the rectangular island, the wooden coffin that it contains.

Frankfort thought that the island, with its two flights of steps, was supposed to represent the first hill of dry land that emerged from the Primeval Ocean at the time of the Creation. He also thought that the large rectangular and square depressions in the surface of the island were for a sarcophagus and canopic chest, but they seem to be much too large for such a purpose. What seems probable is that these depressions

were intended to receive the bases of a large statue and an altar. If so, this again points to an Old Kingdom date when statues were sunk into recesses in the pavements of the temples to make their removal or overthrow more difficult.

It is possible that some ruler of the Old Kingdom, thinking that a mud-brick mastaba tomb was unsuitable for Osiris, rebuilt it in eternal stone? In some of the ancient hymns Osiris is referred to as, "He who sleeps surrounded by water." If he were buried on (or in a still undis-covered chamber, inside) the island, this would certainly be true. Further-more, a stela from a Late Period refers to "the Hill of Thinis, which conceals its Lord." And as we have already said, Strabo mentioned that the Osirion was covered by a hill. It would seem as though some Egyptians regarded it as the Tomb of Osiris although others of their compatriots thought that the Mastaba of King Djer was the holy tomb.

But as the channel surrounding the island has never yet been freed from its water, despite the use of powerful pumps, and probably never will be, it is unlikely that the mystery of the Osirion will be solved. It will always remain one of the most breath-taking puzzles of Egyptology; a challenge for a future generation of Egyptologists who must really make an exceptional

effort before solving its mystery.

A Glimpse of an Old Scandal.

Near the ancient temple at Kom el Sultan was found the only statue, so far known, of King Khufu, the builder of the Great Pyramid of Giza. This is a miniature ivory figure not more than 7.0 centimeters (2.75 inches) high but having all the power and dignity of a colossus. The King is seated and wears the Red Crown of Lower Egypt, and the determined little face seems to have been a portrait as it bears a close resemblance to his son Khafra (Fig. 2-20). It is now in the Cairo Museum (No. 4244).

This figure, with a number of others, some of which dated back to the Ist dynasty, were found by Petrie in a pit near the ancient temple. All had been slightly damaged, and were coated with some dry, brown material. Puzzled by the nature of this material, Petrie sent a sample of it to be analyzed only to learn that it was dry human excreta! The pit in which they were found was evidently the cess-pit of the temple lavatory, and here we get a glimpse of an ancient scandal. It was the custom for kings and nobles to dedicate votive statues to a temple. When these figures became too numerous, or were damaged, a priest would take them away and bury them somewhere in the sacred temple enclosure, and so make room for newer votive offerings. In the case of these statues, the priest was probably a lazy, irreligious wretch, and instead of troubling himself to dig a hole and bury them, he just threw them down the lavatory. And to think that this happened to the only known statue of the great Khufu, of all the pharaohs of Egypt!!! What an unbelievable irony of fate!

Another ivory figure from the same group is now in the British Museum, London. It represents a king wearing the White Crown of Upper Egypt, and a richly patterned cloak. Who is he? We shall never know. But the beautiful, thoughtful face, with its intensely spiritual expression tempts one to think that perhaps we have here a portrait of the Archaic King who was to be later worshiped as Osiris (Fig. 2-21).

By the time of the Vth dynasty, Abydos was quite a big, flourishing town. The old temple was now greatly enlarged and had may priests and lay-workers, as well as lands and cattle, all designated by royal decree of King Nefer-ir-ka-Ra for the protection of these people and the temple property. This decree was inscribed on a limestone stela, and was found by Petrie at Kom el Sultan. It is now in the Museum of Fine Arts, Boston, U.S.A. On it the King says, "I do not permit that any man has the right to take away any priests

Fig. 2-20. Ivory statuette of Khufu, the only figure of this King so far discovered (from Kom el Sultan).

who are in this district except to do service for the God himself in the temple in which he is and to conserve the temple in which they are. They are exempt in the limits of Eternity by the decree of the King of Upper and Lower Egypt, Nefer-ir-ka-Ra.

"I do not permit that any man has the right to take away the necessary equipment for any work in any other temple estate on which there is priestly service by any priest.

"I do not permit that any man has the right to take away any serfs who are on any god's field for the corvée or for any other work in the district.

"As for any man who should disobey this decree," the King orders, "thou

shalt consign him to the temple work-house; he himself being put on any corvee, or to the place of ploughing."

This is really poetic justice, and it must have been a joyous sight to the oppressed to see a fat, pampered, over-fed official grubbing about the mud of a canal, or staggering along in the blazing sun behind a plough! Justice spread its wings at a very early time in the history of mankind in the land of Egypt.

The Triumph of the Common People's Cult.

The annual pilgrimage was firmly established, and by now Osiris was regularly referred to as, "Lord of Abydos." The Cult of the God of the Common People had triumphed and the proud priests of the Solar Cult had to include him in their great religious work now known as the "Pyramid Texts." The earliest known version of these are found on the walls of the passages and burial chamber of the Pyramid of King Unas of the Vth dynasty, at Sakkara. They are also found in the pyramids of the kings and queens of the VIth dynasty and very much later in the tombs of private people.

From these texts we have clear proof that Abydos was regarded as the burial place of the entire body of Osiris. Thus it was considered to be particularly holy ground and many persons, though living elsewhere in Egypt, longed with all their hearts to be buried in Abydos beside the body of their God. And so a large necropolis gradually grew up on the sandy plain between the cultivation and the mountain.

Sometimes family ties or other reasons prevented a person from realizing the wish to be buried in Abydos, and he had to be content with erecting a small cenotaph, or even a memorial stela.

A few years ago, an interesting monument of this kind was found. It was dedicated by two women to their mother. The old lady had passionately desired to be buried in Abydos, but for some reason or other the family had not complied with her wish but had erected a stela there in her name. But her daughters did not forget their mother's wish, and at last they were able to fulfill it. They brought the old lady's body to Abydos and interred it in a modest tomb in the "cool earth of Osiris." They erected this stela at the tomb, and ended its inscription by asking future passers-by to pray for offerings on behalf of their dead mother.

How such small human documents as this bridge the gulf of nearly 5000 years between their time and ours! And we may be sure that there are many more of such small monuments remaining still buried under the sand.

King Tety, the first ruler of the VIth dynasty, left a similar decree to that of King Nefer-ir-ka-Ra. His successor, King Pepy I, married two sisters of Djau, the Nomarch of Abydos. The latter had a stela made for these ladies, both of whom were named Mery-Ra-Ankh-Nes. This stela was found by Mariette Pasha built into the side of a well in the modern village. It is now in the Cairo Museum (No. 1413.)

Apparently Djau did well at the hands of his royal brother-in-law as he managed to accumulate the following official titles: "Real Hereditary Prince, Nomarch, Overseer of the Pyramid City, Chief Justice, Vizier, Overseer of the King's Archives, Priest of the Gods of Buto, Priest of the Gods of Nekhen, Chief Ritualist, Sempriest, Master of the Wardrobe, Wearer of the Seal". He says that he made a stela in "Abydos of Thinis, as one in honor with the Majesty of the King of Upper and Lower Egypt, Mery-Ra (Pepy I) out of love for the nome in which I was born." The inscription ends with a plea that the priests of the Temple of Osiris Khenty-Amentiu shall honor the contract made between them and Djau to the effect that the latter had made an endowment of land to the temple, but out of the income from it, the priests were to provide him with mortuary offerings after his death.

There is little doubt

that Djau and his two sisters inspired Pepy I to take an interest in their hometown. He entirely rebuilt the old temple in limestone, and judging from the fragments which remain, the sculpture was of a very high standard. He also built a limestone portal at Kom el Sultan, the battered remains of which still bear his name.

Pepy II, whose reign of ninety years is the longest in history, added to the temple and left a decree endowing offerings to the priests and to the statues of the two Queens Mery-Ra-Ankh-Nes and their brother Djau.

37996
Ivory figure of a king.
From Abydos.

Fig. 2-21. Ivory King from Kom el Sultan.

CHAPTER THREE

ABYDOS AFTER THE OLD KINGDOM

Abydos Abandoned.

The VIth dynasty ended in chaos. The royal power declined and Egypt was split up into several petty kingdoms each warring against the other. The funerary endowments of both royal and private tombs ceased and a veritable army of mortuary priests, their living gone, began to ransack the tombs that they had previously looked after. Internal security was non-existent and for this reason there is little doubt that pilgrims from distant parts of the country ceased to visit Abydos. If, as we have discussed elsewhere, the Osirion had been built during the IVth dynasty, it now became sanded up as did the plundered royal tombs of Omm el Gaab. But the worship of Osiris continued to grow in popularity, and Abydos retained its sacred reputation.

From the VIIth dynasty to the end of the Xth dynasty, the history of the country as a whole is shrouded in darkness and only here and there as through a break in the clouds, can we catch a glimpse of what was happening. One such glimpse is afforded by the instructions given by King Khati to his son, the future King Mery-Ka-Ra. It shows us Abydos caught in the throes of civil war,[1] in which King Khati, though finally victorious, seems to have suffered some great misfortune which he attributes to the violation of the tombs at Abydos during the war. He says, "Egypt fights in the necropolis by hacking up the graves. I did the same, and the same happened as was done to one who transgresses the way of God.

"Behold a misfortune happened in my time; the Thinite regions were hacked up. It really happened through what I had done, but I knew of it only after it was done. Behold my recompense came out of what I had done."

This seems to be the earliest and perhaps the original version of the "Curse of the Pharaohs" story and even today many people still believe that misfortune dogs the footsteps of those who violate the Egyptian tombs.

But whatever personal misfortune had befallen King Khati, the prosperity of Egypt was on the upswing. The petty kingdoms were again reunited under a strong line of Thebian kings some of whom bore the name of Monthu-Hotep.

....
[1]The many hundreds of bronze and copper arrowheads that are still to be found near Kom el Sultan are perhaps mementos of these battles which continued to rage for quite some time.

At the end of the XIth dynasty, Monthu-Hotep III seems to have added much to the ancient Temple of Osiris at Abydos. But unfortunately only scattered, finely sculptured blocks of limestone remain as witnesses to his activities. Some of these are fragments of a large offering list that mentions "offerings of provisions for the statue of the King of Upper and Lower Egypt, Neb-hepet-Ra (Monthu-Hotep III)."

Abydos in the Middle Kingdom.

The XIIth dynasty was one of the greatest periods in Egyptian history. A line of wise and strong rulers brought law and order and consequently prosperity to the country as a whole. Great irrigation projects and land reclamation in the Fayoum province benefited the national economy. Abydos also shared in this wave of prosperity. The Cult of Osiris had grown; more and more people were now going on pilgrimages and were in a position to record their visits there.

The kings, even though occupied with their great projects in the north including the building of a new capital to the south of Memphis, did not neglect Abydos. It is to this period that we owe the massive brick enclosure walls of Kom el Sultan that surrounded the sacred Temple of Osiris. A great part of these walls are

Fig. 3-1. The interior of the Temenos. The pool marks the site of the 1st dynasty temple. In the foreground (left) red granite blocks from a doorway of a Thotmes III temple. In the center background, a limestone gateway near the site of a later temple.

still standing (Fig. 3-1). This area must by now have been crowded with temples of which, however, only a few sculptured blocks now remain to give us a glimpse of their former beauty. Any effort to restore them, even partially, would be very worthwhile.

Because of the general prosperity of the time, more of the common folk were able to make inscribed monuments to tell us of their hopes and way of life; while the nobles and government officials inscreased their tomb inscriptions and stelae.

The pilgrimage to Abydos was now a very important feature of religious life. It always had been, but now, thanks to the general well-being and internal security, more pilgrims were able to visit the Holy City.

To the present day there is a wide path in the desert leading from Kom el Sultan to Omm el Gaab; this path was beaten hard and flat by the feet of millions of the devout who had come, often accompanied by their families and servants, to fulfill their obligation to Osiris. Standing

on this "Pilgrim's Way" it is not difficult to recapture the scene.

The desert was then (and still is now) already crowded with tombs, rectangular mud-brick rooms, their roofs vaulted on the inner side, and having a small brick pyramid on the flat outer side. In front of each tomb was a walled courtyard and beside the doorway to the chapel, a stela with a stone offering table in front of it (Fig. 3-2). These tombs were whitewashed and to modern eyes would have looked like an immense field of tents.

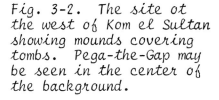

Fig. 3-2. The site ot the west of Kom el Sultan showing mounds covering tombs. Pega-the-Gap may be seen in the center of the background.

27

During all the year, and especially on religious feast days, there would have been considerable traffic here--priests coming and going, attending to their duties at the tombs; family parties visiting the graves of their beloved dead; necropolis guards sauntering along the paths between the tombs, their eyes alert for any suspicious sign of digging that would betray the work of tomb robbers.

But on the days of annual pilgrimage, which coincided with the great Feast of Osiris,[2] the necropolis became like an overcrowded city. Families which had tombs there would be encamped in the courtyards. Early-comers no doubt found accommodation in the inns of the city, and the tardy, for whom "there was no room at the inn," could camp out in the temple courts or take shelter under the massive walls of the Temenos where they would have had to share space with vendors of "souvenirs of Abydos" (scarabs, small bronze figures of Osiris, amulets, etc...).

The Osiris-Tragedy Reenacted.

. . . .
[2]The days of this feast fell on the 23rd of the month of Khiak and lasted until the 30th day. Khiak corresponds to January of the modern calendar. The old name still persists among the modern Egyptian peasantry.

Although it had probably been in existence since very early times, we now find proof and even details of the sacred Mystery Play performed here at this season. This play showed incidents in the life, death and resurrection of Osiris. In this play the part of Osiris was taken by a life-sized wooden statue of the God adorned with gold and semiprecious stones. Horus was traditionally played by the King himself although he sometimes delegated this honor to some important official. The other gods were personified by the priests and priestesses, and it was stipulated that women who played the parts of Isis and Nepthys should be virgins. The "crowd," representing the followers of Osiris and the followers of Set, were played by the pilgrims themselves who fought together with stripped palm branches. How many heads were broken and how many old scores were paid off? History does not tell us! We wish it would one day!

Each episode of the play took place on a separate day and in a special place. Some scenes, such as the murder of Osiris, took place inside the temple with only the King and the priesthood present. The sacred boat of Osiris, called Neshmet, was an important factor in this play, and sailed from Thinis to Abydos bearing the statue of Osiris and the sacred actors. We

can imagine how eagerly it was awaited, how, as it arrived at the stone quay on the great Nif-wer Canal, the hubbub of the crowd ceased. In a silence broken only by the cry of a fretful child or the hastily stilled bark of a dog, the Neshmet touched shore and the gangplank was lowered. First there descended a priest wearing a jackal-head mask and carrying a standard surmounted by a figure of a jackal. This was Wepwawat, the "Opener-of-the-Ways"! No sooner had he stepped ashore than the followers of Set crowded around and threatened to bar his way. They were attacked and driven off by the followers of Osiris. Then the "Gods" disembarked, led by the splendid, glittering King in the guise of Horus. The statue of Osiris was placed in a smaller boat of gold and carried to the temple in triumph on the shoulders of some priests while the crowd shouted themselves hoarse with joy at the God's safe arrival.

As we have said, the murder of Osiris was too sacred, too tragic and harrowing for public presentation, and the next public episode was the search for the body. This was enacted on the banks of the canal where the original incident was supposed to have occurred. The two women impersonating Isis and Nepthys, their hair unbound and their faces and robes smeared with mud, ran wailing along the banks of the waterway. Finally, they "found" the God lying on the ground, and Isis threw herself upon him weeping and lamenting. The two Goddesses then sang the heart-rending "Lament of Isis and Nepthys" which even in modern translation has the power to stir our deepest emotions and invoke our most inward sympathies. The effect on the pilgrims can be imagined. To them it was as if the ancient tragedy was taking place before their very eyes. After all, this was the same canal beside which Osiris was slain; over yonder were the same unchanged mountains to which the real Isis had raised her tear-stained face. Sometimes, even today when the wind blows across the ruins of Abydos, one can imagine that it echoes the sobs and wails of the pilgrims mourning for their murdered God.

The next public episode of the play was the funeral procession of Osiris which was headed by Wepwawat followed by the King as Horus. The statue of the God, again placed in a boat, was carried forth from the temple, along the Pilgrim's Way, to the Tomb of King Djer at Omm el Gaab which was now considered to be that of Osiris.[3] The priests

[3] It was believed that the souls of the dead who

and pilgrims followed in what must have been a very impressive and solemn procession. On the way, the followers of Set attacked the boat of the God but were driven off by Wepwawat and Horus and the followers of Osiris.

The actual resurrection of Osiris was performed inside the tomb.

The next episode was the great triumphal procession of the resurrected God, who himself, having triumphed over death, was the pledge of immortality for his followers. In this episode, the image was placed in a boat called "The Great," and splendidly bedecked, was carried on the shoulders of the priests. The inevitable battle took place, but this time the followers of Set were "slain," not merely driven off. The procession wended its way back over the Pilgrim's Way. The lamentations changed to hymns of praise and to the joyful shouts of men and the shrill, quavering festive cries of the women. Osiris entered his palace in triumph.

We owe many of the details of these events to the ancient inscriptions and especially to .... had ascended the nearby Pega-the-Gap to the Kingdom of Osiris would now return again through it to take part in this solemn occasion.

a certain Ikher-Nefert who lived during the reign of King Senusert I.[4] This man apparently the trusted favorite of the King was sent by his royal master to Abydos to renew the furnishings of the Temple of Osiris. At the same time he was authorized by the King to play the part of Horus in the sacred drama which he did with obvious enjoyment.

A Stairway Leading to the God.

King Senusert III, like all of his family, was greatly interested in Abydos and added to its temples. He built a cenotaph for himself to the southeast of Pega-the-Gap. This must have been an impressive building in its time; it was reached from the edge of the desert by a long flight of stairs. These buildings are now all covered again by the protecting sands of the desert, and all that remains of Senusert's monuments is the lower half of a seated statue of himself. This is beautifully carved from golden brown quartzite sandstone which still retains a glass-like polish.

The stelae of the private people and small officials of this period are so numerous that there

[4] From his stela found at Abydos and now in the Berlin Museum (No. 1204).

is scarcely a museum in Europe and America that does not possess at least one of them. Some of these, such as that of Sisaset,[5] give some interesting information and details of the life of the times. Sisaset says that he came to Abydos with Ikher-Nefert (whose stela gave us much information about the sacred Mystery Play) while King Senusert III was on his way to Nubia to quell an uprising there in the XIXth year of his reign. This explains why the King had allowed Ikher-Nefert to deputize for him in the sacred drama.

Nineteen years later, in the reign of Amenem-Hat III, a second stela was erected for Sisaset at Abydos,[6] "that his name may endure at the Stairway of Gods."

There are many references to this stairway on the stelae, and in the ancient religious literature, sometimes it is called the "Stairway of Osiris" or the "Stairway of the Lord of Abydos." It had its counterpart in the Other World, and the blessed dead were assured that they would receive their daily ration of "bread and beer at the Stairway of the Great God of Abydos."

So far no such stair-

[5]A stela found at Abydos and now in Geneva Museum.
[6]Now in the Louvre, Paris. Sisaset was apparently dead by this time as this is a memorial stela.

way has been discovered. It cannot be the stairway of the Cenotaph of Senusert III as it is another name for Pega-the-Gap under whose sand-slope may lie huge natural steps? All we know is that it was a very sacred place, and that offerings were made there and incense burned and the same was done at Pega-the-Gap. Incidentally, there are few places on earth where the sunset is so dramatized as in this cleft in the mountain. On any evening in January (Khiak) the place is so full of a wistfull serenity that we never fail to find ourselves watching in respectful silence the departure of another day. So if the venerated stairway really does lie under the sand-slope of Pega, it would be a very fitting place for it.

The Works of King Nefer-Hotep.

During the early part of the XIIIth dynasty, Egypt remained prosperous and the kings of that period were still active in the welfare of Abydos.

In the second year of his reign, King Nefer-Hotep wished to renew a statue of Osiris at Abydos.[7] In order to be sure that it was traditionally correct in all its details, he went to a great deal of trouble to look up

[7]From the stela of Nefer-Hotep found at Abydos and now in the Cairo Museum.

the specifications for such a statue which were housed in the archives of the Temple of Ra at Heliopolis. For it was said that in the beginning, when God created the lesser deities, he permitted each one to choose the form in which he or she desired to be known to mankind. Then Ptah, the Master Artisan, "made their statues in every kind of wood, in every kind of stone, in every kind of metal, according to their hearts' desire." These forms were not supposed to be changed although in later times they certainly were.

Having gotten the information that he wanted, King Nefer-Hotep had the statue made and entrusted it to an official to deliver. "Betake thyself southward together with troops and marines. Sleep not night or day until thou arrivest at Abydos."

Evidently the statue was intended for use in the sacred drama because as soon as he heard of its safe arrival, Nefer-Hotep himself went to Abydos and took part in the play.

Another stela of Nefer-Hotep, dated to his fourth year[8] and also found at Abydos, seems to have been the southern one of the four boundary stelae. The inscription on it is very curious. It decrees

[8]Also now in the Cairo Museum.

that the southern end of the necropolis of Abydos shall be held sacred to Wepwawat, and no person was to set foot on it. "As for him whom anyone shall find within there, whether a craftsman or a priest at his business, he shall be branded. As for any official who shall have a tomb made for himself within this cemetery, he shall be reported, and the law shall be executed against him and upon the necropolis guards. [9]

"Now as for any addition to this cemetery, in the place where the people make tombs for themselves, there shall they be buried."

The only place in the southern end of the necropolis (which at that time seems not to have extended more than half a kilometer --0.3 mile-- to the southeast of Omm el Gaab), which

was apparently unoccupied is a spot lying immediately to the west of the later Temple of Sety I, in which we now know that the Osirion exists. Is this an indication that although the latter building was completely hidden under the sand, there was some tradition concerning its whereabouts, and the place was therefore considered to be especially sacred? This is one more of the problems that are always cropping up to give headaches to the archeologists!

King Khendjer, also of the XIIIth dynasty, sent an official named Ameni-Seneb to Abydos in order to "cleanse" (redecorate) the Temple of Osiris that had been built by Senusert I two hundred years previously.[10] Ameni-Seneb was ordered, "Behold, it is commanded that thou shalt cleanse the Temple of Abydos. Artificers shall be given to thee for the contract together

with the lay-priesthoods of the district of the storehouse of offerings."[11]

Ameni-Seneb says that he carried out the royal commands and also had painters retouch the colored scenes "restoring that which the Majesty of the King of Upper and Lower Egypt, Kha-Kheper-Ra (Senusert I) the Justified had made."

A second stela of Ameni-Seneb records King Khendjer's satisfaction with the way in which the job had been done.

....
[9] Evidently those who had not prevented him from building.

[10] From the stela of Ameni-Seneb found at Abydos and now in the Louvre, Paris (No. C.77) A second stela of the same man was found nearby. This is also in the Louvre (No. C.12).

[11] Apparently priests were expected to tuck up their robes and work as assistants to the master craftsmen.

CHAPTER FOUR

ABYDOS AFTER EGYPT'S FIRST LIBERATION WAR

Abydos Weathers the Storm.

At the end of the XIIIth dynasty darkness descended again on Egyptian history and a little later, through the shadows, we catch glimpses of the first great humiliation. Egypt lay under the domination of Asiatic invaders called the Hyksos whom later the great Queen Hatshepsut referred to as "the barbarians who ruled from Avaris in ignorance of Ra." From scattered local references, and the later account of the Jewish historian Josephus, it seems that these people had infiltrated into the Eastern Delta of Egypt during the XIVth dynasty, and finding a period of weak government, seized the royal power as Josephus says, "without a battle."

The Hyksos founded a new capital at Avaris in the Delta; in reality their power did not extend to the whole of Upper Egypt. Descendants of the old royal house continued to rule from Thebes, and their northern boundary lay somewhere between Abydos and Akhmim.

The Hyksos held Lower and Middle Egypt for about one hundred fifty years, and though, no doubt, pilgrims to Abydos from the northern towns were fewer than in previous times, the place continued

Fig. 4-1. Ahmes I as Osiris (from Kom el Sultan).

of great religious importance thanks to the courage and energy of the Thebian kings.

In the XVIIth dynasty, the struggle between the royal house of Thebes and the Hyksos drew to a close. King Ahmes I (Fig. 4-1) finally invaded Lower Egypt, attacking the Hyksos stronghold at Avaris and drove them out of Egypt thus putting an end to a sad episode of humiliation. The Hyksos disappeared and their history remains a mystery.

King Ahmes I Plays a Trick on Posterity.

While still only King of Upper Egypt, Ahmes I had made for himself a splendid rock-cut tomb at Abydos. Its entrance lay close to the mountain nearly opposite to the modern village of Ghabat. Naturally, a rock-cut tomb of any size meant a great accumulation of debris thrown out from its excavation. Left at the site, these heaps of debris would betray the presence and position of a burial, so the wily Ahmes had it all carried away to the edge of the desert, piled up into a great heap and cased with limestone thus transforming it into an excellent imitation pyramid. As Ahmes expected, tomb robbers past and present, as well as modern archaeologists, have thoroughly tunneled into and under the supposed pyramid, expending time and energy in a frantic search for the "royal treasure" which existed only in their imaginations! The heap, from which the casing has now nearly all disappeared, is known locally as Kom Sheik Mohammed.

As it happened, Ahmes was never buried in his tomb at Abydos. He must have been buried at Western Thebes as his mummy was among those of the other kings and queens found in a pit at Deir el Bahari where they had been hidden for safekeeping during the XXIst dynasty.

Ahmes also built a terraced temple against the mountain near his tomb and another Temple of Osiris at Kom el Sultan. The few remaining blocks from the latter show some beautiful low relief work including a portrait head of his mummy which is now in the Cairo Museum.

He has a rather broad, square face with a distinctly humorous twist to the mouth quite in keeping with the character of the man who played such a good joke on the would-be tomb robbers. Besides his indisputable courage, Ahmes must have possessed that fantastic Egyptian sense of humor with a certain predilection for harmless practical jokes that would be accepted with good grace.

Another monument built by Ahmes at Abydos was a small shrine in honor of his grandmother, Queen Teti Sheri, in which he dedicated a limestone stela. The lady was the widow of King Seken-en-Ra who was killed in the liberation battle against the Hyksos. A statue of her in the British Museum, London, shows us a dainty, pretty little lady, (Fig. 4-2) but she must have had a strong, though lovable, character for she made a great impression on her contemporaries, and many private people erected stelae in her honor.

Ahmes was clearly devoted to his old Granny and the warmth of human love shines through the formal phrases of the inscription on his stela. The inscription begins by describing how one day King Ahmes and his wife Queen Ahmes-Nefertari were seated together in the palace talking of the duties of the living towards the dead when the Queen suddenly asked, "Why have these things been recalled? For what reason have these matters been related? What thought has come into thy heart?" And the King said to her, "I, even I, have thought about the mother of my mother and the mother of my father the great wife of the King, Teti Sheri, the Justified (following the Egyptian custom, the parents of Ahmes were brother and sister). She already has a chapel and a tomb upon the soil of the Thebian and Thinite nomes.[1] But I say unto thee that I have decided to make for her another pyramid[2] and chapel in the Sacred Land as a memorial presented by my Majesty. Its lake being dug, its trees planted and its offerings being instituted, equipped with personnel, furnished with land, endowed with cattle, mortuary priests and ritualists engaged in their duties, every man knowing his in-

....
[1]Apparently she had a tomb at Thebes and another, or perhaps a cenotaph, at Abydos.
[2]As we have seen, the tombs at Abydos were surmounted by a small pyramid.
[3]The King intended to endow this monument as though it were a real tomb.

Fig. 4-2. Queen Teti Sheri. A limestone statuette now in the British Museum, London (photo by kindness of the Egyptian Department of the British Museum).

structions.3

"Even as His Majesty spoke these words, these buildings were being carried out with good speed. His Majesty did this because he loved her (Teti Sheri) beyond anything. Never had the kings who were before done the like for their mothers.

"Then did His Majesty thrust forth his arm, and bend his head[4] and make for her a royal offering

....

[4] The ceremonial posture when presenting offerings.

and an offering of Geb and the two enneads (of gods) ...for Queen Teti Sheri."

Queen Teti Sheri was still living during the first years of the reign of her grandson, and we can imagine her surrounded by a group of her great grandchildren all clamoring for tales of the stirring times of her youth and the heroic deeds of her husband King Seken-en-Ra. The picture of "Granny" telling bedtime stories with loving affection to grandchildren, is one that is very near to the heart of every Egyptian.

Ahmes also built a whole new quarter of the city of Abydos in the neighborhood of his tomb. This was to house the workers on his building projects. It was partly excavated by Petrie and showed large villas for the architects and small but neat and well planned houses for the workmen. These houses were occupied until about the middle of the XVIIIth dynasty when, for some unknown reason, the quarter was deserted.

The Oracle of Ahmes I.

Ahmes certainly made a great impression on the people of Abydos; and long after his death he was worshiped there as a demigod and the source of an oracle. A stela from the XIXth dynasty dated to the fourteenth year of the reign of Ramesses II tells how the deceased Ahmes settled a dispute about the ownership of some land.

As we have already seen, it was the custom on religious feast days to place the statues of the gods in model boats and carry them in procession around the city on the shoulders of special priests. Anyone of the population

had the right on these occasions to stop the boat and ask any serious question of the God. The question being phrased to make possible a "yes" or "no" answer.

It so happened that two priests had been disputing over the ownership of some land, and when the feast of the deified Ahmes came round, one of them named Paser stopped the boat and cried, "'As for the field, it belongs to Pai, the son of Sedjem-en-ef and the children of Hayu?' And the God remained still. 'It belongs to the priest Paser, the son of Mes?' Then the God nodded very much in the presence of the priest Pa-iry, the Priest of the Front Yanzab, the Priest of the Front Taya-nefer, the Priest of the Rear Nakht and the Priest of the Rear Thotmes.

"The priest of Ahmes, Pa-iry, called for a scribe to write down the judgement on papyrus thus giving the ownership of the land to Paser. Pa-iry himself signed the document and the four priests who carried the boat (two in the front and two in the rear) also signed as witnesses. God only knows what kind of trick these four priests played to confirm the ownership of this piece of land to their colleague Paser!"

In gratitude, Paser had a small but finely carved stela dedicated to Ahmes I. At the top is a scene showing the actual incident taking place; and below, the inscription

telling the story from which we have just quoted (this stela is now in the Cairo Museum No. 6313).

The Foundation of the Empire.

When Ahmes I drove the Hyksos out of Egypt, they settled down somewhere in Palestine. According to Josephus they settled in Judea and built the city of Jerusalem. However, we can credit that statement with a grain of salt as Josephus was trying very hard to equate the Hyksos with the children of Israel. In reality they must have settled much nearer to the borders of Sinai as Ahmes' son Amon-Hotep I of the XVIIIth dynasty considered their presence a menace, and partly for this reason, and partly for revenge, attacked and utterly defeated them. From that time the Hyksos as a people were wiped off the face of the earth and ceased to exist. Up to now, we have no true idea of the mystery whence these people originally came, what they looked like, or anything about them except that they introduced the horse and chariot into Egypt.

The heady wine of victory set Egypt onto the path of Empire, and the normally peaceful Egyptian farmers became for a period, bold, invincible warriors. What with the spoils of war and the exacted tribute of conquered foreign lands pouring into the treasury, the first half of the XVIIIth dynasty became a time of unparalleled wealth and splendor.

Being the chief God of Thebes and of the royal house, naturally Amon-Ra came in for the lion's share of this new prosperity. But the other gods, and of course Osiris and his Holy City, also prospered exceedingly.

In addition to his military enterprises, Amon-Hotep I went on a great building spree restoring and rebuilding the northern monuments and towns that had been destroyed or neglected during the Hyksos Period. For these projects he employed hundreds of Semitic captives whose principal job was the making of mud-bricks. This sounds suspiciously like the Biblical story of the children of Israel in Egypt; for at this time of great construction, Semitic labor was cheap and they were expert brick makers. Moreover, it is not unlikely that Joseph the Semite might have found favor with one of the last of the Hyksos kings (for at that time he certainly would not have been popular with an Egyptian pharaoh) and with his official Potiphar whose notorious wife had that famous incident with Joseph (see Genesis 39).

Amon-Hotep I added a hall to the Temple of Osiris at Abydos. It measured about 12.0 by 16.0 meters (39 X 52 feet), the roof was supported by six columns and three chapels opened out of its Hypostyle Hall. It was

adorned with fine colored bas-reliefs, and among them was a scene showing Amon-Hotep honoring his deceased father Ahmes the Hero.

Thotmes I, the son of Amon-Hotep I, does not seem to have built at Abydos; but he furnished the existing temples there with golden offering tables, statues, incense burners, dishes and other cult objects. He also made a new, large Neshmet boat of cedar wood from Lebanon and electrum. We know all this from a stela on which he recorded his deeds.[5] The inscription ends with the King's address to the priest. After he had enumerated all that he had done for the temples of Abydos, he says, "This is no lie before you, there is no exaggeration therein. I have made monuments for the gods; I have beautified their sanctuaries for the future; I have maintained their temples; I have restored that which was ruined; I have surpassed that which was done before. I have made the boundaries of Egypt as far as that which the sun encircles. I have made strong those who were in fear; I have expelled all evil from them; I made Egypt the superior of every land."

Thotmes III, usually named the Egyptian Napoleon, seems to have made a great enlargement to the temple of his great grandfather

....
[5]Found at Abydos, and now in the Cairo Museum No. 34007.

Amon-Hotep I, but it is now too ruined to show more than part of the plan of its foundations. However, some large fragments of its red granite doorway still stand in the great enclosure of Kom el Sultan, and slabs of finely carved limestone, including the lintel of a doorway, show the high standard of craftsmanship employed. A few fragments of a large offering list show that Thotmes III had endowed the temple with lands, serfs, equipment and vast quantities of daily food and drink offerings.

The Heb-sed Jubilee; A Very Old Festival.

A block bearing the name of Amon-Hotep II the son of Thotmes III, and mentioning his Heb-sed Jubilee, was also found at Kom el Sultan, but the monument to which it belonged has completely disappeared.

The Heb-sed Jubilee was a very important event in a king's reign. In very primitive times, if a king had reigned for thirty years he was supposed to make this Jubilee. The most vital ceremony demanded that the ruler should run at full speed around a fixed course. If he had grown old and feeble and was unable to make this ritual sprint, he was promptly killed and a young and active man put in his place! This was not only because a young and vigorous ruler was necessary to repel his country's enemies, but was also due to a belief that by means of sympathetic magic, the vigor of the ruler was transmitted to the country as a whole; people, cattle and crops thrived better under a strong and healthy king. Of course in dynastic times this possible ritual murder, becoming hateful to the Egyptians who naturally detested bloodshed, was transformed into a magical ceremony designed to restore the aged ruler's powers. He still had to run the course but he could now take his time over it; and no doubt many an old but popular king tottered up breathlessly to the "winning post" to the wild cheers of his loving subjects (probably also to the whispered jesting remarks of some of them).

The stela of a certain Pe-aake, also found at Abydos, tells how Thotmes IV gave many different kinds of cattle and poultry to Osiris, Lord of Abydos, as well as 1200 stat[6] of land. This king also made a similar endowment for the "Good God" Neb-pehti-Ra (Ahmes I) who, as we have already seen, was worshiped locally as a demi-god.

Amon-Hotep III, usually called "The Magnificent", must have built at least a chapel at Abydos as foundation deposits bearing his name were found at Kom el Sultan. Such deposits usually consisted of small model tools, samples of materials used such as: stone, metal, faience, etc., bearing the King's name. They were placed in small shallow pits under each of the four corners of a temple or chapel, and were supposed by magical means to keep the building in repair.

A statue of Pa-en-In-hert, one of the officials of Amon-Hotep III, (and also found at Abydos) shows him holding the government surveying cord used for measuring the ground for temples. This suggests that he may have been engaged on some building project for this king.[7]

The only real proof we have of any activity in Abydos by the heretical King Akhen-Aton is the removal of the element "Amon" wherever it occurred in the names of his ancestors! A few small limestone blocks bearing parts of scenes sculptured in the "Amarna style" were recently found by the Pennsylvania-Yale Expedition in its excavations to the west of Kom el Sultan. But these blocks seem to have been brought there from other places and reused as building material.

....
[6]One stat equals 2735 square meters or two-thirds of an acre.
[7]Cairo Museum, No. 6135.

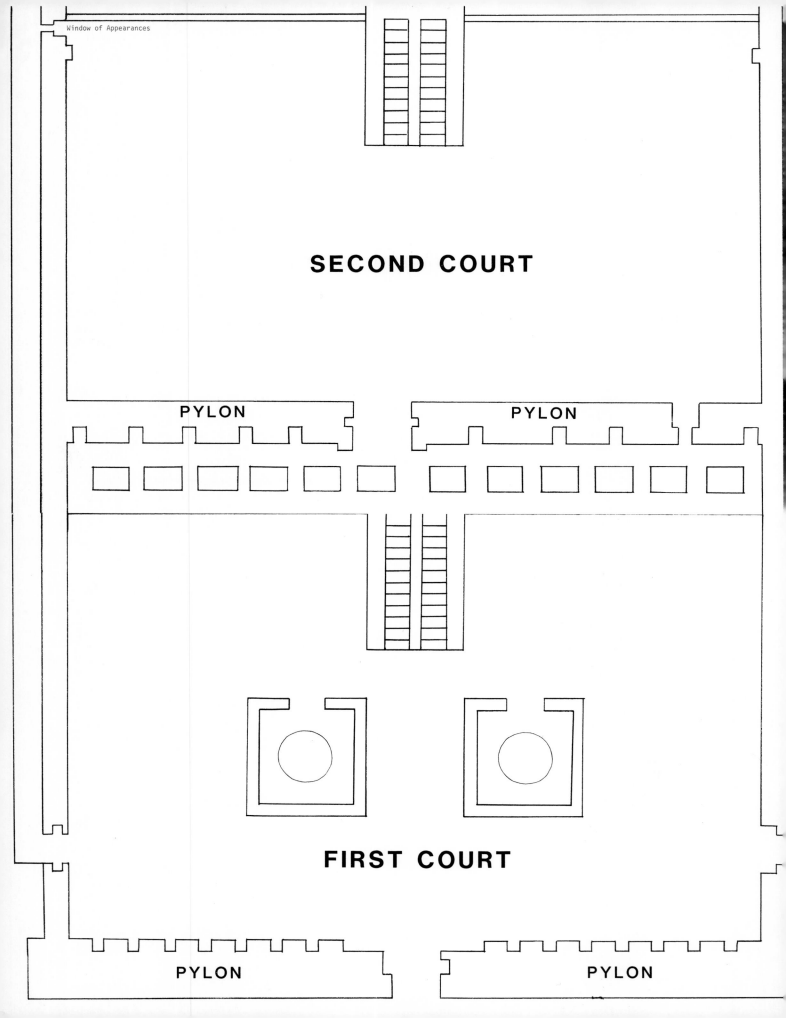

Window of Appearances

SECOND COURT

PYLON   PYLON

FIRST COURT

PYLON   PYLON

AKH

GLORY

PART II

AKH = THE GLORY

CHAPTER FIVE

SETY I. A GREAT KING AND
A TRAGIC LIFE

The Glory of Abydos.

Up to now, the story
of Abydos seems to be
practically the story of
Egypt since the early
days of prehistory. We
have also seen that the
XIIth and XVIIIth dynas-
ties more than any other
period had enriched
Abydos with monuments.
But it was a king of
the XIXth dynasty who
was destined to add a
temple so beautiful in
form and decoration as
to cause the name of
Abydos to ring in the
ears of the ancient and
modern worlds. Travelers
and pilgrims from ancient
Greece and Rome flocked
to Abydos to marvel at
this temple. Pilgrims
from the whole civilized
world now make the long
journey by sea or air
to gaze in wonder and
admiration at this shrine
of incarnate beauty.

Some of the early
tourists, especially those
coming from Greece, left
a few lines scribbled on
the walls of the temple,
and there is also a very
roughly painted "Star of
David" in red ochre. But
this was probably done
in early Christian times
when this symbol was used
to keep evil spirits at
bay. There is no evidence
that there was ever a

Jewish community in Abydos.
Furthermore, there is a
possibility that the
"Star of David" was not
originally a Jewish crea-
tion but was only an
emblem of their short-
lived kingdom borrowed
from some earlier civili-
zation, perhaps from the
Sabaeans who venerated the
starry "Hosts of Heaven"
and who had a community
in Egypt.

The Builder of the Temple.

And what of the builder
of this temple, whose dream
of beauty was made reality
in stone, and whose work
bequeathed to the modern
world a heritage of unsur-
passed relief sculpture?
The man was Sety, the army
officer who became Pharaoh
and ruled Egypt from about
1313 to 1292 B.C. and proved
himself to be one of the
greatest, wisest and noblest
rulers that the country has
ever known.

Sety was not of pure
royal blood; he came
from a military family
which had lived for about
four hundred years in the
Sethorite nome in Egypt's
eastern Delta.[1] His
personal history is closely
linked with that of his

---

[1]At that time, in that part
of the country, Osiris'
evil enemy Set was worshiped
as a War God. Sety's fam-
ily followed this cult;
many bore the name of Sety
which means "Set's Man."
In his youth, King Sety
had once been a priest of
Set, yet his real reli-
gious devotion was to
Osiris.

period.

The kings of the late
XVIIIth dynasty, Akhen-Aton,
Semenkh-ka-Ra, Tut-ankh-
Amon and Ay, were rulers
who were not interested
in the Empire or conquest,
and they had ruined the
internal economy of the
country and had let Egypt's
great Empire slip through
their feeble hands. But
there was one strong man
in the land; this was
the General of the army,
Hor-em-heb, who came
from a good provincial
family from Middle Egypt.
Apparently Hor-em-heb made
a military coup in (or at
the end of) the brief reign
of King Ay, proclaimed
himself King of Upper and
Lower Egypt and founded
the XIXth dynasty.[2] As
there are no records of a
civil war or internal un-
rest, Egypt must have
accepted the new Pharaoh
without opposition. He
was just the right man
appearing at the right
moment.

To legalize his posi-
tion, Hor-em-heb married
a lady of the old royal
family[3] named Nedjem-Mut

---

[2]Hor-em-heb left at least
two monuments at Abydos.
These were statue groups
representing him seated
with the Holy Family
of Abydos: Osiris, Isis,
and Horus. One group
is of limestone and the
other of granite. Both
are now in the Cairo Museum,
Nos. 6018, 6019.

[3]In ancient Egypt the royal
blood was transmitted in
the female line so any man
who married the royal heiress was entitled to rule.

who was apparently the same Nedjem-Mut shown in scenes of the royal family in the tombs of Tel Amarna. If so, she was the sister of the famous Queen Nefertiti and must have been well past middle-age at the time of her marriage. Hor-em-heb was also an elderly man at this time, so as we may expect, the union was childless and Hor-em-heb appointed a fellow officer named Ramesses, who was also his vizier to succeed him.

This Ramesses was already married to a very beautiful lady named Sat-Ra, who was perhaps a sister of Akhen-Aton; by her he had a son named Sety who was also in the army.[4]

At the death of Hor-em-heb, Ramesses ascended the throne as Ramesses I and appointed Sety to be his vizier. At that time, Sety was commander-in-chief of a garrison on Egypt's eastern frontier at a place now called El Kantara, on the Suez Canal, and was apparently fully satisfied with his military life. Ramesses I was already an old man when he ascended the throne, so when a rebellion against Egypt broke out in Nubia, it was Sety who went south

....
[4] We can glean some detail of Sety's family history from the so called "Stela of Four Hundred Years" found in Tanis (San el Hagar) and now in the Cairo Museum, No. 6204.

at the head of the army to successfully crush the revolt.

After less than three years of reign, the aged Ramesses I died and Sety stepped into his place. He married a lady named Tuy, whose father was an officer in the Chariot Corps, and whose mother was a singer in some temple of Isis. As Sety's accession was unopposed, either Tuy or his mother Sat-Ra (or both of them) must have had some of the sacred royal blood in their veins. Tuy is never mentioned on her husband's monuments, and apparently there was no love lost between them. All that we know about her comes from the monuments of her famous son Ramesses II.

In his youth, Sety had married a non-royal woman who died before he became King. After his accession, Sety had her tomb opened and her title "Mistress of the House" hammered out on her stone sarcophagus[5] and replaced by, "King's Wife" so that the housewife in this world became a queen in the next. This kindly thoughtfulness is characteristic of the man.

A Family Tragedy.

By the wife of his youth, Sety had a son who was old enough to accom-

....
[5] "Mistress of the House" is the exact equivalent of the Arabic "Sit el Beit," and used up until now among middle class Egyptians as a title for married women.

pany him into battle in the early part of his reign. However, this boy having a non-royal mother was not entitled to succeed to the throne, and Sety instead, made the young Prince Ramesses his co-regent.

Now we can sense a tragedy in Sety's personal and public life. His elder son apparently committed some great crime; perhaps he plotted against the lives of his father and little brother; probably we shall never know what he did. But whatever it was, it was punishable by death and disgrace in this world and the next. His body was found at the bottom of a deep pit at Medinet el Gurob, in the Fayoum region. It lay in a fine stone sarcophagus from which the inscriptions had all been hammered out. But when photographed by infra-red light, the words "King's son of Men-Maat-Ra (Sety's prenomen), Pa-Ramessu" could be seen. The body was that of a young man with a slightly deformed back. It had never been mummified and was wrapped in a sheepskin; a disgrace accorded only to the worst type of criminal. Some forensic doctors have suggested that the man may have been buried alive. The figures and name of Pa-Ramessu were hammered out of all of Sety's battle reliefs at Karnak, and in some cases were replaced by those of young Ramesses.

We have little doubt that this early tragedy in

the reign of Sety must have left its mark on such a wonderful and sensitive man. We can compare this tragedy with that of King David and his rebellious son Absalom who also was killed. The cry of the bereaved father David echoes painfully from the Bible, "O my son, Absalom, my son, my son Absalom! Would God I had died for thee, O Absalom, my son!"[6] Maybe Sety also suffered the same heart-rending pain.

A New Policy for a Dynastic State.

When he became King, Sety chose as one of his official names, Wehem-musut, which means, "Repeating Births" or in other words "Renaissance"; and this name was a proclamation of his policy. For Sety had inherited a kingdom riddled with corruption despite the unceasing efforts of Hor-em-heb to clean up the government departments. Egypt's Asiatic Empire had vanished, her frontiers were threatened and even her age-old claim on the Sinai Peninsula was disputed by roving bands of armed nomads.

Sety's policy of Renaissance aimed at the full restoration of internal law and order, regaining the lost Empire and stamping out all memory of the unorthodox "Heresy Period" that had preceded Hor-em-heb's coup. In these aims he

6 . . . .
[6]II Samuel 18:33.

was largely successful although he did not extend his frontiers of empire to the same great extent as Thotmes III had done. He had the power to gain enough territory of the Middle East but was sufficiently far-sighted to know that he should not have held it and too humane to indulge in needless bloodshed to gain nothing but pomp and vain glory while internal reform was of more necessity.

An inscription at Karnak Temple tells us that a report reached Sety that the Habiru, whom many historians identify with the Hebrews, had taken to "cursing and quarreling, each man slaying his neighbor. They have disregarded the laws of the palace and have pulled out their tongues at Thy Majesty." Sety's answer to this was to send a division of the army to teach them better manners, which was done so effectively that the Habiru learned to keep their tongues in their mouths, and they do not reappear in history for nearly two hundred years!

Thus most of the first half of Sety's twenty-one years of reign was occupied in settling the unrest in the Middle East. Only then did he feel free to embark on his great building schemes. His monuments are numerous and all are characterized by good taste and careful workmanship. They extend

from the east of Jordan to Sesebi in Nubia. To him we owe the completion of the building of the great hypostyle hall at Karnak (begun by Hor-em-heb), the Temple of Gourna and additions to many existing temples. But his greatest artistic triumph into which he had put his whole heart, soul and energy is his beautiful temple at Abydos. The whole building stands as a witness to his reverence for the gods and his love of sheer beauty. Moreover, he apparently inspired his workmen with his own passion, for every figure, every hieroglyph seems to have been created in reverence and love. Their beauty is unique, sublime.

Sety also restored many ancient, ruined monuments and organized a veritable army of gifted sculptors to recut the names of Amon and the other gods which had been hammered out wherever they occurred by the fanatical King Akhen-Aton. It is characteristic of Sety that in all these restorations he never attempted to claim an older monument as his own but merely added modestly, and almost timidly, small hieroglyphs that it had been restored by his orders.

Sety and the Gold Mines.

To meet the cost of these projects without endangering the ecomony of the country, Sety

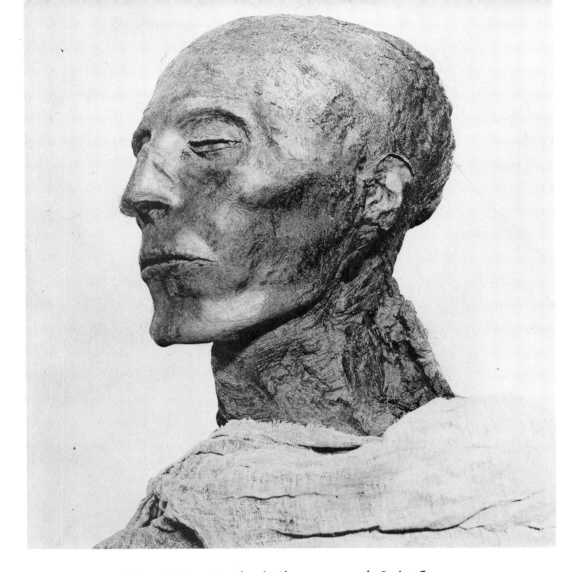

Fig. 5-1. Head of the mummy of Sety I.

reorganized the working of the gold mines in Egypt's eastern deserts. It is to these mining projects that we owe the existence of the earliest known map; it was drawn on papyrus and shows the location of some of the mines, water supplies and desert tracks, the latter being represented by a band of human footprints.

In the ninth year of his reign a report reached the King that a certain mine, which was worked by convict labor and lay about fifty kilometers (30 miles) to the east of Edfu, was not producing its proper quota of gold, and that workers were dying of thirst and hardship. As we might expect, Sety insisted on going personally to investigate the complaints in spite of the protests of the Governor of the district who warned him of the dangers and discomforts of the journey. Apparently the Governor had not exaggerated, for the King exclaims, "How evil is the way which is without water![7] The traveler whose mouth is parched; how shall his throat be cooled, how shall he quench his thirst?"

The King had a well dug at the mining station to insure a plentiful supply of water, and made various humane provisions for the welfare of the convict laborers and free officials. It is remarkable that in those days a king should inconvenience himself for the welfare of felons. The usual attitude

....
[7]Inscription in the rock-cut Temple of Hedesieh. For a full translation see: Breasted, "Ancient Records of Egypt" Vol. III. 81 ff.

of ancient rulers in such cases was, "So what? If they die, there are plenty more to replace them." But not Sety.

Having provided for their bodily needs, he then had a rock-cut temple made for their spiritual welfare. Then having gotten the project working successfully, Sety dedicated the entire output of gold from these mines to his Temple of Abydos and begged the gods to protect his endowment "for the things which you desire, may you speak to those who are still to come, whether kings or princes or common folk that they establish for me my work in this place on behalf of my beautiful temple in Abydos made by the oracle of the God, the Existent One, that they may not subvert my plan. Say you that it (the temple) was done by your oracle for you are the Lords. I have spent my life and my might for you to attain my acceptability from you. Grant that my monuments may endure for me, and my name abide upon them."

Following that beautiful plea to the gods, Sety makes definite rules concerning the working of the mines, the treatment of the workers and the conveyance of the gold to his temple at Abydos. The inscription terminates in a terrible curse on any future king or official who should divert the gold

to any other use. "Osiris shall pursue him, Isis shall pursue his wife, Horus shall pursue his children...and they shall execute their judgement with him."

At Nauri, in Nubia, Sety had a great stela cut in the cliff overlooking the river. On it was inscribed a decree stating that all the revenue from the customs duty on goods entering Egyptian territory from the south should be paid to the temple at Abydos.

He also orders that if any priest or employee of the temple complains of an injustice, the complaint must be promptly investigated and redress given to the plaintiff. If the proper official fails in this duty to protect the oppressed employee, "Osiris will be after him, after his wife, after his children to wipe out his name, to destroy his soul and prevent his corpse from resting in the necropolis."

Sety also built for himself a small palace at Abydos which he named "Heart's Ease in Abydos." A name clearly expressing his love for this place. Here he used to come unannounced, from time to time, to personally supervise the work on the temple. This palace has not yet been discovered, but it probably lies under the high mound of sand and debris to the north of the temple. A small flake of limestone was found

near the temple on which was written a list of food and drink ordered for one of these royal visits. Beer was not a minor item on this ancient "grocery list"!

The Tomb of Sety is one of the largest and certainly the most beautiful in the "Valley of Kings" near Luxor. The well-known family of Abdel Rassoul have a tradition that the funerary treasures of Sety are still in this tomb. An exciting attempt to locate this supposed treasure chamber was made by Sheik Abdel Rassoul but was stopped prematurely because of the fragile nature of the rock on which the men were working.

The perfectly preserved mummy of Sety is now in the Cairo Museum and proves that the beautiful faces of his reliefs at Abydos are indeed true portraits of him (Fig. 5-1).

It is a moving experience to gaze upon the mummified but still handsome features of this great man so regal in the calm majesty of death. This man who was a brave warrior, a wise statesman, a pious worshiper of the gods, and was above everything else a merciful Lord and protector of the common folk (even to the wretched felons condemned to a life sentence of hard labor). In many ways he represented all of the magnificent magnanimity that the word "pharaoh" can convey.

CHAPTER SIX

THE TEMPLE OF SETY I
DESCRIPTION OF ITS OUTSIDE

The Exterior.

Before attempting a description of the Temple of Sety I, it must be pointed out that there are some unique features (apart from the exquisite perfection of its sculpture) which set it apart from any other Egyptian temple.

First of all, the plan of the building is not the customary rectangle but is shaped like a capital letter "L" (see page 9). But this does not seem to have been premeditated. The width of the short arm of the "L" is exactly the width of the main part. Moreover, the chambers in it should normally be at the extreme western end of the building behind what is now called the "Osiris Complex." Furthermore, the thickness of the wall dividing the Chapel of Sety, and the chapels of the Statue Hall from the Hall of Soker and its chapels is the same as that of the outer southern wall of the two hypostyle halls and the two courts. In other words, that was the original southern exterior wall of the building; and all of the rooms to the south of it are additions.

The reason for this change of plan is, as we have seen, the rediscovery of the Osirion. Had the temple been continued westward, as it should

have been, it would have covered the roof of the older building. This was something the architect wanted to avoid at all costs. The Osirion was by no means just one of those old temples to be built upon!

The second unique feature is the Seven Vaulted Chapels arranged in a row at the western end of the Second Hypostyle Hall (see pages 9 and 50). Normally an Egyptian temple of the New Kingdom has a main sanctuary for the god to whom the building is dedicated and two subsidiary chapels, one for the wife and one for the son of the principal god.

Here the three chapels to the north are for the Holy Family of Abydos: Osiris, Isis and Horus. The central chapel is for Amon-Ra of Thebes.[1] Next comes Ra-Hor-akhty of Heliopolis, followed by Ptah of Memphis. Thus these latter chapels are dedicated to the chief gods of the three most important cities in ancient Egypt. The last chapel to the south was for Sety's own memory.

There are two posible reasons for these extra chapels. One is that Abydos, being a place of pilgrimage, received priests and pilgrims coming from those cities

....
[1]Amon-Ra is given this prominent place as being the King of the Gods although the temple really belongs to Osiris.

who would find their own local deities held in honor here. But it may also mean that the great gods themselves were coming as pilgrims to the Holy City of Osiris.

The third unique point is that in normal temples of this period, the roofs of the various halls become lower as one penetrates further into the building. This temple, being built on rising ground, has the same effect but obtained by a reverse process. Instead of the roof being lowered, the ground is gradually raised, and it is not until we reach the extreme western end of the building that the actual roof is lowered.

This arrangement, entailing the leveling and banking of the different planes, must have meant an enormous amount of hard work before a foundation block was ever set in place. As there were plenty of level sites in Abydos, it bears out the statement made by Sety that the temple was built in accordance with the demands of a divine oracle. This may also explain why Sety abandoned the traditional temple site at Kom el Sultan (which must have been very overcrowded by this time). So far as we know, this was the first temple to be built outside the great Temenos of Osiris.

The Approach to the Temple.

During the XIXth dynasty, pilgrims journeying to Abydos on the river would have left the Nile at a town called Per Djada (nowadays Abu Shusha) and sailed northwest on the Nif-wer Canal which connects the temple to the Nile. Their first glimpse of the Temple of Sety would have been the south-eastern angle of the great bastioned Temenos Wall looming over the flat roofs of the surrounding houses. Their boat would have put in at the quay, built of huge blocks of red granite, opposite to the eastern side of the Temenos Wall.

A wide open space lay between the canal and the temple; from its western side a broad, double stair-way of limestone ascended to a terrace of the same material. The present-day staircase, of limestone, is a modern restoration built of the foundation of its ancient predecessor and having the same form.

The front wall of the terrace was adorned with some very lively battle scenes relating to the wars of Ramesses II.[2] Here we are shown the invincible Pharaoh in the heat of battle; enemies falling dead and dying beneath the hooves of his spirited chariot horses.

A delightfully human touch is a group of soldiers

. . . .

[2]The entire building of the temple is the work of Sety I. But as he died before all the decoration was completed, the First Hypostyle Hall and most of the exterior owes its sculpture to Ramesses II.

led by their standard-bearer. These are real "other ranks," the "GI's" of their day with no attempt made to idealize them. They are swinging along in fine style, their chins up, their mouths open. Are they shouting the praises of their bold young pharaoh or are they singing the bawdy songs with which soldiers, ancient and modern, love to while away their marches?

Scrutinizing these faces, one gets the immedi-ate impression of the present day, good natured Upper Egyptian peasants singing a folk song in a wedding feast or on their way back from the "Souk" or "market day" after a fruitful, eventful morning.

Immediately to the west of the terrace, which also serves to keep its foundations from slipping, stands the towering First Pylon built of limestone and hard brown quartzite sandstone. Its twin towers bear scenes of the victori-ous pharaoh "slaying" his enemies in the presence of the gods. Two tall masts, cut from the famous cedars of Lebanon, stand in grooves in the face of each tower. From the top of the masts, brightly colored pennants stream out in the wind.

The great Central Gateway is closed by a massive door. It is also of cedar wood and covered with sheet copper and flanked by colossal statues of Sety. That is how the pilgrims saw it. Today the proud pylon is in

ruins, but its massive, scattered blocks show us its former glory and the beauty of its sculpture. Of the colossi of Sety there remain only the limestone foundations of their bases and a statement made by Ramesses that he had them set up in their places. This statement occurs in his great in-scription on the facade of the temple.

The Audience Hall and the Storerooms.

To the south of the pylon a small doorway of limestone pierces the mighty Temenos Wall. In-side was a small lodge where a priestly doorkeeper kept an eye on all comings and goings. The back door of the lodge opened into a passage running westward, and if visitors intended to enter the temple court, they passed through another small doorway in its northern wall (see page 38). The passage continued westward; opposite to the Second Pylon, a splendid monumental gate-way sculptured in relief opened southwards into an imposing colonnaded hall. The walls of this hall were made of mud-brick, faced with mud-plaster but painted with geometrical designs and bands of in-scriptions in bright colors. Against the southern wall was a limestone platform approached by three low steps of the same material. Here, on the days of the royal visits, the King sat enthroned in splendor to give audience to the

people, great and humble alike. The center of the hall was open to the sky; a limestone colonnade surrounded all the walls and was supported on polyangled columns of limestone inscribed with the names of Sety and those of the gods by whom he was beloved (Fig. 6-1).

This hall may also have functioned as the "House of the Morning," the royal robing room. Here the King, assisted by the Sem-priest, would change into the various ceremonial costumes required of him when, as honorary High Priest of every god, he took part in the temple services.

From this hall, four sculptured limestone doorways opened into storerooms, two on the western and two on the eastern sides. These were long, vaulted tunnels of mud-brick with

Fig. 6-1. The Audience Hall showing the place of the throne (center). Polyangled columns are on the right.

whitewashed walls (Fig. 6-2). They were lit by barred window-grills of limestone set over the doorways.

Two similar doorways, one on each side of the throne platform, led into two long narrow corridors running south. Their walls were also decorated with panels of geometrical patterns composed mostly of conventionalized lotus flowers and spirals and framed by bands of inscriptions. Eight vaulted storerooms

Fig. 6-2. The mud-brick magazines (looking southwest). Note the remains of the vaulted roofs at the far right of the picture. The Temple of Sety 1.

with limestone doorways and window-grills led out of the western wall of the western corridor. They resemble the well preserved storerooms of the Ramesseum at Western Thebes.

Was it the Palace?

Some Egyptologists wish to identify this complex of buildings with the palace "Heart's Ease in Abydos" which Sety is known to have built here. But although its position to the south of the temple corresponds with that of other known palaces, the type of rooms it has do not seem to be adapted to such a purpose.

So far as the present-day ruins tell us, there are no signs of a kitchen or other "modern conveniences" of which even a great pharaoh must have been in need. Also, the two long painted corridors could hardly have been sleeping apartments. Are we to suppose that His Majesty's slumbers were to be disturbed by priests running in and out getting supplies from the storerooms? No, it is far more likely that we must look elsewhere for the missing palace; it may be under the high mound of sand to the immediate north of the temple courts.

Passing the doorway to this complex of buildings, the passage continues west until it reaches the eastern wall of the southern wing of the temple. Here it turns southward at right angles and passes through a large limestone gateway. In the center of the western wall a doorway leads into the Slaughter Court. At its southern end, the passage opens into what once was the Temple Garden. Here were found formal beds of earth once gay with flowers. Tree and vine roots interspersed with water channels were also found; and the well that fed these channels still contains water.

All the buildings described above are contained in the space between the "L" shaped temple and its rectangular Temenos Wall (see page 38).

The Gateway of the First Pylon.

Return again to the gateway of the First Pylon. Like all ancient Egyptian gateways, it had a name which was inscribed at the bottom of its outer jambs and reads, "The great gateway called 'King of Upper and Lower Egypt User-maat-Ra-Setep-en-Ra' makes Benefactions in the Palace of Eternity."

However, Mer-en-Ptah the son of Ramesses II, could not be satisfied with this lengthy name so he gave it another one. He had it inscribed below that of his father; this was "The great gateway called 'Ba-en-Ra-Mery-Amon' is beloved of Osiris Lord of Eternity."

On the southern side of the gateway, Ramesses made an inscription which for many years misled Egyptologists into believing that he had really built the pylon. He says, "Live Horus, the Mighty Bull, beloved of Maat, Favorite of the Two Ladies,[3] Subduer of the Foreign Lands, Golden Horus, rich in years, King of Upper and Lower Egypt, User-Maat-Ra-Setep-en-Ra; he made it as his monument for his father King Men-maat-Ra, making for him a great gateway of white stone as a marvel which I made for him,[4] namely I, the son of Ra who makes benefactions, the Lord of Diadems, Ramesses Mery-Amon, beloved of Amon-Ra, King of the Gods."

The definite statement that he made the gateway is one of those little (let us say) "embroiderings of the truth" for which Ramesses II is rather famous. Incidently the gateway is not of "white stone" but is of brown quartzite sandstone (Fig. 6-3).

That Sety really completed the entire building was proven in 1954 when excavations by the Antiquities Department of Egypt uncovered his cartouche inscribed on the southeastern and southwestern corners of the southern tower of the pylon. Originally these cartouches were completely hidden by the pavement of the terrace.

Following in his father's footsteps, Mer-en-Ptah was

....
[3] The two Goddesses of Upper and Lower Egypt, Nekhbet and Wadjet.
[4] In Egyptian texts we often find an abrupt change from the third to the first person, or vice versa.

Fig. 6-3. A main entrance to the First Pylon (see pages 38 and 50) of Sety's temple showing the remains of the old Nif-wer Canal. The Temple of Sety I.

stupid enough to make the unblushing claim to having built the gateway and put his inscription immediately underneath that of Ramesses. After the usual royal titulary he says, "He made it as his monument for his father[5] King Men-maat-Ra, beloved of Osiris, Lord of Abydos".

The First Court of the Temple.

On feast days, the great copper sheathed door of the Central Gateway stood open and worshipers passed through into the spacious First Court (see page 38). The sight must

[5]This is an example of the Egyptian custom of calling a grandfather, or even more remote ancestor "father."

have been dazzling to the eyes, for the vast space was then paved with gleaming white limestone;[6] the walls of the same material were adorned with colored reliefs. Nowadays the once white limestone has turned a beautiful creamy shade and so the reliefs (their original colors having vanished) appear as though carved in old ivory.

Two pillared porticos, one against the eastern wall[7] and the one at the west, gave welcome shade on hot days. Shaded by the eastern colonnade, the

[6]This has long since disappeared, for after the downfall of the old religion, the temple was used as a quarry.
[7]Only the foundations of the pillars of this colonnade remain.

western faces of the two towers[8] were each adorned with seven niches containing colossal statues of the King in the form of Osiris. As these statues form an integral part of the building, they must be intended to represent Sety, but their kindly, impersonal faces are not portraits. In any case, Ramesses has inscribed four out of the seven statues with his own name! The upper parts of these statues are now missing, but three of the best preserved heads may be seen standing at the northern end of the portico in front of the facade of the temple (Fig.

[8]The northern tower is almost completely ruined and only the foundations and parts of the lower courses of masonry remain.

49

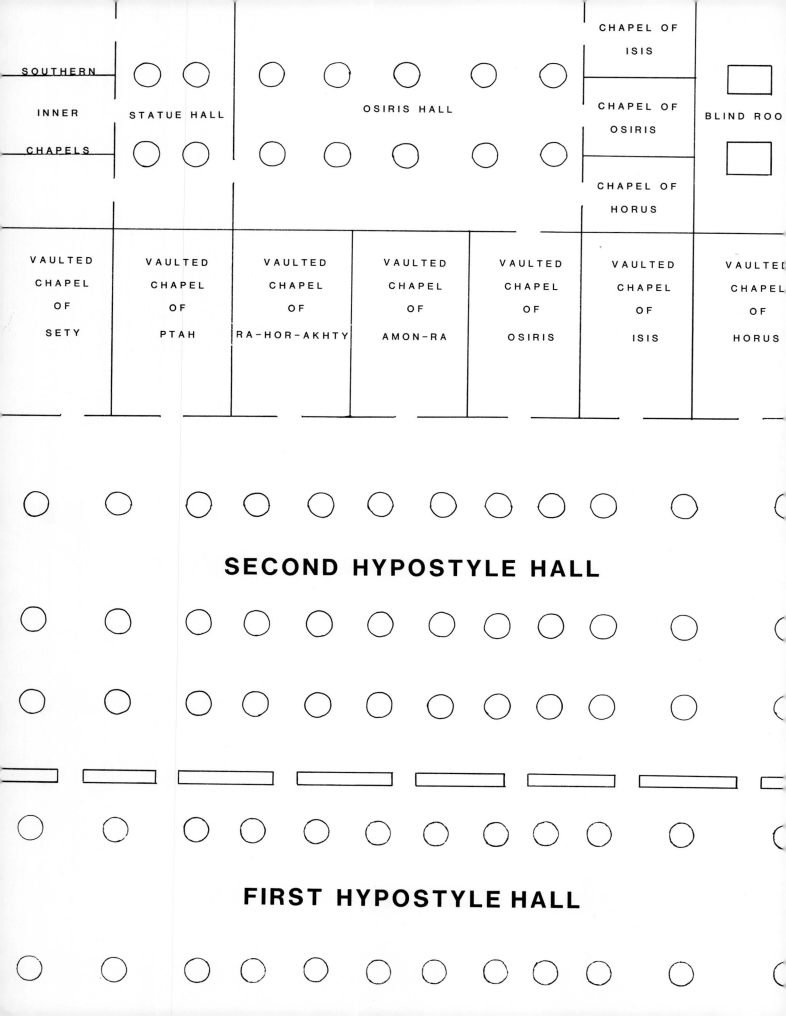

SOUTHERN

INNER

CHAPELS

STATUE HALL

OSIRIS HALL

CHAPEL OF
ISIS

CHAPEL OF
OSIRIS

CHAPEL OF
HORUS

BLIND ROO

VAULTED
CHAPEL
OF
SETY

VAULTED
CHAPEL
OF
PTAH

VAULTED
CHAPEL
OF
RA-HOR-AKHTY

VAULTED
CHAPEL
OF
AMON-RA

VAULTED
CHAPEL
OF
OSIRIS

VAULTED
CHAPEL
OF
ISIS

VAULTED
CHAPEL
OF
HORUS

SECOND HYPOSTYLE HALL

FIRST HYPOSTYLE HALL

6-4). One of these heads had the top of the crown carved upon a separate block of stone, now missing, and the resulting effect of a flat-topped headdress leads many visitors to think that it represents Queen Nefertiti! One hopes that the spirit of Sety cannot overhear such an innocent remark!

The Southern Wall.

At the eastern end of the southern wall is a scene showing military scribes counting the severed hands of enemies slain in battle. Whenever an Egyptian soldier killed an enemy, he hacked off the right hand of the corpse, tucked it in his belt and turned it in at the end of the battle to be counted. In this way they were sure to keep track of the enemy losses. Soldiers who turned in a good haul of hands were rewarded with a share in the spoils of war. This procedure cannot be compared with what the Israelites did by cutting away the genital organs of their captives or to the savage and outrageous mutilations the Assyrians usually did as a matter of course to their victims.

Here the counting of the hands is taking place in front of Ramesses, but only the lower part of this scene remains. However, there is enough to show that he was sitting on the rail of his chariot with his back to the horses. His foot wearing a sandal with the sole turned up in a point is very naturally drawn. Five toes are shown instead of the conventional single great toe, and these are slightly bent as though they are taking some of the weight of the King's body. Underneath the royal foot is the head of a bearded Asiatic who apparently lay doubled up on the floor of the chariot to serve as a footstool.

Fig. 6-4. Three sandstone heads from the Osirid statues on the western face of the First Pylon. Note the sandals of Ramesses II on the wall above the heads. The Second Portico. Northern wall. The Temple of Sety I.

Fig. 6-5. First Court (southern wall). Asiatic enemies falling from a fortress (details).

The pair of chariot horses are impatiently pawing the ground, and their charioteer stands beside them holding his whip while a groom stands at their heads holding them by the reins. A soldier armed with a spear and dagger looks on.

Next comes a small doorway that opens into the southern passage.

Ramesses Storms a Fortress.

To the west of the small doorway is a large, spirited battle scene. Ramesses is shown storming an enemy fortress which is strategically built upon a hill. The King has left his chariot and is attacking the enemy on foot. He is striding over vanquished foes who lie bound back to back in pairs. An inscription in front of the King likens him to the War God Monthu.

The occupants of the fortress seem to have come from different city states. Pierced by the King's arrow they topple over the ramparts (Fig. 6-5). One man, his mouth open as though screaming, is still in midair. Judging by his high, feathered headdress, he is a Philistine. Another man who is just reaching the ground wears a turban and a short robe dipping to a point in front. A man wearing bushy shoulder-length hair, falls backwards but still keeps hold of his dagger.

A small figure of an Egyptian officer, following Ramesses, carries a whip and has a quiver slung over his shoulder. A damaged inscription tells us that he is a "King's Son of His Body...." Unfortunately his name is lost so we do not know if he was the brother or son of Ramesses. He was probably the former. A vertical inscription explains the scene: "Ramesses Mery-Amon is trampling upon the cowardly chiefs of the Rethenu" (i.e. Syria and Palestine). Ramesses made war upon the Rethenu in the fourth, fifth and eighth years of his reign; but this scene may be more symbolic of the King's warlike prowess than a representation of an actual historical event.

In the next scene Ramesses fights from his chariot, but only the lower part of the car and the legs and bellies of the horses remain. The enemies are of the same types as those in the fortress and are dramatically rendered as they fall before the victorious Pharaoh. One unlucky fellow is lying under the chariot wheel!

A smaller chariot, also belonging to the Egyptian army, follows the King; it probably carries one of his brothers or sons.

The Return of the Conqueror.

The rest of the wall is taken up by a scene of the King's triumphal return to Egypt. The composition is dominated by the colossal figure of Ramesses in his chariot. Again, only the lower part remains. The horses are trotting in a very natural manner; and the King's pet lion runs beside them. Ramesses is known to have had his pet lions accompany him into battle. We only hope that they were trained to distinguish friends from foe!

Two small chariots follow Ramesses. In one of them two men stand side by side. The nearer one is driving and his companion is a shield-bearer. The former is inscribed:

"The King's Son of His Body, the Hereditary Prince..." (once again, his name is missing).

In spite of the faulty anatomy of the horses, the action of their trotting legs and the spirited tossing of their heads have been faithfully caught by the ancient artists.

Ramesses drives before his chariot two groups of living prisoners from "the rebellious foreign lands."[9] They have their arms bound together at the elbows and are linked together by a long rope that passes around the neck of each man; the ends of the rope are held by Ramesses. The men are of different types. Among them can be distinguished a pigtailed Hittite and bushy-bearded Semites. Although they are all bound at the elbows, they hold their arms in front of themselves or over their heads.

It is usually explained that the prisoners were intentionally bound in these contorted attitudes as a form of torment. But because of the known humane character of the ancient Egyptians and the fact that such prisoners were destined to work as slaves on the royal and temple estates, it is unlikely that they would be unnecessarily harshly treated. Their contorted attitudes
. . . .
[9]There was originally a third group, but this has disappeared with the destruction of the upper part of the wall.

probably represent their attempts to loosen their bonds.

The Spoils of War.

The final scene shows Ramesses presenting the spoils of war to the temple; again only the lower part remains. The King is leading a group of bound prisoners behind him and has set down some precious gold vessels in front of the two gods. These are supposed to be treasures captured as the spoils of war. But although the gold may well have come from the Pharaoh's Asiatic campaigns, the forms of the vessels suggest that it had been reworked by Egyptian goldsmiths. At the top is a large bowl supported on a central stem rising from a flat base (very much like a modern fruit bowl). A graceful vase with a conical cover has long stemmed lotus flowers for handles. The "Pièce de résistance" is a shallow bowl with a central stem. Figures of two bound Asiatic prisoners kneel upon the flat base and support the bowl upon their heads. Inside the bowl, or perhaps forming its upper part, is a model of a Syrian fortress which rises in two stages its ramparts lined with shields.[10] On the upper
. . . .
[10]Possibly this fortress representation was really engraved inside the bowl. Often Egyptian Art showed the contents of bowls and baskets as standing upright upon the rim.

Fig. 6-6. The "Fortress-bowl" (First Court, southern wall).

stage, miniature figures of Semitic defenders raise their arms imploring for mercy; while from the lower stage more enemy heads peep out timidly, their faces set in comical expressions of dismay. This piece is certainly the work of Egyptian goldsmiths (Fig. 6-6). The two gods who promise "all valour and victory, like Ra" to Ramesses are too badly destroyed to be identified.

The Northern Wall of the Court.

The first ten meters (33 feet) of the northern wall of the court are completely destroyed; the remainder is in a bad state of preservation. The remains of a small doorway, opposite to that in the southern wall, perhaps led to the missing palace "Heart's Ease in Abydos."

To the west of the doorway is a large scene showing Ramesses, accompanied by his chariot and infantry, setting forth for battle. The inscription over the chariots records the promise of Amon-Ra, "I have come to thee that thou mayest destroy the evil ones, the rebels, as a Lord of Power for ever and ever."

The leading chariot is driven by a prince. Standing beside him is a standard-bearer.

The infantrymen precede the royal chariot and are armed with curved battle-axes. Only the lower part of the King's chariot and the legs of its trotting horses now remain; grooms run beside them.

The westernmost scene on this wall is a very splendid composition (Fig. 6-7). Ramesses is in the act of mounting his chariot. He wears the blue war helmet. He grasps the reins and the front rail of the chariot with his left hand and the curved

the remarkable beauty of his youthful face resembles the profile of the famous statue of Ramesses in the Turin Museum.

The Ablution Basins.

Like the Moslems, the ancient Egyptians performed ceremonial ablutions before praying. It was for this

They are built of limestone blocks which would have allowed the water to seep away through the joints into the underlying sand.

The chambers in which they lie are built of sandstone. Their pavements slope gently down to the central basin. Water was poured in from outside and ran through a channel cut

Fig. 6-7. Ramesses II mounting his chariot (First Court, northern wall).

battle-ax with the right one. His left foot is already on the floor of the chariot, and the right one, shod with a sandal, is stretched out behind him to give impetus to his leap into the car. The action is vividly lifelike. The King's head is entirely undamaged;

purpose that two large circular stone basins in rectangular chambers were constructed in the north and south of the central axis of the First Court (Fig. 6-8, also see page 38). Each basin measures about 3.0 meters (10 feet) in diameter and about 1.0 meter (3.3 feet) deep.

under the wall. The walls, not one of which is preserved to its original height, were sculptured with scenes and inscriptions by Ramesses II; the lintels of the doorways were inscribed during Sety's reign and bear his names and titles. As these chambers are about 9.0 meters (30 feet)

Fig. 6-8. The First Court showing the two Ablution Basins in center.

square; it is unlikely that they were ever roofed. All of the scenes on the walls are of a religious nature and show Ramesses offering to the various gods or performing ceremonies for them.

The water used in these basins came from a well which lies a few meters to the north of the northern basin. It was apparently repaired during Roman times. It still contains water and has never been known to run dry. Similar arrangements for ablutions were made at Solomon's first Temple to the Lord with the "Molten Sea" in front of its entrance.

The Second Pylon and its Portico.

The Second Pylon and its portico stand upon a limestone terrace raised about 1.5 meters (5 feet) from the pavement of the First Court. It is reached by a double flight of steps with a central ramp between them. On the western face of this terrace are two long but somewhat damaged inscriptions of Mer-en-Ptah "who seeks excellent things for the Abydos Nome of Eternity, the Divine Place of Eternity." These inscriptions seem to have been intended to commemorate the fact that Mer-en-Ptah had celebrated the Feast of the New Year in his grandfather's temple.

The Second Pylon is really only a pylon shaped wall measuring only 5.7 meters (18.7 feet) thick and of solid masonry; whereas the First Pylon is 10.5 meters (34.4 feet) thick and its hollow interior had a staircase ascending to its roof. In place of the grooves for flag masts in its eastern face, it has nine niches for

Fig. 6-9. Some of the sons of Ramesses II. (From the left:) Prince Sa-Ptah, Prince Sa-Amon, Prince Monthu-em-Wast and Prince Amon-em-Ipt (First Portico, southern wall). The high regard held by Ramesses II for his family and the temple record of them are of great interest. Temple of Sety I.

statues; the walls of which are all sculptured with scenes of Ramesses adoring various gods. For some unknown reason, the carving of these scenes is very rough and in marked contrast to the fine work on the surface of the wall.

There were two gateways in this pylon. The great Central Gateway closed by a double-leaved wooden door and a smaller one in the northern tower. Originally inscribed by Ramesses, they seem to have been regarded as a "visitor's book" by later kings and we find there the inscriptions of Mer-en-Ptah, Ramesses III and Ramesses IV.

Probably the Central Gateway and the Main Entrance to the temple were only opened on special occasions. The daily traffic to and from the temple and its courts, priests going about their duties, worshipers coming to bring offerings and pray, etc. would have been through the

Fig. 6-10. Prince Monthu-em-Wast (First Portico, southern wall). Temple of Sety I.

smaller doorways.

In front of the eastern face of the pylon stood a portico, its roof supported on twelve rectangular pillars of sandstone and limestone none of which are now complete. Their lower parts are decorated with designs and imitation wooden paneling above which are horizontal inscriptions of Ramesses II of no particular interest.

The Walls of the Portico.

Ramesses II, who was later to be famed for his family of one hundred and eleven sons and sixty-nine daughters, already had a quiver full when early in his reign he decorated this pylon and portico. Like any proud father, he was determined to immortalize his children here. He had the figures and names of his sons carved on the southern wall of the portico and on both sides of the southern tower of the pylon while his very charming daughters occupy the same places on the northern tower and wall.

The figures of the five princes on the southern wall of the portico are the best preserved (Fig. 6-9). They are all represented almost exactly alike and are not attempts at individual portraits. They are handsome young men, obviously "taking after father." They wear elaborately curled wigs with the hanging side tresses that were the badges of princes of the royal house. They are clad in long transparent robes of fine linen over which is a kilt formed of a folded strip of linen tied in front. Each boy raises his right hand in adoration, and in the left hand each carries a long-handled fan formed of a single ostrich plume. This was the insignia of the office of "Fan-bearer of the Right of the King"; an honorary title held only by royal princes and very high ranking nobles. Tied to the handle of each fan is the crook of royal authority from which hang ribbon streamers (Fig. 6-10).

In front of each figure a vertical inscription gives the prince's name and titles. For example, the first boy to the east is "The King's Son of His Body, his be-loved Sa-Ptah." Next come Sa-Amon and Monthu-em-Wast "The God Monthu in Thebes," Amon-em-Ipt, and Hor-her-wenemy-ef ("Horus is on His Right Hand"). This last boy is also known from inscriptions at the Ramesseum and the Nubian Temples of Wadi el Seboua, Abu Simbel and El Derr.

The figures continue on the eastern face of the pylon (which is also the western wall of the portico) on the surfaces between the niches. Here the first name is destroyed. The second is Monthu; then come Monthu-em-hekau, Ramesses-sa-Atum, and Sa-nakht-en-Amon (who is also mentioned in the Nubian temples). There were some others but they have all been destroyed.

Underneath all the figures of the princes is a long horizontal inscription of Mer-en-Ptah in which he unblushingly claims to have built this pylon "as his monument for his father," King Sety!

The Daughters of Ramesses.

On the eastern face of the northern tower of the pylon, commencing immediately after the Central Doorway, are some representations of the daughters of Ramesses. These were also all alike; their faces are a softer, feminine version of that of their handsome father. They wear long transparent robes of fine linen, and on their heads are close-fitting

Fig. 6-11. *Some of the daughters of Ramesses II. (From the left:) Princess Pipui, Princess Baket-Mut, Princess Renpet-Nefert ("Happy Year"), Princess Neferu-Ra and Princess Meryt-neter (First Portico, northern wall). The Temple of Sety I.*

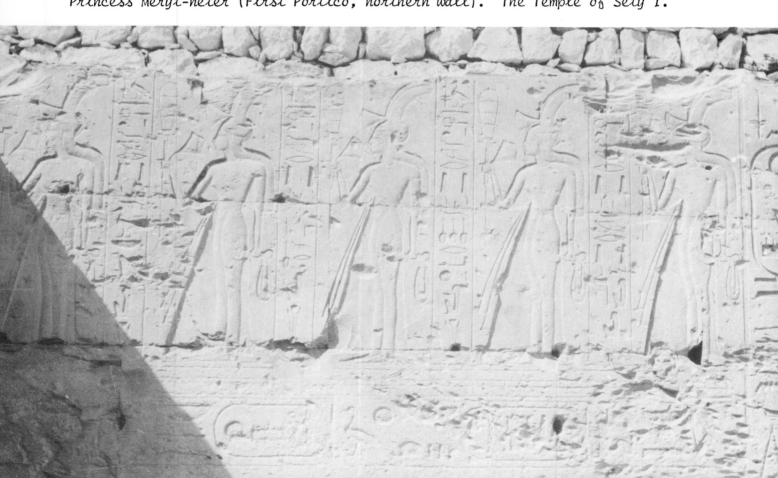

wigs with side tresses similar to those of their brothers', but their long natural hair hangs daintily down over their shoulders. The wig is bound by a band of ribbon in each side of which is stuck an ostrich plume; a lotus flower hangs over the brow. They also wear sandals. Each girl carries a sistrum (a sacred rattle) and carries the mystic menat necklace. The girlish figures are beautifully carved and are a combination of youthful grace and royal dignity.

The names of the first two girls and most of their figures have been destroyed. Number three is Wert-Hekau-nebet-Tawi ("Great of Magic Mistress of the Two Lands). What did they call her for short? Then comes Ta-qedet-mert, Nebet-Iwnt, Wer-nu-Ra (who also appears in the Nubian temples), Nefertari (probably named after the favorite wife of Ramesses), Isit-Nefert (also named after a wife of Ramesses). The name of the tenth girl was Iny-nehat, but those of the following three are lost and the fourteenth is incomplete. Number fifteen is destroyed, but number sixteen has the lovely name of Khesbed, meaning "Lapis-lazuli." Next comes Shepses-her-itef-es ("Honored by Her Father). The next girl's name is missing but her sister is called Meryt-mi-Hapi ("Loved Like the Nile"). Number twenty has the good old IIIrd dynasty name of Meryt-itef-es ("Beloved of Her Father"). Number twenty-one is Nub-em-Iwnt ("Gold

in Heliopolis") who is followed by Henut-sekhumu ("Lady of Powers"), Henou-pa-houry-Ra and Henut-ikhep.

Five more figures of princesses whose figures and inscriptions are very well-preserved are on the northern wall of the portico (Fig. 6-11). The first one of these is "The King's Daughter of His Body, his beloved Pipui." The next girl is Baket-Mut ("Servant of Mut") who is also mentioned in the Nubian temples. Following her is Renpet-Nefert whose name meaning "Happy Year" suggests that she was born on New Year's Day (Fig. 6-12). The next girl is Neferu-Ra ("Beauty of the Sun") and the last has the lovely name of Meryt-neter ("Beloved of God").

Under all the figures of the princesses is another long inscription of Mer-en-Ptah in which he again claims to have built the pylon, established "good laws throughout the two riverbanks" (Egypt) and giving "offerings to the gods through love of them"! But let us now leave Mer-en-Ptah to his overbearing boasting and pass through the Central Gateway into the Second Court.

The Second Court, the Eastern Wall.

The Second Court (see page 38) was also originally paved with limestone. Like the First Court it measures about 51.5 meters (169 feet) wide and 31.5 meters (103 feet) from east to west.
The eastern wall of

the Second Court is also the western face of the Second Pylon. On the southern tower are more representations of the sons of Ramesses, but they are not well-preserved. They are dressed in the same way as on the eastern face of the pylon, but here their fans are slung over their shoulders leaving their hands free to carry offerings.

The figures of the daughters of Ramesses on the northern half of the wall are all badly damaged. They appear to have been carrying offerings, and numbers 4, 7, 9, 10, 13, 15, 17, 19 have already appeared on the eastern face. Apparently Ramesses was short of daughters when this work was in progress!

The Northern Wall of the Second Court.

The scenes on the northern (and southern) wall of this court show a change in character from those in the First Court. The latter were concerned with this world and the military conquests of Ramesses, but here we are drawing nearer the temple and the world of the gods, and so Ramesses has left aside his prancing horses, his comrades-in-arms and his living prisoners of war and turned his thoughts to religious matters.

In two registers[11] of finely sculptured and once colored scenes, Ramesses worships his gods. At the

....

[11]The upper register is mostly destroyed.

eastern end of the wall he offers a symbolic image of Maat to Atum. The face and figure of the King are well-preserved. He wears the blue war helmet; and because he is still in the court of the temple, we can see that his feet are shod with sandals.[12] The second and third scenes are badly damaged. In the fourth scene, Ramesses anoits a god with perfumed ointment, but the name of the deity is lost. Next the King presents flowers to the Goddess Nut who here wears the moon disk and cow horns as her headdress in place of her usual name-sign, the round jar. But her name "Nut the Great" identifies her. In the next three scenes Ramesses offers to the Holy Family of Abydos, Osiris, Isis and Horus.

In this latter scene, the King wears a curious form of the war helmet which is here flanked on both sides by ostrich plumes. We shall see this form of the crown again inside the temple.

Another scene shows Ramesses offering wine to his deceased father Sety who holds the crook and flail emblems of royalty. The crook as a reminder that he should be a good shepherd to his subjects,[13] the flail a symbol of his power to punish the rebellious.

. . . .
[12]Sandals were always removed before entering the temple.
[13]So also the pastoral staff of the Christian bishops.

Fig. 6-12. Princess Renpet-Nefert ("Happy Year"), daughter of Ramesses II (First Portico, north wall).

The Northern Stela.

Following the ninth scene on the northern wall is a large stela which is built as part of the wall of the court. On its originally rounded top is the lower part of a scene showing Ramesses offering to Osiris behind whom stood Isis, Horus and Sety I. Below are nine lines of inscription in which Ramesses is said to "make great the Abydos nome among the nomes, doing excellent benefactions for eternity, making monuments in the temple of his father; the Sovereign living in truth, beloved as one carrying a happy face."[14]

A curious alteration

60

Fig. 6-13. *Ramesses II offers an image of Maat (damaged) to Atum (the Second Court, northern wall).*

was made to the western-most scene of the northern wall. Here the entire surface of the stone has been cut away to a depth of about 2.0 centimeters

....
[14]His cheerful expression is characteristic of all the good portraits of Ramesses and even his mummy is smiling.

(three-fourths inch) and a colossal figure of a pharaoh carried over the two registers of smaller figures. This large figure which was never completed shows the King leaning forward, his legs straddled. Both arms are held forward with the elbows bent, the hands closed and near together as though tying

something. A possible explanation is that the King was supposed to be binding a group of prisoners of war.

The Southern Wall of the Second Court.

Opposite to the stela of the northern wall is another of the same type but in better condition. The scene on the rounded top shows Ramesses offering a symbolic figure of Maat to Osiris behind whom are Isis, Horus and Sety I (Fig. 6-13). In the inscription below, Ramesses claims to have "created his excellent monuments, provisioning the offering tables, increasing the drink stands of his fathers, the Lords of the Sacred Land, doubling their offering bread in tens of thousands, for ever and ever."

The Window of Appearances?

Immediately to the west of the stela is an opening in the wall now used as a door to the magazines and Audience Hall (see page 38). It was originally a window and was reached from the passage running south of the wall of the courts. It overlooked the Second Court and the terrace of the portico. A damaged scene on its western side showed Ramesses burning incense and pouring a libation to his deceased father Sety.

This seems to have been the "Window of Appearances" usually found overlooking a court in an important temple. From such windows the King could show himself to the people assembled in the court and on certain occasions would hand down golden collars and other golden ornaments to officials whom he wished to reward. These gifts were called, the "Gold of Praise" and were highly prized by their proud possessors both for the value of the metal and the honor which they conferred. A person so honored was said to have been gilded by the King. All of his family, friends and neighbors often assembled at the ceremony and gave vent to their gladness by shouting and even leaping for joy.

Near the southwestern end of this court is another well but this is now dry.

The Portico of the Temple, the Northern Wall.

At the western end of the Second Court is a platform about 1.25 meters (4.1 feet) higher then the original pavement. On this platform stand twelve rectangular pillars supporting the roof of the portico. Like those of the two courts, the walls and pillars of the portico were all decorated by Ramesses II in incised relief; these are very good in both style and execution.

Two scenes adorn the northern wall. The scene to the east represents Ramesses "slaying" a bunch of Asiatic prisoners of war whom he grasps by their hair. The wretched enemies

are forced to their knees and raise imploring arms to beg mercy from their mighty conqueror.

Originally the ceremonial slaughter of captured enemies may, though it is very doubtful, have been an actual fact. But by the time of the New Kingdom it had become merely a symbolic gesture. The prisoners were brought to the temple, knelt before the King who, in the presence of the gods, tapped them lightly upon the head with an archaic stone-headed mace. In this scene the King's head and upraised hand holding the mace are destroyed; and the figures of the enemies have been wantonly damaged. Ramesses is performing this ceremony in the presence of Amon-Ra who extends to him the curved battle-ax as a symbol of victory. In an inscription in front of him, Amon-Ra says, "I give to thee all foreign lands under thy sandals."

The second scene, which is under the roof of the portico, retains much of its original color. Here Ramesses, carrying a horizontal incense burner[15] and the Key of Life (not yet shown) in his left hand, raises the right one in the

....

[15]This type of incense burner was called "Hand of Horus" because one end terminates in the head of a falcon of Horus while the end which supports the bowl of glowing charcoal is shaped like a falcon's talon or a human hand.

Fig. 6-14. Ramesses II recites the offering formula for Osiris. Three heads from the Osirid statues on the western face of the First Pylon (the Second Portico, northern wall).

conventional gesture of a person speaking or reciting. In this case he is reciting the traditonal offering formula which begins with "An offering which the King gives" on behalf of the God Osiris who stands before him. Osiris wears the crown of Upper Egypt and stands upon an oblong pedestal the outer end of which is a steep slope or ramp. This is one of the symbols of "Truth and Justice"; when seen under the feet of a god it denotes that the deity's authority is founded upon these two qualities. Osiris promises to give the King "all lands and rebellious foreign countries under his sandals" (Fig. 6-14).[16]

[16] Note that Ramesses is wearing sandals. This shows that he is supposed to be still outside the temple.

The Western Wall.

The western wall of the portico, which is also the facade of the temple, has much of its original color preserved. At the northern end is a small doorway leading eventually to the Cult Chapel of Horus. At the top of its lintel hovers the winged sun disk of Horus of Edfu; below are two lines of inscription giving the titles and names of Ramesses. On the wall above the door, the King offers round loaves of bread to Horus, Isis and the deceased Sety I.

Ramesses Goes to the Temple of Ra-Hor-akhty.

To the south of the doorway is a fine large scene showing the ram-headed God Khnum and the falcon-headed Horus taking Ramesses by the hands and leading him to the Temple of Ra-Hor-akhty at Heliopolis. Much of the original color remains, especially on Khnum and Ramesses; and the figure of the latter is one of the very few which retains the black pupil of the eye giving a very "alive" look to his handsome face. Horus looks back over his shoulder at the King and holds the Key of Life to his nose (Fig. 6-15).

In the next part of this scene Ramesses receives the crook and flail from Ra-Hor-akhty while Osiris stands approvingly in the rear. The King stands in front of the sacred Persea tree of Heliopolis and the God Ptah of Memphis is writing the name of Ramesses upon the leaves. For every leaf bearing his name, the King would reign for one year. As Ramesses II reigned for sixty-seven years, Ptah must have been somewhat busy! The ibis-headed Thot, here in his role of Measurer of Time, is making notches on a stripped palm branch, also recording

Fig. 6-15. The Gods Horus (left) and Khnum lead Ramesses II to the Temple of Ra-Hor-akhty at Heliopolis (the Second Portico, western wall). Temple of Sety I.

the length of the King's reign.

As this wall of the portico marks the limit to which lay folk were allowed to come, this scene really means that Ramesses is letting everybody know that his ascension to the throne was officially approved of by the great gods!

The scenes are now interrupted by the doorway leading to the Cult Chapel of Osiris. This was once blocked up by Ramesses but was subsequently re-opened as can be proven by the incomplete figure of Horus to the south of the doorway and the arm, hand and part of a foot of another figure on the northern side. Behind the incomplete figure of Horus stands his mother Isis who tenderly raises her hand to his shoulder. The deceased King Sety brings up the rear.

Now comes the Main Entrance to the temple which also leads to the Cult Chapel of Amon-Ra. On its lintel was a colored double scene showing the King dancing in front of Osiris and Isis (right) and in front of Amon-Ra and Mut (left). On each of the jambs of the doorway three small scenes show Ramesses offering to various gods.

To the south of the Main Entrance is another large scene in which Ramesses (wearing sandals) offers the symbolic image of Maat to Osiris, Isis and the deceased Sety I who here seems to be taking the

place of Horus in the Holy Family of Abydos.

The rest of this wall is taken up by a long but very interesting inscription in which Ramesses tells future generations what a good son he was to complete his father's monuments.[17] He tells how he visited Abydos in the first year of his reign and found that the work on Sety's temple had ceased as well as the work on another temple which the late King was building in Abydos in honor of his predecessors from ancient times.[18] Ramesses called together all the important officials of his court, the Clerk of Works and the architects, and expressing his anger at the neglect, ordered them to immediately get busy on the completion of his father's monuments. He speaks of the love between him and his father and says, "When my father appeared in public, I being a child between his arms, he said concerning me, 'Crown him as King, that I may see his beauty while I live with him.[19] Place for him the crown upon his head; let him administer;

17..........................
For a full translation of this inscription see Breasted, "Ancient Records of Egypt" Vol. III pp. 104 ff.
18This is probably the temple to the west of Kom el Sultan.
19This refers to the co-regency between Sety and Ramesses which took place when the boy was about ten years old.

let him show his face to the people.' So spake he because the love of me was so great in his heart." In addition to making him Commander of the army, Ramesses says that Sety provided him with beautiful girls as wives and concubines. He then enumerates all the work which he intends to do for the Temple of Sety, and explains why we find his own name inscribed there by saying that the monument "shall bear my name and the name of my father, for the son is like him who begat him."

Of course, all the courtiers and officials were loud in their praise of the young King's decision likening him to Horus and saying that Isis had never loved any king except Ramesses and her own son. Ramesses also endowed the temple with offerings, lands, slaves, cattle and a fleet of merchant ships and increased and enriched the priesthood. He then calls upon the spirit of his dead father to witness what he has done and promises to take care of all Sety's monuments and especially this temple. "I will take counsel for thy temple every day. If I hear of any damage about to happen I will command to remove it instantly. Thou shalt be as if thou wert still alive as long as I reign."

The spirit of Sety then appears to Ramesses speaking to him "as a father on earth speaks to his son." He praises Ramesses for his energy and devotion and says that he has begged the

God Osiris to double for him "more than the duration of thy son Horus." He prophesies for him a long, happy and prosperous reign which really did happen!

Although in this inscription Ramesses by no means minimizes his own good qualities, modesty and humility being the very last of his virtues, yet we can detect under the bombast the very deep and genuine love existing between Sety and his handsome, arrogant son. In the sentence where he says, "Thou shalt be as though thou wert still alive, as long as I reign," one can sense that the young King was still grieving for the loss of his father and missing his companionship.

The Southern Wall, the Pillars of the Portico.

At the western end of the southern wall of the portico are the last two rows of the long inscription of Ramesses and a large figure of the King who is supposed to be reciting it.

The eastern end of the wall is very badly damaged; it originally bore a scene similar to that on the eastern part of the northern wall. Here being on the southern wall, Ramesses was shown "slaying" his southern enemies also in the presence of Amon-Ra.

Originally the twelve rectangular pillars supporting the roof of the portico stood about 7.6 meters (25 feet) high but,

none of them are now complete and their upper parts, the architraves and roof, are modern restorations. The ancient roof was edged by a cavetto cornice many blocks of which still lie in the temple courts. It is hoped that they may one day be replaced in their original positions, and so give a true impression of what the facade looked like in the ancient days.

Each of the four faces of the pillars bear scenes and inscriptions in incised relief which, like the walls of the portico, are the work of Ramesses II; most of the scenes show him being affectionately embraced by a god or a goddess. Artistically speaking, they are very well done. Worshipers and pilgrims, seeing them from the court, were probably greatly impressed by the obviously friendly relations existing between the gods and their own King! The diversity of the gods shown in these scenes is very interesting as it bears out the pantheistic nature of this temple.

In the long inscription on the western wall of the portico, Ramesses claims to have erected these pillars. He says that he found that "the pillars were not erected upon their platform." There is every reason to believe him this time because they were clearly set up after five of the seven doors of the temple had been blocked up; this blocking had been done by Ramesses. Had the pillars dated from the

reign of Sety, they would have been arranged in pairs like the columns in the hypostyle halls so as to flank the doorways. As they now stand, they would have almost blocked all but the Main Entrance.

The Scenes and Inscriptions on the Pillars.

The most interesting scenes on the pillars are as follows:

On the western face of pillar number one (from the north) is a scene showing Ramesses embraced by a very unusual form of the God Thot. This God of Wisdom and Learning is usually depicted as an ibis-headed man, but here he is in full human form and bears the large yellow disk of the full moon upon his head.[20] The name of the God is destroyed but the epithet "the youth who is in Khemenu, (Ashmunein) the Great God" identifies him as Thot. In the horizontal inscriptions underneath the scenes, Ramesses claims to have "put in order the temple of his father, King Men-maat-Ra who is justified before the great God."

As the western faces of all the pillars were protected by the roof of the portico, they have all retained much of their original colors.

On the eastern face of pillar number two, Ramesses is embraced by another anthropomorphic god that is crowned
....

[20]In the scenes in this temple, the lunar disk is colored yellow and the solar disk is red.

65

with a large disk. As no color is preserved, we cannot say if it is a solar or lunar disk, and to make matters worse, the god's name is destroyed. He may be either Khonsu, the Moon God Iah, a very rare form of Ra-Hor-akhty, or Min-Ra!

The scene on the western face of the same pillar is very beautiful and its colors are well preserved. It shows Ramesses and the God Nefer-tem, the third person of the Memphite Triad. Appropriately enough, as he is in the presence of a northern god, Ramesses wears the Red Crown of Lower Egypt. This contrasts nicely with the blue wig of Nefer-tem, the colored lotus flower on his head and his green tunic.

In the inscriptions below the scenes, Ramesses claims to be "great in monuments like his father King Men-maat-Ra." For once Ramesses is overly modest! By the end of his long reign he had erected many more monuments than his father although none of them ever quite reached the same high standard of those of Sety.

On the northern face of pillar number four, Ramesses is embraced by a goddess whose name is lost. Her hair is dressed in a style fashionable during the XIXth dynasty. She also wears a headdress of disk and cow's horns (Fig. 6-16).

Pillar number six is by the Main Entrance to the temple; on its southern face is a single figure of Ramesses facing west as though about to enter the building. He wears the Red Crown of Lower Egypt, and his feet are shod with sandals. His right hand is raised as though he were speaking, and indeed he is supposed to be reciting the prayer for offerings before entering the temple. The inscription in front of him reads, "Making offerings of everything good and pure."

On the lower course of both this pillar and number seven are three horizontal inscriptions, the upper one being of Ramesses II who claims to have "made benefactions for his progenitor, King Men-maat-Ra." The second line was added by Mer-en-Ptah and the third by Ramesses III of the XXth dynasty.

On the western face of pillar number six, Ramesses is embraced by a king who wears the Archaic royal tunic upheld by a single shoulder strap. This may be a personification of the ancient kings of Egypt whose names are recorded inside the temple and whose tombs lie to the west at Omm el Gaab. Ramesses had dedicated a chapel in his own temple to their funerary cult.

On the northern face of pillar number seven is a figure of Ramesses which is almost identical to that on the southern face of pillar number six. Here he wears the crown of Upper Egypt. As this pillar is immediately to the south of the Main Entrance, the crowns on the two figures are in their correct geo-

Fig. 6-17. Pillar number seven. Ramesses II about to enter the temple. Note the way his long robe partly hides two hieroglyphs but without obscuring their meaning (the Second Portico, northern face). Temple of Sety I.

graphical positions. Apparently the artist who drew the design for this scene misjudged the space required for the King's full skirt and the vertical inscription; but instead of altering it, he turned it into a very natural detail by allowing the royal skirt to partially hide the hieroglyphs meaning "everything" and "pure" without in any way obscuring their meaning (Fig. 6-17).

The scene on the western face is also very beautiful, and shows Ramesses offering a bunch of lotus flowers to Osiris. He holds the flowers to the face of the god, inviting him to smell them.

On the northern face of pillar number eight, Ramesses is embraced by the Goddess Mut the wife of Amon-Ra. As Queen of the Gods, she wears the Double Crown. Above her is inscribed, "Mistress of Isheru." Isheru being the name of her temple at Karnak (Fig. 6-18).

In the scene on the northern face of pillar number nine, Ramesses is embraced by the Goddess Hathor who wears her hair in the fashionable XIXth dynasty style (Fig. 6-19).

On the eastern face of pillar number eleven, the God is Geb and his wife the Sky Goddess Nut. Nut embraces the King on the southern face. As her headdress she wears the round jar which is the hieroglyph for her name. Her epithet, "Mistress of Heaven, Who Bore the Gods" is inscribed above her.

A single figure of the deified Sety I adorns the northern and southern

Fig. 6-18. Pillar number eight. Ramesses II embraced by the Goddess Mut (the Second Portico, northern face).

68

Fig. 6-19. *Pillar number nine. Ramesses II embraced by the Goddess Hathor (the Second Portico, northern face).*

faces of pillar number twelve (Fig. 6-20).

All these pillars bear much graffiti (mostly scratched upon the background of the scenes). These are usually the names of ancient pilgrims and tourists. But among the Greek graffiti are (we regret to say) some very rude words scratched in hieroglyphs!

The Temple Schools.

On many of the sandstone bases of the pillars are round depressions just the right size and shape to hold an ancient round-bottomed drinking jar, and this is probably the purpose that they served. Most of the important temples had schools annexed to them, and classes were usually held under the colonnades. These temple schools taught children between the ages of five and twelve years and we can imagine the priestly teachers seated at the bases of the pillars, the water (or beer?) jar close at hand while the children squatted on the ground in front of them. There were also classes for older pupils who wished to become priests, doctors or judges. Education was free to all, and there were no class distinctions. This is the earliest known example of the democracy of education.

But to return to the scenes on the pillars, as we have said, they are well executed and are far superior to the later work of Ramesses II. All the main details

69

are carved in the stone and the modeling of the faces and limbs is admirable; most of the finer details of the clothing and ornaments are in paint only. When compared with the work of Sety I in this temple, the figures are somewhat formal and the faces, though good portraits of Ramesses, lack the variation of expression seen in those of Sety. In scenes where Sety is shown offering to a god, he either kneels or stands bowing slightly from the hips as he reverently extends the offering to the deity. Not so with Ramesses. He was too arrogant to do the same. Take for example the scene on the western face of pillar number seven where Ramesses offers flowers to Osiris. Instead of adopting Sety's reverent attitude of becoming a worshiper before his God, Ramesses stands squarely upright smiling gaily into the face of Osiris as one equal to another! This is characteristic of the work of Ramesses, and is probably a reflection of his personal character, that of a cheerful, self-confident man, somewhat arrogant but kindly and full of personal charm. He is sometimes quite difficult to understand and yet it is hard to deny that he has quite an engaging personality.

Had he not considered himself to be one of the gods as pictured at Abu Simbel? His progression to godhood was "right now" according to him.

Fig. 6-20. Pillar number twelve. The dead and deified King Sety I (the Second Portico, northern face).

70

CHAPTER SEVEN

HYPOSTYLE HALLS

The Inner Temple, the First Hypostyle Hall.

To pass through the great Central Doorway and enter into the Temple of Sety I is like entering a "Time Machine" of science fiction. One leaves the modern world outside in the glare of the sunshine and in the soft, subdued light of the interior, enters the world of the past which, for a time, becomes the present. It is also a world of magic such as the modern mind and particularly the western mind has difficulty in understanding.

Most people think of the temples of Egypt as being something like churches or cathedrals where people came to public worship and to make their personal prayers and petitions. But temples are not and never were like this. In ancient Egypt, that kind of worship belonged to the temple courts and porticos, to the small temples of local gods and to the wayside shrines, for the Egyptian was always pious by nature.

The interiors of the great temples were in truth the holy houses of the gods where emanations of the divine spirits worked ceaselessly day and night to ward off from the universe the ever threatening return of chaos and to maintain the divine order of the

world and the welfare of Egypt, the "beloved Land." Prayers, hymns and sacrifices were certainly made here. Ceremonies and ordinances were performed and offerings laid upon the altars. These were done not by ordinary people but by priests trained in voice and gesture to perform the magically important ceremonies in exactly the correct manner that would render them acceptable and serviceable to the gods.

The ordinary folk were never permitted to enter the interior of the temple, and it is doubtful if any of them have dared to do so! Every element in the scenes on the walls had a magical significance. Nothing is there merely for the sake of a good presentation or for beauty alone. If they are beautiful as well as being magically potent, it is because they were conceived by men of vision and taste and brought into being by men who, even though working for wages, were above all proudly participating in two momentous projects. They were helping to create a suitable dwelling-place for the gods in the midst of their own city. They were honored to have a share, however insignificant in the great work being carried out by their God-King, their "Horus Upon Earth."

The scenes on the walls were magically active in two ways. They were supposed to make permanent the action shown

being performed. If the pharaoh offers a loaf of bread to Osiris, that loaf will continue to be presented so long as the representation remains both in this world and in the world of the gods. Likewise, if one stood before a figure of a god and uttered his name, a portion of the divine spirit would animate the stone, and the deity's attention would be upon the speaker, upon his actions and upon the hidden thoughts of his heart.

One could imagine that these beliefs held and practiced in this temple for over a thousand years have charged the very stones of the building with their potency. To be alone in the Temple of Sety is to feel surrounded by invisible presences, to feel watched over by benevolent all-seeing eyes and to know an overwhelming sense of peace and security.

As one passes through the great doorway, one is greeted by a large figure of Osiris standing in gracious dignity as the Master of the House receiving his visitors. Ramesses makes offerings and burns incense before him, and below him are added inscriptions of Ramesses II, Meren-Ptah, Ramesses III and Ramesses IV (Fig. 7-1).

Inside the Great Hall, twenty-four gigantic papyrus-bud columns uphold the painted ceiling where the vultures of Nekhbet spread their wings in protection over the holy place. On the massive architraves, large

Fig. 7-1. First Hypostyle Hall. Southern side of the Main Entrance. Ramesses II burns incense to Osiris.

colored hieroglyphs proclaim the names of Ramesses and his father.[1]

The two rows of columns are arranged in pairs forming aisles leading to the seven doorways in the western wall (see page 50), and on their shafts are scenes showing Ramesses adoring the gods to whose Cult Chapels the aisles eventually lead. At certain times of the day, the light so shines that these normally brown sandstone columns seem to become greenish and translucent. Here and there a square patch of sunlight from an opening in the roof spotlights the cheery face of Ramesses or the calm and kindly countenance of one of the deities. The whole place seems then to be full of benevolence, serenity and love.

The Eastern Wall.

Built of sandstone, the eastern wall really consists of six massive piers separating the original seven doorways in the facade of the temple. Each pier bears an upper and lower scene, and below them the Nile Gods kneel with vases of water and trays of offerings, each God bearing on his head the standard of the nome through which he flows. The Gods, plump and prosperous, are represented as bearded men with the breasts of a
....

[1]Each block of the sandstone architrave weighs fifteen tons. The original roofing slabs weigh about six tons each.

woman. This naive representation of the Nile as both Father and Mother of Egypt, the Begetter and the Nourisher, does not fail to attract the attention of visitors. Even the casual observer is intrigued by what seems to be a deformed masculine figure.[2]

On the first pier to the south, the upper scene shows the King running and towing behind him the sacred Henu-boat of the God Soker which is placed upon a sledge. The action of the King's figure is beyond praise; the squared shoulders taking the weight of the boat, the flying legs, the feet scarcely touching the ground, the robe billowing out, all create an illusion of rapid movement that could hardly be improved upon.

In the lower scene Ramesses recites the offering formula for the ithyphallic God Min. In front of the God is a curious looking figure like a mummified ape (Fig. 7-2).

On the second pier, Ramesses offers the standard of the God Nefer-tem to Ptah. This is a long pole surmounted by a lotus flower from which spring two tall plumes. A beau-

....
[2]The Nile is in truth the begetter of Egypt, for without it there would be no life in the region. It is also the nourisher, for it is the source of all food for men and animals dwelling all along its banks.

Fig. 7-2. First Hypostyle Hall, eastern wall. Ramesses II and the God Min. Note the curious figure of an ape. In front of the King is inscribed, "Making the offering formula for his father, that he may cause him to live." Below are the Nile Gods carrying vases of water and trays of food offerings. This proxy deed for an ancestor is of considerable interest. Temple of Sety I.

tiful composition on the third pier shows Ramesses between the Gods Atum and Amon-Ra who extend to him the emblems of Life, Endurance and Prosperity. The grace-ful, perfectly balanced figures of the Gods and the lithe vigor of the King make this scene one of the masterpieces of incised relief (Fig. 7-3).

A similar but not so

Fig. 7-3. First Hypostyle Hall, eastern wall. Ramesses II receiving the blessings of Life, Endurance and Prosperity from Atum and Amon-Ra. Temple of Sety I.

well-balanced scene is on the fourth pier (to the north of the Central Doorway). Here Amon-Ra holds the Key of Life to the King's face while Osiris-Andjty brings to him the emblem of the Heb-sed Jubilee. This is in the form of a small pavillion containing two thrones and set upon the sign of a basket meaning, "Feast". It hangs from a stripped palm branch. Ramesses II celebrated the Heb-sed in his XXXth and LXth years of reign and then every alternate year until he died after ruling for sixty-seven years!

On the upper part of the fifth pier Ramesses is digging the ground in front of Osiris for the foundation trench of the temple. Below, he and the Goddess Seshat (or as she is often called, Sefekh-abui), who is here in her role as Goddess of Architecture, are driving stakes into the ground. Cords tied to these stakes will be used to mark out the plan of the temple. This foundation ceremony is also carried out in front of Osiris, the Lord and Master of the Temple.

A scene on the sixth pier shows Ramesses dedicating a chapel to Horus. The interesting part of this scene is the representation of the chapel (Fig. 7-4). Its rectangular doorway and vaulted roof are identical with the Cult Chapels of the temple, but in accordance with rules of Egyptian art, the interior and exterior of the chapel are shown in one drawing, the vaulted roof appearing like an inverted "U" with the doorway inside it.

The Northern Wall.

The northern wall being of limestone allows for even finer sculpture than the sandstone piers; the first scene from the eastern end is another masterpiece of balanced design and inspired carving.

We have already remarked that only the King and the priesthood could enter the inner temple, and even they had to be ceremonially purified by water and natron.

In this scene, Ramesses is being purified by the Gods Horus and Thot. The King is wearing a priestly costume with the white robe of the Ritualist over his shoulder. The Gods holding aloft slender, golden vases, pour the magically purifying liquid into two symmetrical streams over the King. But instead of the water being represented as a long zigzag line as was customary, it is here shown as two chains of emblems of Life and Prosperity (Fig, 7-5). Much of the original color remains on these figures, and by painting the parts of the King's legs that are covered by his robe light pink, in contrast to the brick-red of the exposed flesh, the artist has achieved the desired effect of semi-transparent linen.

In the next scene, the purified King, his hands held by the Gods Horus and Wepwawat, is led into the temple. He is met by the Goddess Hathor who welcomes him saying, "Come in peace, O Good God. Lord of the Two Lands, beloved of Ra. My two arms make obeisance before thy beautiful face, and thou art enriched with life, endurance and prosperity." On the oustretched hands of the Goddess are two zigzag lines standing both for "water" and the letter "N." The meaning is twofold; her hands are ceremonially pure and the two letters "NN" stand for the word "nini" meaning to make "obeisance."

Above this scene is a rectangular window once having a stone grill. It is very unusual to find such windows in the outer walls of temples. It was probably cut in order to give light to the hall after Ramesses had blocked up five of the seven outer doorways. There is a similar window in the same place in the southern wall.

In the last scene on this wall Ramesses is offering the "Henty" to Osiris. This means that he is pre-

Fig. 7-4. First Hypostyle Hall, eastern wall. Ramesses II dedicating a chapel to Horus. Temple of Sety I.

Fig. 7-5. *Ramesses undergoing purification prior to entering the temple. Note how the water is represented here as a chain of emblems of Life and Prosperity. In front of the God Thot is inscribed: "Making purifications for the King of Upper and Lower Egypt, User-maat-Ra Setep-en-Ra by Thot who dwells in Abydos. Thy purification is the purification of Horus; thy purification is the purification of Geb (repeat)." To be recited four times. Temple of Sety I.*

senting to the God the title-deeds of his temple, a papyrus roll on which would be written the dimensions of the building and of all the land belonging to it. The document is supposed to be rolled up inside a golden case shaped like a column, its cover in the form of a falcon's head crowned with a solar disk. The column stands upon a rectangular base and is supported by a statuette of the King kneeling. Underneath is the gilded chest in which this beautiful "Henty" would be kept in the temple archives On its cover lies a recumbent jackal and below are poles for carrying it (Fig. 7-6). Osiris is enthroned, and behind him stand Isis and Horus, the Holy Family of Abydos (Fig. 7-7).

The Western Wall.

Again the wall is formed by six sandstone piers which separate the doorways leading into the Second Hypostyle Hall.

On the upper part of the first pier from the north, Isis suckles Ramesses in the presence of Horus. This act on the part of the Goddess means that she had adopted the King as her son this being the legal form of adoption in ancient Egypt.

In the lower scene Horus presents the Double Crown to Ramesses while Isis offers him the royal uraeus (sacred cobra) and the mystic menat and sistrum.

On the second pier Osiris-Andjty gives to Ramesses the emblem of the Heb-sed and Horus and Isis stand behind the King.

On the third pier Ramesses offers perfumed ointment in an ornamental holder to Amon-Ra and Mut, and a similar scene is shown on the fourth pier.

On the fifth pier, Ramesses holding a folded cloth in his hand, stands before the God Ra-Hor-akhty. The latter is in his usual form of a falcon-headed man. Behind the King stand the Goddesses Hathor and Iusaas.

Unfortunately the scene on the sixth pier is damaged; it was of unusual beauty, and much of its original color remains. Ramesses adores the God Ptah and his wife the Goddess Sekhmet who has the zigzag sign "N" on her hands showing that she is about to make

Fig. 7-6. Ramesses presenting the "Henty." To the left, the vertical inscription reads, "Giving the Henty of the august temple to his father that he may grant that its name exists as the lifetime of Heaven forever and ever."

77

obeisance. Her leonine head is colored green and she is crowned with a red solar disk. Behind Ramesses stands the Goddess Mut wearing the Double Crown. Her hair is arranged in a New Kingdom style.

The Southern Wall.

The southern wall is in poor condition; most of its surface is eroded by the action of salt in the stone which must have oozed as a result of heavy showers of rain over the years. This unfortunate mishap has also spoiled the world-famous Nefertari Tomb in Western Thebes.

At the eastern end of the wall is the purification scene similar to that in the same place on the northern wall.

The remainder of the wall is occupied by a large scene showing the divine creation and nurture of Ramesses. Conscious of his nonroyal ancestry Ramesses is here representing the polite fiction used in such circumstances. (He was undoubtedly an amusing bombast!) To the west we are shown the ram-headed God Khnum fashioning the King's physical body as though it were a statue, and Ptah supplies the color by painting it.

Next, Isis cuddles the infant King, patting him lovingly under the chin before handing him to be suckled by four forms of the Goddess Hathor. Here the King is shown as a bigger child who stands before his divine wet-nurse. The figures of the Goddesses as they bend down and embrace the child-like King are very natural, and still retain some of their beautiful colors in spite of the damage that they have suffered.

The Seven Doorways to the Second Hypostyle Hall.

Seven imposing door-ways open into the Second Hypostyle Hall. They are exactly opposite to the original doorways in the facade of the temple and to the doorways of the Seven

Fig. 7-7. *Continuation of the scene of presenting the Henty. The God Osiris (right), the Goddess Isis and their son the God Horus. Temple of Sety I.*

Vaulted Chapels. These doorways like the columns in the First Hypostyle Hall were partly decorated in bas-relief by Sety. But most of this was erased and re-cut in incised work by Ramesses.

On the eastern side, the lintel of each doorway is surmounted by a palmetto cornice and a torus moulding. In the center of each cornice is a solar disk cut in very high relief and flanked by two crowned uraei. The serpent on the northern side appropriately wears the Red Crown of Lower Egypt while its companion to the south wears the White Crown of Upper Egypt. This patient, meticulous attention to minute details is characteristic of the work of Sety I. Each "frond" of the cornice bears an incised cartouche of Ramesses.

The lintels and outer jambs are all adorned with scenes of Ramesses and the gods, and at the bottom of each jamb Thot, pen and palette in hand and accompanied by the personification of "Hearing" or "Doing," writes an inscription of good wishes for the King. For example on the southern jamb of the northern door, Thot writes: "The years of eternity in life and prosperity for the Lord of the Two Lands, Men-maat-Ra, given life." Below was once the name of the doorway, inscribed by Sety. But these have all been purposely erased and were not replaced except on the Central Doorway where a large roughly cut inscription proclaims the name of Ramesses III.

At the bottom of each of the inner jambs, Sety had inscribed dedication texts. All of these have been effaced except one on the southern jamb of the third doorway from the north and this reads, "Live the Good God, Lord of the Two Lands, Men-maat-Ra, the son of Ra, Sety Mer-en-Ptah, given life. He made it as his monument for his father Osiris Khenty-Amentiu who dwells in the House of Men-maat-Ra; making for him a door of electrum called 'The King of Upper and Lower Egypt Men-maat-Ra Makes Festive the Nome of Abydos.'"

This refers to the great double-leaved door that once closed the doorway. These doors were made of thick planks of cedar wood, sheathed in electrum, a natural alloy of gold and silver, of which the ancient Egyptians were very fond. What a sight these doors must have presented with their gleaming surfaces of precious metal! And no wonder that they have long since disappeared!

The sides of the doorways against which the door-leaves opened were all inscribed by Sety with six vertical lines of dedication speeches relating to the gods whose Cult Chapels were opposite to the doorways. All of these inscriptions were incised for a very practical reason. Had they been carved in bas-relief, Sety's favorite style for interior sculpture, they would soon have been damaged by the door-leaves banging against them. This arrangement is used throughout all those parts of the temple that were decorated by Sety. When the entrance was closed by a single leaf door, we find that the side where the door opens is sculptured in the incised style while the opposite side is in bas-relief.

As an example of these dedication inscriptions, let us take the first line on the northern side of the northern doorway which reads: "Live Horus the Mighty Bull, Kha-em-Wast, the King of Upper and Lower Egypt, Lord of the Two Lands Men-maat-Ra. He made it as his monument for his father Horus who dwells in the 'House of Men-maat-Ra' making for him a great chapel of gold, that he may give him life."

CHAPTER EIGHT

STEPS TO GODHOOD

The Second Hypostyle Hall.

If by some terrible catastrophe the Temple of Sety had been largely destroyed and only those parts which we have already described had been preserved, it would have still been hailed as a masterpiece of Egyptian art and architecture. Certainly no later sculpture of Ramesses ever rivaled the grace and purity of line and masterly carving of his reliefs here. But happily the remainder of the temple has survived. Damaged it is true by malice, carelessness and ignorance much more than by time, and yet it still is of such breathtaking beauty as to cause no lesser man than M. Jean Capart, the great Belgian Egyptologist and art critic to exclaim, "It is perfection. There is nothing more to say!" All the other Egyptologists almost without exception held the same opinion.

Passing through any one of the seven doorways brings one into a hall where walls, columns, architraves and ceiling are all covered with exquisite bas-reliefs. Every figure and even every hieroglyph is modeled with skill and minute attention to detail. And yet the effect is grand and impressive, not finicky or overcrowded as is the case in some later temples.

The art displayed here has a dignified, majestic style of its own. Sety's policy was to return to the orthodox ways and art of the pre-heresy period. But the impact of the Akhen-Aton Period was so great that the artists and sculptors had become accustomed to the more naturalistic style of the so-called "Amarna Art." So while obeying Sety's demand for orthodox representations, they unwittingly infused into them the grace, softness and facial expressions not found in the formal relief work of earlier times.

The King's Portraits.

Thanks to the perfect preservation of his mummy (see Fig. 5-1, p. 43) we are able to check the excellence of the King's portraits. How this startling likeness was obtained we do not know for certain. Undoubtedly Sety was far too busy to sit for every portrait! Perhaps a head of him sculptured from life was used as a model. Or perhaps a plaster cast was made from the King's living face from which many extra casts could be made and distributed to the artists. Anyway the likeness is most remarkable.

The idea of a great pharaoh with his face slathered in plaster is a rather startling one, but it had been done before.

Certainly King Tety of the VIth dynasty had submitted to this inconvenience. The mold of his face was actually found in his Mortuary Temple at Sakkara where it had apparently been used as a model for the reliefs.[1] It seems to have been made by laying a piece of very fine linen soaked in oil over the king's face and them pouring the wet plaster over it. The result is extraordinarily natural.

In the eastern part of the hall, twenty-four papyrus-bud columns uphold the roof. These are also arranged in pairs to form aisles. The pavement of the western part of the hall is raised to a height of about 55 centimeters (22 inches) and here stand twelve more columns. These have round shafts and no capitals, the architraves resting directly upon the abaci. Six limestone ramps and a central stairway ascend to the higher part of the hall.

The Eastern Wall.

Here again the eastern wall is formed by the western faces of six sandstone piers separating the seven doorways. All bear scenes in relief similar in subject to those on the eastern and western walls of the First

....
[1] It is now in the Cairo Museum (No. 97B) where it is, quite without foundation, described as a "death mask."

Fig. 8-1. *Second Hypostyle Hall. Eastern wall. King Sety wearing an unusual form of the war helmet. In front of the King is inscribed, "Placing things (offerings) for his father Ptah that he may give him life like Ra." Note the full length transparent robe. Temple of Sety I.*

the King wears the most unusual form of the blue war helmet flanked by feathers and further adorned by a solar disk (Fig. 8-1).

The first scene on the second pier shows Sety pouring a libation to Ptah. The King's figure is of extraordinary grace and reverence as he bows towards the God. Such a pose could have easily looked top-heavy, but the sensitive artist has avoided this by placing the King's right foot elegantly and sufficiently in advance to balance the forward movement of the shoulders (Fig. 8-2).

In the second scene Sety offers perfume in an ornamental holder to Ra-Hor-akhty. The reliefs on the third, fourth and fifth piers were damaged by fire.

In the first scene on the sixth pier Sety again pours a libation for Isis and the Goddess shakes a sistrum before him. In the second scene he makes offering to Horus.

The Northern Wall.

On this wall, which is of limestone, the art of the period is displayed in all its glory. Although the upper part of the upper register of scenes is destroyed, the remainder is in almost perfect condition. No words can describe the beauty of the scenes on this wall.

Had King Sety lived longer, all the scenes would have been colored, but for some reason Ramesses

Hypostyle Hall; but here there are two scenes on the lower parts of each pier.

Beginning from the south, the first scene shows the Goddess Sekhmet presenting to Sety the lily and papyrus wands of Upper and Lower Egypt. In the companion scene Sety makes offering to Ptah. Here

Fig. 8-2. Second Hypostyle Hall. Eastern wall. Sety pours a libation to the God Ptah.

Fig. 8-3. Second Hypostyle Hall. Northern wall (upper register). Sety about to prostrate himself before the God Amon-Ra.

Fig. 8-4. *Sety burning incense and pouring a libation of water into three vases shaped like hearts (the Second Hypostyle Hall, northern wall).*

Fig. 8-5. *Second Hypostyle Hall. Northern wall. Osiris and his son Horus.*

did not have the painting completed. Therefore the creamy surface of the limestone reveals uninterrupted the exquisite modeling of the figures.

The scene in the upper register at the eastern end of the wall shows Sety about to prostrate himself before a god and goddess (probably Amon-Ra and Mut). He kneels on his right knee with the left leg and foot stretched out behind him; his body leans forward and both hands are raised in adoration. So full of life and humility is this figure that one expects to see the King suddenly throw himself prostrate before the god. It is one of the most expressive scenes of adoration in all Egyptian sculpture (Fig. 8-3).

In the lower scene Sety burns incense and pours a libation before Osiris and Horus. The libation is poured from three slender vases which are joined together, and the triple stream of water falls into three vases shaped like human hearts (Fig. 8-4). This is a play on an Egyptian expression "Washing the Heart," which means to fulfill a long desired wish or ambition. In his subtle way Sety proclaims that he is fulfilling his great desire to adore Osiris here in his own beautiful temple.

Horus stands behind his father (Fig. 8-5). He is clad in a close-fitting tunic of scale work, and his figure is remarkable for the anatomical details in the arms and legs. The modeling of some of the muscles is so delicate as to be more perceptible to the touch than to the eye.

In the next scene Sety has an incense burner in his hand and he is adoring Osiris under fourteen different names or epithets which are inscribed in a panel in front of him (Fig. 8-6). These may perhaps symbolize the fourteen pieces of the body of Osiris, for at this period Egyptians believed that Set had mutilated the corpse of his brother after he had murdered him.

Fig. 8-6. Temple of Sety I. Sety adores Osiris under fourteen different names. Second Hypostyle Hall. Northern wall.

A Real Chef d'Oeuvre.

The next scene has long been hailed as the masterpiece of Egyptian relief sculpture. It represents the adoration of Osiris by five Goddesses (Fig. 8-7). Osiris sits enthroned, majestic and dignified, but the most remarkable thing about his figure is the way in which the sculptor has suggested the details of the arms, knees and ankles under the enshrouding mummy wrappings.

In front of Osiris stands the Goddess Maat wearing a robe patterned like feathered wings folded around her graceful body (Fig. 8-8). Between her and Osiris is inscribed, "Adoration four times by the goddesses." Behind Maat stands Renpet, Goddess of the Year (Fig. 8-8).

Isis stands behind Osiris; on her head she wears her name-symbol, the throne, and she also wears a wing-patterned robe like that of Maat. She rests one hand on the shoulder of Osiris and the other is raised in a tender, caressing gesture (Fig. 8-9).

Behind Isis stands Amentet, the personification of the West (Amenty), the Kingdom of Osiris and the Home of the Dead. On her head is the symbol of Amenty, a falcon perched upon a semicircle (Fig. 8-10).

Lastly comes Nepthys, the sister of Osiris and

Fig. 8-7. Second Hypostyle. Northern wall. Osiris and the five Goddesses. Below is the dado of Nile Gods.

Isis. She wears a plain robe covered by a network of beads.

It is impossible to find words to describe the beauty, dignity, charm and gracefulness of these God-desses. With the exception of Isis, they all stand with both arms hanging at their sides, a simple pose. But what unnamed genius made of this whole scene the epitome of tender, graceful dignity? "It is out of this world!" exclaimed a world-known photographer. "No, these are not just ordinary human beings of our poor planet; these are real gods and goddesses!" ex-claimes another.

One of the very remark-able features about the sculpture here is the uni-formed excellence of the work. The lower register of sculpture is of course, easily seen; but only keen scrutinity could discern the

Fig. 8-8. Temple of Sety I. The Goddesses Maat (left) and Renpet (right). The Second Hypostyle Hall, northern wall (see Fig. 8-7).

Fig. 8-9. The Second Hypostyle Hall. Northern wall. Isis and Osiris.

Fig. 8-10. The Second Hypostyle Hall. Northern wall. Amentet, Goddess of the West.

Fig. 8-11. Sety pouring a double libation (the Second Hypostyle Hall, northern wall).

details in the upper register especially in the ancient days when the temple was darker than it is today,[2] and yet the work in the upper register is as fine as in the lower one.

We have already remarked on the astonishingly lifelike figure of the praying King on the eastern end of this wall. We see this excellence again (above the figure of Osiris and Isis) where he is pouring a libation upon an offering table (Fig. 8-11).

The Mysterious Column.

Following the above mentioned scenes is a pilaster (opposite to the third row of columns) which bears an interesting representation of the Djed Pillar once the symbol of Osiris and of his resurrection. The origin of this emblem and what it really represents is still a mystery. Some Egyptologists say that it represents the backbone of Osiris but others say the sternum. Other scientists see in it a conventional representation of a tree while others say that it is a sheaf of corn! In appearance it is usually a tall pillar, widening slightly at the base and having four

. . . .

[2]The modern doors of iron bars let in more light than did the old solid doors. Also the apertures in the modern roofing slabs admit more light as these slabs are only 15.0 cms. (6 inches) thick while the original slabs were over one meter (3.3 feet) thick.

Fig. 8-12. The decorated Djed Pillar on a pilaster (the Second Hypostyle Hall, northern wall).

Fig. 8-13. Temple of Sety I. Second Hypostyle Hall. Northern wall (pilaster). Figures of the King wearing the Red Crown of Lower Egypt, supporting the Djed Pillar.

Fig. 8-14. Second Hypostyle Hall. Northern wall. Sety kneels to receive emblems from the God Horus. The coloring of the scene was unfinished at the time of the King's death.

Fig. 8-15. Temple of Sety I. Sety offers the symbolic image of Truth (Maat) to Osiris. Second Hypostyle Hall. Northern wall.

crossbars at its upper end. As a hieroglyph, the Djed stands for Endurance, Stability and the like. In this representation it personifies the God himself. The summit was originally crowned with a divine headdress; great human eyes look out from under the top crossbar and it is adorned with a wide collar and pectoral pendant which hang from the lowest crossbar (Fig. 8-12).

Supporting the Djed Pillar are two figures of the King, probably statues. As this pilaster is at the northern end of the hall, the King wears the Red Crown of Lower Egypt. There is a pilaster opposite to this at the southern end of the hall. It bears the same representation (Fig. 8-13), but the figures of the King are wearing the White Crown of Upper Egypt.

More Masterpieces.

In the upper register to the west of the pilaster, Sety kneels before Horus (Fig. 8-14) who hands to him the crook and flail of kingship and the curved battle-ax emblem of conquest. Isis is seated behind Horus and a goddess whose distinguishing headdress is destroyed stands behind Sety. She holds a stripped palm branch, emblem of long years of reign, and perhaps she is Seshat.

The artists had just begun to paint this scene. They had gotten as far as coloring the upper parts of the figures brick-red for Horus and Sety and yellow for the goddesses and the overwrap of the kilt of Horus. But the lower parts of all the figures are uncolored. It is a mystery why they were not finished.

What happened? Did a swift messenger reigning on his sweating chariot horses cry aloud the terrible news, "The good God has flown to heaven"![3] Did the artists, hearing the piercing death wails of the townswomen of Abydos, drop their brushes and pots of color and rush out of the temple to find out the cause of the outcry never to return and complete their work? Nobody can really tell for certain, but the work remains just as they left it.

It is very difficult to see why the work on the temple should have stopped at Sety's death. There was no question about the succession as Ramesses

: . . . .
[3]In Ancient Egypt, "death" was never mentioned in the connection with the King except in a negative form.

had been co-regent with his father since early childhood. The endowments made by Sety in respect to this temple cannot have been diverted to other ends, so that there would have been no doubts about the payment of the workers' wages.

As Ramesses was already building a neighboring temple here, perhaps the fawning officials had called off the work of his predecessor hoping to please their young new Lord. If so, they made a great and unpardonable mistake as we can see from the long inscription of Ramesses on the facade of the temple.

The lower scene on the western end of the wall is yet another one of singular beauty and is very well known. There is hardly a book on Egyptian history or art that does not publish it as an illustration. And we shall follow suit (Fig. 8-15)! It shows Sety presenting a small image of Maat, here symbolizing Truth, to Osiris. The inscription under the King's arm says, "Presenting Truth to the Lord of Truth."

The figure of the King is beyond praise in its grace and dignity. So skillful is the carving that one forgets the hardness of the stone; the semitransparent linen of the King's clothing looks soft to the touch and seems to respond to the movements of his body. This kilt, which just un-

covers the knees in front and droops to mid-calf behind, was the "uniform" of army officers, and we see many representations of Sety wearing it. As an ex-officer, he may have preferred it to other styles, but it soon became a fashion for gentlemen of high rank who had no military connections at all.

Osiris is enthroned in a shrine, and in front of him is a pedestal offering table carrying a large bouquet of lotus flowers. The God wears the Itef crown and gazes at the King with gracious kindliness. Behind him stands Isis crowned with the lunar disk and cow's horns. With her usual tender gesture, she places one hand on the shoulder of Osiris, and lovingly caresses him with the other. Horus, holding the scepter of Prosperity and the Key of Life, stands behind his parents (Fig. 8-16) completing a beautiful representation of the Holy Family of Abydos.

The Western Wall of the Second Hypostyle Hall.

The western wall of the Second Hypostyle Hall consists of six piers, but here they are of limestone and are decorated with colored bas-reliefs. They separate the doorways of the Seven Vaulted Chapels.

The Doorways.

The outer sides of these doorways are surmounted by palmetto cornices in the center of which is a solar disk and crowned uraei in high relief similar to those over each doorway between the two hypostyle halls. Above each doorway was a window with a stone grill.

The outer jambs of each doorway bear three scenes showing the King adoring the deity to whom the chapel is dedicated. The fourth and lowest scene shows the God Thot accompanied by "Doing" or "Hearing" writing an inscription. Below is a dedication text which also gives the name of the doorway.

Each doorway was once closed by double-leaved doors of cedar wood plated with gold or electrum and inlaid with semiprecious stones.

What a wonderful sight they must have presented, these seven great gleaming doorways, "giving forth radiance like the sun," as one of the inscriptions claims! We sincerely feel there is no exaggeration whatsoever in such a claim.

The Niches.

In the center of each of the limestone piers is a niche, each wall of which bears a scene of Sety and the gods. Their ceilings are decorated with yellow five-pointed stars on a blue ground representing the sky. Their lintels all bear splendid emblems of the winged sun disk of Horus of Edfu and inscriptions giving the names and epithets of Sety and the gods by whom he is beloved.

Similar inscriptions adorn the jambs, and every hieroglyph in them is a miniature work of art.

As the floors of these niches are only 44 centimeters (17 inches) higher then the pavement of the hall, they cannot have been intended to house statues; they were probably for the token offering of a loaf of bread and a jar of beer.

In ancient Egypt, bread and beer were a synonym for food and drink in general. A meal was often referred to as a "Bread-beer"; a young man was now old enough to "earn his own bread and beer."

With the exception of a few burnt offerings, offerings were left in place for a short while and then removed by the priests to be eaten by them or placed on the offering tables of the dead. This was because they believed that all things animate or inanimate had a Ka.[4] The Kas of the gods or of the dead consumed the Kas of the offerings. The material substances could then be eaten by the living.

Above each niche is a large scene covering the whole width of the pier and showing Sety between two deities. These are so arranged that each god is shown beside his own chapel. Below on each side of the niche a smaller scene shows the King in

....
[4]The Ka is sometimes called the material soul, or the spiritual double.

Fig. 8-16. The Second Hypostyle Hall. Northern wall. The God Horus.

the presence of a god or goddess.

In the upper scene on the first pier from the north, Horus presents Sety with the Heb-sed emblems and the lily and papyrus wands. Behind Sety stands Isis also offering the Heb-sed emblem and holding out the menat necklace which she is wearing around her neck.

In the northern lower scene Sety is embraced by Horus who here wears the Itef crown in place of his more usual Double Crown of Upper and Lower Egypt.

The southern lower scene has unusual beauty. Sety stands in front of Isis who holds the Key of Life to his face. This usually is a banal theme, but the artist transformed

Fig. 8-17. The God Khonsu, crowned with the full and crescent moons, gives "Life" and "Prosperity" to Sety. The Second Hypostyle Hall. Western wall.

it into one charged with emotion. The King wearing a short wig adorned with a simple golden uraeus on the brow is clad in the military kilt. Both arms hang at his sides; the left hand holding a mace and the Key of Life. The expression on his face suggests weariness and disillusionment as though having tasted the Wine of Power, he found it bitter and repugnant. He leans slightly forward towards Isis like a son about to throw himself into the comforting arms of an all-understanding mother. By contrast, the figure of the Goddess is a picture of slim grace and serene dignity seemingly imbued with the divine power to heal and comfort. Her calm and beautiful face smiles with tender under-standing, and she assures the King that he is to her "as Horus who was in my body."

In the upper scene on the second pier, Sety kneels before the enthroned Osiris to whom he is burning in-cense. Behind the King, Isis who is also seated holds a palm branch with a pendant Heb-sed emblem.

In the northern lower scene, Horus grasps the King by the hand and offers him the combined emblems of Life, Endurance and Prosperity. Sety raises his free hand to accept the gift. He is clad as a priest and wears the white pleated robe of a ritualist.

In the southern scene the jackal-headed God Wepwawat embraces Sety. A lesser artist could easily have given the canine face of the God a wolfish grin instead he has the kindly expression of a friendly dog.

The upper scene on the third pier shows the King, wearing the divine headdress, kneeling before Amon-Ra who hands him the crook and flail and a stripped palm branch. Behind the King, Osiris sits enthroned in austere dignity.

The northern lower scene shows Sety seated like a little child on the lap of Isis; the Goddess places one hand behind his head and with the other tenderly raises his face as though about to kiss him. She addresses him as her beloved son whom she brought forth and nursed "that his limbs might be strong."

In the southern lower scene the God Khonsu in the form of a falcon-headed man crowned with the full and crescent moons holds the emblems of Life and Prosperity to the King's face (Fig. 8-17).

On the upper part of the fourth pier is a very interesting scene. Sety is kneeling before Amon-Ra. In his left hand he holds a bird that sym-bolizes the rekhyt, the common people of Egypt. His right hand is raised to accept the mace and curved battle-ax which Amon-Ra extends to him. In the inscription behind him, the God promises to give Sety "all the foreign

Fig. 8-18. The Goddess Mut suckles Sety showing that she has adopted him as her son. The Second Hypostyle Hall. Western wall.

lands under thy feet."

This group means that Sety as ruler of Egypt holds his subjects safely in his hand, but Amon-Ra also gives him the weapons of war, symbols of conquest and promises to restore the Egyptian Empire which was one of the King's chief aims after solving internal problems.

Behind Sety is a very unusual figure of Ra-Horakhty here shown as a ram-headed man wearing a solar disk between his horizontal horns. He extends his hand in blessing towards the King.

The northern lower scene is also very beautiful in spite of wanton damage to the faces of the figures. Here the Goddess Mut is suckling the King, and the scene is similar to that on the first pier in the western wall of the First Hypostyle Hall. The Goddess embraces the King with her right arm and with her left hand holds her breast to his mouth. The pose of this hand with three fingers hidden behind the swell of the breast is very natural and is one of the few examples of perspective in Egyptian art. The King stands as a little child in front of her holding her left forearm in his hand and gazing up trustingly into her face. The whole pose of Mut and the way in which she bends her head down towards the little King is a masterly depiction of maternal affection (Fig. 8-18).

In the southern lower scene the Goddess Iusaas of Heliopolis offers the emblems of Life and Prosperity to Sety who is again shown as a young child.

In the upper scene on the fifth pier, Sety kneels beside the Tree of Life of Heliopolis while Ra-Horakhty writes his name upon its leaves. Ptah seated on a throne extends to

the King the emblem of "Millions of Years" in the form of a kneeling man holding a stripped palm branch in each hand. Sety raises his hand to accept the gift.

In the northern lower scene the Goddess Hathor holds out the emblems of Life and Prosperity to the King saying, "To thy nose O this good God, Lord of the Two Lands." Here the Goddess wears a most unusual crown. Above the normal "Vulture crown" worn by queens and goddesses is a circle of uraei on which stands the figure of a falcon. The bird's wings are half extended forwards and shelter two more uraei one wearing the crown of Upper Egypt and the other wearing the crown of Lower Egypt.

In the southern lower scene, the lioness-headed Goddess Sekhmet grasps the hand of the King with her left hand and with her right one holds out to him the menat necklace that she is wearing. This scene is very similar to that of Sety and Isis in the same place on the first pier but lacks its emotional character.

The upper part of the sixth pier has been destroyed and with it part of the scene. It shows Sety offering flowers to Ptah who stands in a golden shrine; Sekhmet stands at the back of the shrine holding a papyrus wand and the Key of Life.

In the scene to the north of the niche, Mut extends her menat necklace

to the King who again holds the common people of Egypt. This means that the Goddess is bestowing her blessings on both the King and his subjects.

In the southern lower scene, Sety is embraced by the God Nefer-tem.

The Southern Wall and the Second Hypostyle Hall.

The western end of the southern end of this wall is occupied by the doorway of the Hall of Soker. Next comes the southern pilaster with its Djed Pillar decoration and then the doorway to the famous "Corridor of Kings." To the east of the latter, the wall bore two registers of uncolored scenes; the upper part of the top register is lost; the surface of the wall bearing the lower register is in a rather bad condition.

The first scene shows Horus offering some emblem (now destroyed) to the enthroned King behind whom stands Wepwawat. Next, Thot dedicates a great quantitiy of food and drink offerings to the King. Above the offerings is inscribed the offering list.

The last scene is in very bad condition. It shows Sety standing in a shrine; two male figures, perhaps the Iwn-mut-ef priest and Thot, stood in front of him.

Around the lower part of all the walls of this hall the benign Nile God kneels with his life-giving offerings of water and food.

CHAPTER NINE

THE SEVEN VAULTED CHAPELS

The Seven Vaulted Chapels,
General Structure and
Function.

As mentioned before,
seven chapels with vaulted
roofs open out of the western wall of the Second
Hypostyle Hall (see pages
50 and 120). Six of these
chapels were intended to
be used for the daily cult
ceremonies of the Gods
Horus, Isis, Osiris, Amon-
Ra, Ra-Hor-akhty and Ptah.
The seventh was for the
Mortuary Cult of Sety himself who had become a god.

These chapels were the
very holy places of the
temple where the gods,
incarnate in their statues,
took up their abode at will.

The barrel vaulted
roofs were first built as
corbelled roofs with each
course of masonry projecting inwards. The angles
were then cut away and the
underside of the spanning
stone hollowed out. Two
small rectangular skylights
in the roof gave ventila-
tion and light. Each chapel
was divided into two halves
by a gilded wooden screen
topped by a frieze of uraei
and having a door in the
middle. A representation
of this screen appears
in the upper register of
scenes at the western end
of every chapel where it
appears to be enclosing a
sacred boat. In reality
the boat was behind it.

In the western wall of
every chapel, except that
of Osiris', is a large
false-door of sandstone.
This represents the door
between our world and
the Hereafter; such doors
also occur in tomb chapels.
Offerings were placed in
front of them and it was
believed that the spirits
of the gods and the dead
could pass through them
at will and partake of
the offerings set out
before them.

In the front part of
the chapel stood a golden
shrine containing the
statue of the god to whom
the chapel was dedicated.
This statue wore real
crowns and ornaments and
was clad in a real linen
scarf or shawl rather than
an actual garment.

For the morning cere-
mony the priest first broke
the clay seal on the doors
and entered the chapel
carrying an incense burner
and a golden libation vase.
He next broke the seal on
the door of the golden
shrine, opened the door
and knelt to pray. In-
cense was burned and li-
bations of water and
natron poured out. The
ornaments and clothing of
the statue were removed,
and the statue itself
then washed, dried and
anointed with perfumed
ointment. It was then
clad in new clothing[1] and
the crowns, ornaments and
scepters replaced.

....
[1]The castoff clothing
was never washed and
replaced but was dis-
tributed to the faithful
who treasured it for use
in their own funerary
wrappings.

Strips of linen were of-
fered and more libations
and incense. Clean sand
was poured all over the
floor of the chapel, and an
offering meal was served.[2]
The door of the golden
shrine was then bolted and
sealed, and finally the
priest walked out of the
chapel sweeping behind
him with a broom to remove
his own footprints from
the sanded floor. Then
the great doors of the
chapel were closed and
sealed, and the daily cult
ceremony was complete.

These rites are the
subject of the scenes on
the walls of the six cult
chapels of the gods, but
instead of being performed
by a priest, Sety himself
is officiating. As honor-
ary High Priest of every
god, he may actually have
performed some of these
rites when visiting the
temple.

The inscriptions ac-
companying the scenes re-
cord the words to be spoken
during the performance of
each ceremony.

Behind the screen in
the western end of the
chapel stood a rectangular
pedestal of gilded wood.
Here, on the feast day of
the god, the sacred golden
boat was brought from the
special hall in which it
was usually housed and

....
[2]A remainder of this
custom still persists
among the modern Egyp-
tian peasants who pour
clean sand in front
of a house when an
important visitor is
expected.

placed on the pedestal. A statue of the god was then put in the veiled cabin-shrine amidships, and small figures of the King knelt in adoration and also held the great steering-oars. Then the boat was fastened to two long carrying-poles, and, borne on the shoulders of the priests, was carried out of the temple into the courts and from thence in a procession through the city. During the Great Feast of Osiris, all the boats were carried out together in a great procession with music and singing. What a sight that was, especially when the Pharaoh himself in all his glittering glory was walking at the head of the procession! Judging by the importance of this feast, hundreds of thousands of people may have participated in these grand parades.

The Cult Chapel of Horus.

This is the first of the Seven Vaulted Chapels (from the northern side of the temple). Unfortunately its northern and western walls are in very bad condition. The presence of salt in the stone has caused the surface to flake away, and added to that, the chapel was, until recently, infested with large, noisy fruit bats who have splashed the beautiful reliefs that are there.

The outer jambs of the doorway bear three scenes in which the King is shown offering to the God Horus. In the fourth lowest scene, Thot accompanied by his assistant, who holds his waterpot, writes an inscription decreeing many Heb-sed feasts for the King. Below this is a dedication text which also gives the name of the doorway and following the royal names and epithets reads, "He made it as his monument for his father Horus, the son of Isis, who dwells in the house of Men-maat-Ra" making for him a great seat shining in the faces of men. Its door is like a great illumination by the side of his mother Isis, (it is called) "Men-maat-Ra is the Avenger (or Protector) of His Father."

Inside the chapel, the lower scene to the north of the doorway shows the King entering the chapel in order to perform the daily ceremonies. He carries a libation vase and an incense burner. In the upper scene Sety is embraced by the God Horus.

The Northern Wall of the Chapel of Horus.

In the first scene in the lower register, the King is breaking the clay seal upon the door of a golden shrine containing an imposing statue of the God Horus. The God is seated on a throne and wears the Itef Crown. Above in the upper register, the King opens the door of the shrine.

In the second and third scenes, the statues of Horus are purified with water and incense, and in the fourth, Sety kneels in adoration before the God.

In the lower register the second, third and fourth scenes all show the King burning incense in front of Horus. But a text describing the latter scene says that Sety is "entering the Great Place." This same text occurs in the same place in all of the six divine cult chapels, and it is immediately in front of the place of the wooden screen that once divided the chapel in half. "The Great Place" must refer to the western half of the chapel which seems to have been considered especially sacred.

The surface of the western end of the wall is almost entirely destroyed. In the upper register one may see a badly damaged representation of the King making offerings to the sacred golden boat of Horus. In the lower register only faint, ghostly traces of figures of the King and his God remain.

The Western Wall of the Cult Chapel of Horus.

On the northern side of the false-door, the upper scene is badly eroded and shows Sety standing before Horus while in the lower scene he is disrobing a statue of the God.

The false-door is well preserved but begrimed with smoke and the droppings of bats. As the false-doors are the same in all of the chapels, we will describe only the one in the Chapel of Amon-Ra which is in the best condition.

Fig. 9-1. Cult Chapel of Horus (southern wall, upper register). Sety pouring sand on the floor of the chapel in front of Horus.

Fig. 9-3. The Cult Chapel of Horus (southern wall, upper register). The sacred boat of Horus. Temple of Sety I.

The Southern Wall of the Chapel of Horus.

This wall is in a much better state of preservation though still somewhat disfigured by the droppings of bats. The sculpture is very fine indeed; the faces of the King being full of life and expression. The figures of Horus are sternly majestic, but the awe-inspiring fierceness of the falcon's face is softened by the tenderness of his gestures towards the King. How skillfully the artist has combined the bird's head with the human body creating a convincingly natural looking figure from two such diverse elements!

The first scene on the upper part of this wall shows Sety pouring clean sand on the floor of the chapel. The sand is in a basin and the

Fig. 9-2. Sety burns incense in front of the sacred boat of Horus. Vaulted Cult Chapel of Horus (southern wall).

action of the King's hands as he holds it and tips out the sand is as natural as one would find in any good modern drawing (Fig. 9-1).

The remainder of this part of the wall is occupied by a large scene in which Sety burns incense in front of the sacred boat of Horus (Fig. 9-2). Falcons' heads adorn the prow and stern posts of the vessel, and behind the prow is a small sphinx standing on a pedestal followed by a standing statuette of the King. Two more royal figures kneel before and behind the cabin-shrine which stands amidships and is partly concealed by a veil. Another figure of the King acts as helmsman working the great steering-oars (Fig. 9-3).

Fig. 9-4. The Cult Chapel of Horus (southern wall, upper register). The prow of the sacred boat of Horus with a falcon figure-head. Note the incense burner placed crosswise on the jar stand and the libation vase shaped like the Key of Life.

Fig. 9-5. The Cult Chapel of Horus. Southern wall. Sety presents a leather strap and counterpoise to Horus.

Fig. 9-6. Cult Chapel of Horus (southern wall, upper register). Horus purified by Sety. Temple of Sety I.

Presenting Bouquets, an Old Egyptian Custom.

The boat fastened to its carrying-poles rests upon a rectangular pedestal, and under the front pole a kneeling statuette of the King serves to hold a formal bouquet of flowers. There are also stands bearing vases some of which have covers in the form of disk-crowned falcons' heads. Under the hind carrying-pole are two bowls of offerings and two statues of the King holding sacred standards (Fig. 9-4).

In those chapels in which the scenes are colored, all the stands, vases, etc.

as well as the boat itself are painted yellow denoting that they were made of gold while the small figures of the King were of silver with golden headdresses and kilts.

In the lower register the first scene to the west shows Sety offering perfumed ointment to Horus, and in the second scene he presents a pair of wide bracelets, the crook, flail and scepter of Prosperity to the God. Isis is seated behind her son and affectionately grasps his upper arm.

In the third scene, the King, wearing the dress of a priest, deftly adjusts

the Double Crown on the head of Horus.

The fourth scene shows the presentation of a leather strap and a counterpoise for a heavy necklace to Horus. These leather straps, usually red in color, were worn over mummy wrappings (Fig. 9-5).

On the eastern end of the wall Sety purifies a statue of Horus with water and incense and also offers to the God "incense of the north" and "incense of the south" (Fig. 9-6).

Below he offers a golden collar and three different kinds of linen.

The ceremonies are now complete; to the south of the doorway Sety leaves the chapel taking his libation vase with him and carefully obliterating his own footprints as he goes.

The Cult Chapel of Isis.

The three upper scenes on the outer jambs of the doorway show Sety offering to Isis (Fig. 9-7); in the lower scene it is Seshat (Sefekh) instead of Thot who writes the inscription of goodwill for the King (Fig. 9-8). Is Seshat represented here because she too is a Goddess? The doorleaves are described as being "glittering with every costly stone, its door gilded with electrum

giving forth radiance like the sun."

The lower scene on both inner jambs shows the graceful, naked figures of the "Mert" goddesses kneeling on the sign of "gold" and raising their outstretched arms to the cartouche of the King. The Mert on the northern jamb is of Lower Egypt, and her sister of Upper Egypt is on the southern jamb.

The interior of the chapel has suffered badly from the burning of the temple; the greater part of the surface of the southern wall being either destroyed or very damaged. The northern wall is in a

better state but is marred by holes cut in the stone. These may have been done at some later time when the temple was used as a dwelling.

To the north of the doorway Sety stands in the presence of Isis; above, he breaks the clay seal on the door of a shrine containing her statue.

The subject of the scenes on the northern wall are similar to those in the corresponding place in the Chapel of Horus, but they are even more beautiful; the artists seemingly have taken special pride in the rendering of the figures of the lovely and gracious Goddess and the deferential

Fig. 9-8. The Cult Chapel of Isis. Outer doorjamb. The Goddess Seshat writing an inscription on behalf of the King. Behind her the personification of "Doing" holds her combined palette and pen-case.

Fig. 9-7. Cult Chapel of Isis (southern inner jamb of doorway). Sety offers wine to Isis.

Fig. 9-9. Cult Chapel of Isis (northern wall). Sety kneels in adoration before Isis. Temple of Sety I.

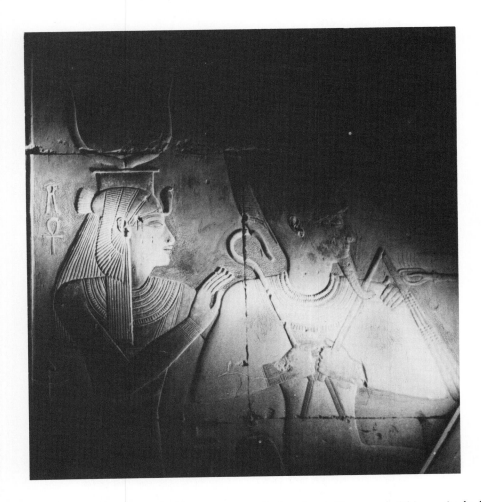

Fig. 9-10. Cult Chapel of Osiris (northern wall). Osiris and Isis. The face of the Goddess has escaped mutilation by the early Christians. The Temple of Sety I.

The Cult Chapel of Osiris.

As this is the most important of the cult chapels (being dedicated to Osiris, the Great God of Abydos, and Master of the Temple), it was among the first parts of the building to be painted, and despite the passing of the years, and the savage, fanatical destruction wrought by the early Christians, the colors are wonderfully well preserved.

But unfortunately the fanatics displayed their religious zeal (or their guilty fear of their deserted gods) by disfiguring the faces of the deities and the King in all the scenes in the lower register with but one exception (Fig. 9-10). One wonders what type of mentality could plan and carry out such senseless destruction of pure artistic beauty. Most probably real fear was behind all this since all the figures are destroyed in one and the same way.

Inside the chapel the scene to the north of the doorway shows the King burning incense to Osiris and Wepwawat.

The Cult Chapel of Osiris, the Northern Wall.

In the first scene in both registers on the northern wall, Osiris is shown as a living God and not in his usual form of a mummy. The former is the way in which he was worshiped in Busiris (now Abusir el Malek) where he was identified with a local God named Andjty.

Another scene in the lower register shows Sety

but dignified King.

Sety Kneels for Once Before Isis.

The fourth scene in the upper register is very unusual. It shows the King kneeling before Isis (Fig. 9-9). There are many scenes in which he appears kneeling before gods, but goddesses are another matter! He bows to them in dignified homage, but he does not kneel! So this scene showing him on his knees before Isis proves how greatly he revered her.

The sacred boat of the Goddess is shown in the upper register of both southern and northern walls (at the western end).

The western wall is much disfigured, but on each side of the false-door Sety disrobes and reclothes the statues of Isis.

The scenes on the damaged southern wall are very similar to those in the Chapel of Horus. Finally, the King leaves the chapel with his libation vase and broom.

burning incense before Osiris and Isis. By a happy chance, the lovely face of the Goddess has escaped the wanton disfigurement of all the others, and she gazes at her husband with a gentle, melancholy smile as though she were remembering all the sorrows that they had once suffered but had overcome.

The sacred boat of Osiris is shown in the upper register of the western half of the wall. This is a replica of the famous Neshmet boat (Fig. 9-11). The figure-head on the prow is a portrait-head of Osiris, but the sternpost curves gracefully inwards and terminates in a lotus flower. Miniature figures of the King kneel in adoration before and behind the cabin-shrine or, accompanied by Isis and Nepthys, stand and hold large feather-fans.

A Curious Modern Belief.

Many of the inhabitants of modern Abydos who know nothing at all of the ancient Egytian religion claim to have seen a golden boat floating on a pool (the remains of the old sacred lake) in the nighttime. One man actually waded out towards the boat hoping to get some of the gold for himself. But before he reached it, he said that a "soldier" came out from behind the cabin and shook his fist at him in a very threatening manner. The would-be robber made a hasty retreat. Up till now he refuses to pass this spot after sunset even though it is a convenient short-cut to his home! This man in particular has nerves of steel; he is very practical, unimaginative, a realist, and certainly not the type to see things that do not exist! We leave the story for the reader's conclusion.

The Western Wall of the Cult Chapel of Osiris.

The western wall of this chapel seems to be different from the others. Instead of the dominating false-door, it is largely occupied by a real portal leading to some other halls and chapels nowadays known as the "Osiris Complex." We shall describe the "Osiris Complex" later. The northern jamb of this door has been entirely destroyed, and the southern one appears to be badly damaged.

Fig. 9-11. The Cult Chapel of Osiris (northern wall, upper register). The Neshmet boat of Osiris. The Temple of Sety I.

Fig. 9-12. *The standard of Abydos. Cult Chapel of Osiris. Southern wall. The Temple of Sety I.*

The Southern Wall of the Cult Chapel of Osiris.

The large scene at the western end of the upper register is very interesting. Instead of being a repetition of the King honoring the sacred boat, here Sety offers incense to the sacred standard of Abydos (Fig. 9-12).

The standard, surmounted by a curious round-topped object, crowned by a solar disk and plumes is fixed into a rectangular stand where it is held in place by the forequarters of two lions. On the upper surface of the stand are small figures of the King in gold and silver. The figures extend their arms to support the pole of the standard while similar figures kneel in prayer. Like the sacred boats, the standard is also fixed to carrying-poles, for this

holy emblem was also carried in procession on the feast days of Osiris. On these occasions the emblem was preceeded by some smaller sacred standards, and these are shown in front of it in this scene (Fig. 9-13). These are the standards of "Wepwawat of the South" surmounted by a standing jackal; that of "Wepwawat of the North" has a recumbent jackal, the standard of Thot surmounted by an ibis, that of Horus topped by a falcon, and lastly the standard of In-hert terminating in a statuette of that God holding a spear.

Beside the standard of Thot is a large golden baton called "Kherp." Such batons were used in the temple to consecrate the offerings by tapping them with it. As a hieroglyphic sign, "Kherp" means "guide" or "direct." In this scene the baton represents the God Thot

himself, one of whose epithets was "Guide (Kherp) of the Gods." This is made plain in the accompanying inscription which reads, "Thot, the Guide (Kherp) of the Gods, he gives all health, all gladness of heart."

The three scenes in the upper register of the wall are well-preserved and beautifully colored. They show the King offering natron to Osiris who is accompanied by Thot, kneeling before Osiris, and burning incense to Osiris and Wepwawat.

In the lower register a beautiful scene shows Sety offering a golden collar to Osiris. Isis stands behind her husband, and attached to her arms are two great wings which she extends on each side of the God like a mother bird protecting her young. Even the horrible disfigurement to the faces of

Fig. 9-13. *The smaller divine standards. Cult Chapel of Osiris. Southern wall.*

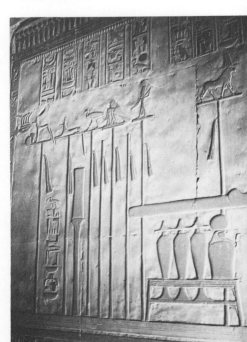

the three figures has failed to destroy the artistic and emotional beauty of this scene. The final scene of sweeping away the footprints has been omitted, and in its place is a scene showing the King offering a conical loaf of white bread to Wepwawat.

The Cult Chapel of Amon-Ra.

Although the entire temple was dedicated to Osiris, Amon-Ra as being

Fig. 9-15. The King about to cleanse the statue of Amon-Ra. Note how the priestly robe has slipped down over the King's shoulder; notice pleats on lower portion. The Vaulted Chapel of Amon-Ra, northern wall.

Fig. 9-14. Sety adjusts the crown of Amon-Ra (here represented as the God Min). The vaulted Chapel of Amon-Ra, southern wall. The Temple of Sety I.

the King of the Gods, and the Chief Deity of the Empire is honored by the fact that his cult chapel occupies the central position on the row directly opposite to the Main Entrance to the temple (see page 38).

Here also the scenes have been colored and are fairly well preserved especially in the western end of the chapel and in the upper registers.

The interior scene to the north of the doorway shows the King carrying a pot of incense as he enters the chapel.

A curious point concerning the figures of the God in this chapel is that while he is sometimes

Fig. 9-16. The Cult Chapel of Amon-Ra showing the false-door in the western wall. Temple of Sety I.

represented in his normal form of a living deity wearing a flat-topped crown surmounted by two high feathers of a falcon, his flesh being colored blue as a mummy, more curiously he is represented as the ithyphallic God Min (Fig. 9-14). In this latter form, the inscriptions usually refer to him as "Amon-Ra, Bull of his Mother."

The finest scenes on the northern wall of this chapel occur in its western end; the entire upper register being occupied by a representation of the sacred boat of Amon-Ra behind which are the boats of his son Khonsu and his wife Mut. Beautiful as it is, this scene is completely outshone by the replica of it on the southern wall.

In the lower register, Sety stands humbly in the presence of Amon-Ra. He wears the costume of a ritualist priest and the carving of his finely pleated white linen robe is beyond praise (Fig. 9-15). A very natural, little detail is the way in which the white robe has slipped down over his shoulder causing the pleats to open somewhat and makes the robe wider at this part. The modeling of the King's legs and thighs under the pleats of his long skirt give the impression that we are looking at soft, transparent linen. The Greeks at their best could never have depicted drapery with such uncanny craftmanship and realism.

Fig. 9-17. Cult Chapel of Amon-Ra (southern wall, upper register). The King burns incense before the sacred boat of Amon-Ra (details). The Temple of Sety I.

Next, Sety performs the rite known as "Laying the hands upon the God," who is here again in the form of Min; lastly he removes a fringed shawl from a mummiform statue of Amon-Ra.

The False-door.

The false-door which occupies most of the western wall of the chapel is very well preserved (Fig. 9-16). As in the other cult chapels, it is of sandstone and it is in the form of a double-leaved door with an openwork transom above it; the whole being surmounted by a cornice of uraei.

The transom has a rounded top on each side of which is a sacred "Eye of Horus" guarded by a uraeus whose tail forms the "eyebrow."

Under the curve of the top on each side, the King in the form of a sphinx, is seated on his haunches in front of a cartouche.

Next come two rectangular panels in each of which the God Heh of Eternity is kneeling on the sign of "gold." Below in the center is a panel containing a fanciful writing of the King's prenomen. It consists of a falcon-headed god crowned with a solar disk and holding an ostrich plume and seated on a sign of a gaming board which, as a hieroglyph, has the sound value of "Men." The ostrich plume has the value of "Maat," and the disk crowned God is "Ra," "Men-maat-Ra."

A double inscription on the lintel reading from the center outwards gives the titles and names of the King who is "beloved of Amon-Ra."

Fig. 9-18. The pedestal of the sacred boat of Amon-Ra decorated with figures of the King supporting the sign of "Heaven." The vaulted Chapel of Amon-Ra. Southern wall.

"Venetion Blinds," an Ancient Egyptian Invention.

The two "doors" are divided by a frame down the center of which is a papyrus wand surmounted by a crowned uraeus. Apparently the umbel of the papyrus was of gold because it has disappeared, and only the hollowed out place in which it was set remains.

The two door-leaves are topped by the winged disk of Horus of Edfu, and below them are representations of an early form of a "Venetian blind." These were made of smoothed pieces of palm ribs fastened together with lengths of cord. In hot weather they could be let down in the open doorway to admit air but exclude sunlight. When not in use, they were rolled up and fixed at the top of the doorway as represented here. Such blinds were known during the Old Kingdom and are still used in the houses of some of the villages of Upper Egypt.

A scene in a square panel on each door-leaf shows Sety offering wine to Amon-Ra.

Something to Take One's Breath Away.

The most beautiful scene in the whole chapel is that of the sacred boats which occupies the whole upper register on the western half of the southern wall. It is almost perfectly preserved;

Fig. 9-19. The figurehead on the prow of the sacred boat of Amon-Ra. The vaulted Chapel of Amon-Ra. Southern wall, upper register.

the colors are as bright as on the day when the artists finished their work. As mentioned above, this scene shows the King burning incense in front of the sacred boats of Amon-Ra, Khonsu and Mut. The King, who stands in front of a great pile of offerings, is using his thumb and forefinger to flip pellets of incense into the firepot of the censer (Fig. 9-17).

The boat of Amon-Ra is really magnificent. It is of gold, and the figureheads on the prow and stern are in the form of rams' heads emerging from polychrome lotus flowers below which is a wide golden collar. In addition to the curved, natural horns of the ram, each head has a pair of twisted, horizontal horns supporting a solar disk. These heads were apparently made of gold inlaid with semi-precious stones.

Amidships, the cabin-shrine has its sides decorated with colored inlaid figures which read alternately, "Men-maat-Ra" and "beloved of Amon." As the dominant figures in each group are those of Amon-Ra, they again spell out the name of the God Amon-Ra. The shrine is partly hidden by a white veil.

As in the other boats, there is a sphinx on a pedestal and small statuettes of the King.

The pedestal on which the boat rests is decorated with four polychrome figures of the King all raising their arms to support the blue sign of Heaven (Fig. 9-18). The leading figure of the group is clad as a priest, but the others wear the blue war helmet and the royal kilt.

In front of the boat, a tall, golden pedestal supports a kneeling statuette of the King which holds a large formal bouquet of flowers. The basis of this floral arrangement is a large Key of Life which, in the ancient language, was called "ankh," and the same word also meant a bouquet or garland of flowers. This charming association of life with flowers illustrates the cheerful optimism of the ancient Egyptian. From the underpart of the pedestal hangs a charmingly natural decoration of vine leaves and bunches of grapes (Fig. 9-19). Under the carrying-poles are the usual collection of golden stands and vessels and statuettes of Sety.

Behind the boat of Amon-Ra are two smaller golden vessels, but these lack much of the colored decoration of the larger boat. The upper one is that of Khonsu, and its figureheads are those of falcons crowned with the full and crescent moons. The lower boat is that of Mut whose head, wearing the Double Crown, adorns the prow and stern.

One cannot look at this wonderful scene without feeling a sense of gratitude to the men who left us this legacy of beauty, and to the fortunate chance that has preserved it almost intact after the

Fig. 9-20. An early form of the Trinity. Kheperi-the scarab, the Morning Sun God; Ra-the disk, the Noonday Sun God; Atum-the Bearded God, the Evening Sun God. One in three and three in one. The Vaulted Chapel of Ra-Hor-akhty. Northern wall, lower register.

passing of all these years. It must have escaped those early Christians' wanton destructions by a very narrow shave!

107

Fig. 9-21. *The sacred boat of Ra-Hor-akhty showing typical "Solar Boat" prow. The vaulted Chapel of Ra-Hor-akhty. Northern wall, upper register.*

Below the scene of the boat, Sety offers perfume to Amon-Ra. The accompanying inscription gives the speech to be recited on this occasion and has been taken bodily from the Pyramid Texts of the Vth dynasty! Even more remarkable is the fact that this text mentions the name of the evil God Set three times, and yet, as we have mentioned, the element "Set" has been deleted from all the cartouches containing the King's personal name!

The Cult Chapel of Ra-Hor-akhty.

The scenes in this chapel were never colored but are of very great beauty and are also of very significant theological interest. They show that the various forms of the Sun God were regarded, at least by the educated people, as a single Entity.

To the north of the doorway Sety burns incense to the God who is in full human form and crowned with a large solar disk. The inscriptions refer to him as Atum-Kheperi, the combined form of the Evening and Morning Sun God.

On the northern wall the King adores Ra-Hor-akhty in the form of a ram-headed man. An interesting figure appears at the western end of the wall; the name being given as "Ra-Hor-akhty-Kheperi." In reality this is an early conception of the Holy Trinity, the three Gods who are one and one in three. The human figure is Atum, God of the Evening Sun; the disk on his head is Ra, God of the Noonday Sun; and the scarab in the disk is Kheperi, God of the Rising Sun (Fig. 9-20).

The sacred boat of Ra-Hor-akhty is a true "Solar Boat" and follows the classical form known since the time of the Old Kingdom (Fig. 9-21). Seated on a platform on the prow is the God Shu supporting the symbol of "heaven" above which rests the disk of the sun. Behind the prow, two goddesses hold

Fig. 9-22. *Cult Chapel of Ra-Hor-akhty (northern wall, upper register). The Ka of Ra-Hor-akhty and the Ka of Atum represented as sphinxes under the sacred boat.*

a solar disk on their outstretched hands, and in front
of them squats Thot in the
form of a baboon holding
an "Eye of Horus." The
usual royal figures are
seen before and behind the
cabin-shrine, and two figures of Horus work the
steering-oars.

The sternpost termi-
nates in two backward
curving horns that emerge
from a wide collar.

Among the objects
shown under the carrying-
poles are two figures of
sphinxes which are very
interesting. The pair
of raised human arms on
their heads show that they
each represent the Ka; the
inscriptions refer to them
as the Kas of Ra-Hor-akhty
and Atum. So far as we are
aware, these are the only
examples of a Ka being
represented as a sphinx.
It is undoubtedly a unique
feature (Fig. 9-22).

There is another un-

Fig. 9-23. The sacred boat of the God Ra-Hor-akhty.
This is in the Cult Chapel of Ra-Hor-akhty. The
Southern wall. Temple of Sety I.

usual detail in the scene
where the King is cleaning
the statue of the God; the
cloth that he is using for
this purpose is so long
that he has to twist it
around his forearm.

A scene which shows
Sety offering incense to
the disk-crowned God proves
that the sculptors took
as much care with the

figures in the upper reg-
ister as they did with
those at eye level. To
the north of the false-
door, the King disrobes a
beautiful statue of the
Goddess Hathor, and on the
southern side, he clothes
a statue of the Goddess
Iusaas.

The scene of the
sacred boat is badly dam-
aged (Fig. 9-23) in its
upper part, but the boat
itself seems to have been
similar to that on the
northern wall. Two rather
interesting objects under
the carrying-poles are a
dismembered calf (Fig.
9-24) and a statue of the
King as a sphinx whose
human arms present a bowl
of offerings (Fig. 9-25).

Undoubtedly the most
beautiful scene in the
whole chapel occurs in
the lower register of the
southern wall. Sety pre-
sents the scepters and
bracelets to Ra-Hor-akhty
who in return holds the
Key of Life to the King's
nose. The face of the

Fig. 9-24. A dismembered calf under the sacred boat of
Ra-Hor-akhty. The vaulted Cult Chapel of Ra-Hor-akhty,
southern wall. The Temple of Sety I.

109

Fig. 9-25. The King represented as a sphinx under the sacred boat of Ra-Hor-akhty. The vaulted Cult Chapel of Ra-Hor-akhty, southern wall.

Fig. 9-26. Sety offers scepters and bracelets to Ra-Hor-akhty as the latter presents a Key of Life to Sety. This is the reciprocal nature of covenant making. Vaulted Cult Chapel of Ra-Hor-akhty, southern wall. The Temple of Sety I.

Fig. 9-27. The Goddess Iusaas (detail). The vaulted Cult Chapel of Ra-Hor-akhty, southern wall. The Temple of Sety I.

Fig. 9-28. Cult Chapel of Ra-Hor-akhty (southern wall). Sety adjusts the crown of Atum (detail). The Temple of Sety I.

latter, upturned towards the God, is a masterpiece of modeling. The expression on his face is one of trustful reverence, and one can almost see the nostrils quiver as he inhales the breath of life from the sacred symbol (Fig. 9-26). Behind the God sits the beautiful and gracious Goddess Iusaas (Fig. 9-27).

The scene where Sety adjusts the crown of Atum is also very fine, and one must particularly admire the deft and graceful movements of the King's hands (Fig. 9-28).

The Cult Chapel of Ptah.

On the well-preserved doorway of this chapel, the dedication text tells us that the door was "Gilded with electrum." Except for willful damage

done when this chapel was used as a quarry, its walls are in very good condition. The surfaces are clean and light in color and unblackened by smoke. The reason for this happy state of affairs is that they had all been coated with plaster which had only been completely removed in recent years. When and why this plastering was done is a mystery; from the fact that there is no trace at all of smoke blackening suggests that it must have been done before the temple was burned.

Another peculiarity about this chapel is the quality of the reliefs. Although the composition and drawing of the scenes are as faultless as all the other work in the building, the actual sculpture seems to be less inspired. The figures lack some of the exquisite modeling of those in the other chapels, and the faces of the King, though faithful portraits, lack individual expression. For example, compare the scene on the southern wall where Sety presents scepters and bracelets to Ptah (Fig. 9-29), with the same scene in the Chapel of Ra-Horakhty. What a difference! In this chapel, the composition seems to be cold and lifeless. Ptah sits aloof and impersonal in his shrine, and Sety's ex-

Fig. 9-30. *Detail of the Iwn-mut-ef priest. The vaulted Chapel of Sety I. Northern wall, lower register. Temple of Sety I.*

pression is coolly polite!

The most interesting scene here is that of the sacred boat on the western end of the northern wall. The figurehead on the prow of this vessel is in the form of two Djed Pillars on which are perched two human-headed falcons crowned with disks. Such human-headed birds were the symbol of the soul, and in Chapter XVII of the Book of the Dead they appear in this form but with a Djed Pillar on each side of them. They are referred to there as "The double divine soul which dwells in Djeddu,"[1] and are variously explained as being the souls of Ra and Osiris, Horus and Set, or Shu and Tefnut. Clearly they represent some very

....

[1] In the ancient writing, the name of the city of Djeddu was written with two Djed Pillars.

Fig. 9-29. *(Left) King Sety presenting emblems and bracelets to Ptah, and adjusting the skullcap of the God. The vaulted Chapel of Ptah, southern wall.*

Fig. 9-31. The Gods Osiris, Thot and Isis. Note that here Thot has a human head in place of his usual ibis head! The vaulted Chapel of Sety I, northern wall.

ancient belief which had been forgotten or misunderstood by the time of the New Kingdom.

The same motif of the soul birds on Djed Pillars is seen again surmounting a standard held by a statuette of Sety which stands under the carrying-pole of the boat. The companion figure holds a standard surmounted by the leonine head of the Goddess Sekhmet.

The Vaulted Chapel of Sety I.

Many people suppose that because Sety has a chapel along with those of the other great Gods, he intended that he too should be worshiped here. But this is not so. A glance at the walls of this chapel shows that it had another purpose than that of the other six. Here there are no daily cult rites, and in their place are a number of symbolic repre-

sentations of the coronations, the Heb-sed Jubilee, and as in any tomb chapel, the deceased seated before his offering table.

In short, this chapel was for the performance of Mortuary Cult of the King and to keep alive his memory in this his most beloved

Fig. 9-32. King Sety enthroned between the Goddesses of Upper and Lower Egypt (Nekhbet and Wadjet). Horus and Thot tie the lily of Upper Egypt and the papyrus of Lower Egypt to the sign of Union, symbolizing the union of the Two Lands (from the vaulted Chapel of Sety I, northern wall). The Temple of Sety I.

Fig. 9-33. (Left) Sety I conducted into his chapel by Ra-Hor-akhty and Atum. The vaulted Chapel of Sety I. Northern wall, upper register.

monument.

The dedication text on the doorway says, "He made it as his monument for his fathers, the Gods who dwell in the 'House of Men-maat-Ra.'"

At the bottom of the inner jamb of the doorway, the King is shown in the form of a sphinx lying upon a pedestal; a small human figure stands in front of him, and it extends the Key of Life to his face.

On the inner wall to the north of the doorway, the Iwn-mut-ef priest burns incense in front of Sety, and on the southern side, the little Mert Goddess of Upper Egypt raises her arms to the King and cries, "Come, bring! Come, bring!" She is a charming little lady crowned with a clump of lilies of Upper Egypt and wearing her hair in a long plait down her back. Sety gazes upon her with a kindly, indulgent smile.

The Northern Wall of the Chapel of Sety.

The first scene on the lower part of the northern wall shows the Iwn-mut-ef priest (Fig. 9-30) praying on the King's behalf to nine

Fig. 9-34. (Left) The jackal-headed Souls of Nekhen. The vaulted Chapel of Sety I. Northern wall, upper register.

Fig. 9-35. The Ka of King Sety I. The vaulted Chapel of Sety I.

Fig. 9-36. Chapel of Sety I (northern wall). Sety seated at his offering table. The Temple of Sety I.

Fig. 9-37. Chapel of Sety I (northern wall). Part of the offering list.

mummiform deities. These are Amon-Ra, Mut, Khonsu, Ra, Shu, Tefnut, Osiris, Thot and Isis (Fig. 9-31).

The following scene is exceptionally beautiful. Sety wearing the Itef crown is seated between the Goddesses Nekhbet of Upper Egypt and Wadjet of Lower Egypt who are embracing him (Fig. 9-32). Thot and Horus are binding the lily and papyrus plants to the symbol of Union on the pedestal under the King's throne so reaffirming the union of Upper and Lower Egypt under the rule of Sety.

The composition of this scene is most artistic. The graduation in the heights of the figures from the apex of the tall Itef crown in the center to the heads and arms of Thot and Horus at the sides makes almost a pyramidal design.

In the upper register, Monthu and Atum hold the King by the hands and lead him into his chapel (Fig. 9-33).

The western end of the second scene is almost destroyed. Next come the jackal and falcon-headed "Souls of Nekhen " all of whom carry libation vases (Fig. 9-34). They together with Thot and the Iwn-mut-ef priest, are advancing

Fig. 9-38. The Nile Gods on the pedestal of the sacred boat. The vaulted Chapel of Sety I. Southern wall, upper register. Note the Key of Life with human arms (right of picture) carrying a standard. The Temple of Sety I.

Fig. 9-39. Statuettes of Sety I, Ramesses I and Queen Satra (Father and Mother of Sety I) underneath the sacred boat of Sety. Vaulted Chapel of Sety I, Southern wall, upper register. The Temple of Sety I.

towards the King, but the royal figure has been destroyed.

The lower part of the western end of the northern wall is occupied by a large offering scene. The King with his Ka (Fig. 9-35) standing behind him, is seated at a table laden with conventional slices of bread (Fig. 9-36).

Next comes a long list of food and drink offerings together with the prescribed formula which should be recited when each item on the list is offered. Many of these formulae are copied from the Pyramid Texts. Here they are supposed to be recited by the Iwn-mut-ef priest (Fig. 9-37).[2]

The upper part of the wall is destroyed. The western wall of the chapel is in a rather bad state of preservation, but on the lower part of its southern side is a figure of Sety preceded by two standards. The latter are carried by the emblems of Prosperity and Life, each provided with a pair of human arms (Fig. 9-38).

The Southern Wall.

The King's statues also had a sacred boat for their

2....................
[2]This scene is repeated on the southern wall. Here Thot recites the offering formulas.

Fig. 9-40. Personified emblems of "Life" and "Endurance" carrying the sacred standards (the vaulted Chapel of Sety I, southern wall).

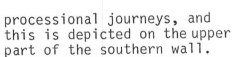

Fig. 9-41. Thot and the Iwn-mut-ef priest in front of the sacred boat. The vaulted Chapel of Sety I. Southern wall, upper register. The priest is wearing an animal skin garment.

Fig. 9-42. The Iwn-mut-ef priest burns incense before Sety who is being carried by the falcon-headed Souls of Nekhen. The vaulted Chapel of Sety I (southern wall, lower register). The priest again wears the animal garment. The Temple of Sety I.

processional journeys, and this is depicted on the upper part of the southern wall.

On both prow and stern the King's head, crowned with the Itef diadem, serves as a figurehead. The pedestal on which the boat rests is decorated with four figures of the Nile God carrying vases of water.

Under the carrying-poles are three statuettes; the first of which represents Sety himself, the second is of his father Ramesses I, and the third is his mother Queen Sat-Ra (Fig. 9-39). They are preceded by a Key of Life whose human arms carry a standard topped by a royal portrait head (Fig. 9-40). In front of the boat, Thot and the Iwn-mut-ef priest dedicate a great pile of offerings (Fig. 9-41).

In the lower part of the eastern half of the wall is a large scene of one of the ceremonies of the Heb-sed. The King, seated on a throne which rests on the sign of "Feast," is carried by jackal-headed and falcon-headed Souls of Nekhen and Pe (Fig. 9-42).

The Goddesses of Upper and Lower Egypt, in the form of crowned uraei, fan him with single ostrich feathers.

The Iwn-mut-ef priest (perhaps young Ramesses himself) walks in front of the Souls of Pe and Nekhen but turns backwards in a very natural way.

Heading the procession are eight sacred standards (Fig. 9-43) which are carried by the emblems of Life, Endurance and Prosperity. These are represented as miniature surrealistic human figures clad in full kilts but having the upper part of each emblem replacing the human head.

Above is shown the coronation of Sety; the ceremony being performed by Horus and Thot in the presence of the Goddesses of Upper and Lower Egypt.

118

Fig. 9-43. The upper parts of some of the sacred standards (the vaulted chapel of Sety I, southern wall). Temple of Sety I.

SECOND HYPOSTYLE HALL

CHAPEL OF ISIS

BLIND ROOMS

CHAPEL OF OSIRIS

CHAPEL OF HORUS

VAULTED CHAPEL OF HORUS

VAULTED CHAPEL OF ISIS

VAULTED CHAPEL OF OSIRIS

VAULTED CHAPEL OF AMON-RA

VAULTED CHAPEL OF RA-HOR-AKHTY

VAULTED CHAPEL OF PTAH

VAULTED CHAPEL OF SETY

OSIRIS HALL

SOUTHERN INNER CHAPELS

STATUE HALL

CHAPTER TEN

THE OSIRIS COMPLEX AND RELATED CHAPELS-- DEIFICATION OF THE DECEASED SETY

The Osiris Complex.

As already mentioned, the "Osiris Complex" is the modern name given to a group of halls and chapels lying at the extreme western end of the building, behind the Seven Vaulted Chapels (see page 120). They are reached by going through the doorway in the western wall of the Cult Chapel of Osiris (page 101) and consist of a large hypostyle hall; the roof of which is supported by ten "tree trunk" columns arranged in two rows of five each. Three chapels open out of the northern end of this hall, and at its southern end is a Statue Hall with four "tree trunk" columns and three more chapels in its southern end.

The walls of the larger hall originally bore two registers of finely colored reliefs, but most of the upper part of the western and southern walls have been systematically destroyed.

Here also, the terrible mutilation of the divine and royal figures is appalling. Even the hands and feet have been battered away. The mutilation of the faces was done to destroy the identity of the being represented while the destruction of the hands and feet were intended to magically prevent the actions shown from being carried out, and also to render those beings helpless and therefore harmless to those who have committed such a senseless destruction.

The three small but beautifully decorated chapels that open out of the northern end of the hall are dedicated to Horus, Osiris (with whom the dead King is identified) and Isis. In the Statue Hall, five niches in each of the eastern and western walls are decorated with colored reliefs, as were the walls of the hall along with the three southern chapels. But unfortunately this part of the building had been used as a quarry after the downfall of the old religion, and so most of the walls are destroyed.

It is thought that this group of halls and chapels was used for some rites in the mysteries of Osiris and were the setting for some of the episodes in the sacred Miracle Play performed annually during the Great Feast of Osiris.

The Large "Osiris Hall."

According to inscriptions on some of its columns, Sety claims that he built this part of the temple on the ruins of an ancient building. This was proven true when it recently became necessary to remove some of the pavement to examine the foundations of the columns. Sure enough, these foundations consisted of ancient stones, which in accordance with the Egyptian custom, were used as the foundations for the new building.

The Osiris Hall, though badly mutilated in a very systematic and distressing fashion, is yet most important from a theological point of view, and so we shall describe it in some detail.

The Northern Wall.

Most of the northern wall of this hall is occupied by the doorways of the three chapels; all the outer jambs of which bear small but beautiful scenes of the King offering to the Gods. The lintels that are still preserved bear double scenes of similar subjects to those on the jambs.

A scene on a jamb of the doorway of the Chapel of Horus is a miniature masterpiece. The King offers two bouquets of blue lotus flowers and papyrus reeds to Horus. The contrast between the deferential attitude of Sety as he holds out the offering, and the divinely majestic pose of the falcon headed God is a triumph of character portraiture (Fig. 10-1).

On the short space of wall between the door of the Chapel of Osiris and that of Isis, the upper scene shows Sety burning incense before Osiris, and in the lower one he again offers the symbolic image of Maat.

The Western Wall.

In ancient times, a stone offering bench ran

Fig. 10-1. Sety presents lotus flowers and papyrus umbles to Horus (the Osiris Hall, northern wall).

Fig. 10-2. The sacred standard of Abydos, here regarded as the God Osiris. The Osiris Hall. Western wall. Isis anointing standard of Abydos. The Temple of Sety I.

the whole length of the hall at the base of the western (and eastern) wall. This has long since disappeared, but the roughness of the pavement on which it stood is still visible, and the stains left by the dirty water, made when the priests washed the upper surface of the offering bench, remain on the wall! At the northern end of the wall, the first scene shows the King anointing the sacred standard of Abydos (Fig. 10-2). Its upper part, the tall headdress of which is destroyed, resembles a heavy wig framing a human face. This has led many Egyptologists to believe that this emblem represents a reliquary containing the embalmed head of Osiris. But in reality, it is more likely that it is conforming to an idea expressed in some other scenes namely that the emblem here is not a symbol of the deity but actually is the deity. This is much like the Christian belief in the Host.

Opposite to Sety stands Isis caressing the sacred standard and two small statuettes of the King kneeling and supporting the standard.

In the second scene, the King burns incense to Thot, who is here in the form of an ibis (Fig. 10-3). Next he offers a conical loaf of white bread to the same God now in the form of a Kherp baton as we have already seen in the Cult Chapel of Osiris (Fig. 10-4).

Between the King and the Kherp is a beautifully carved offering table laden with bread, fruit and poultry and decorated with flowers. Among the fruits offered are sycamore figs which are shown to have small notches cut in them. This practice is still followed at the present day and is said to help the fruit to ripen and to improve its flavor. Under the table are two jars of beer decorated with lotus flowers.

Two interesting scenes show the annual ceremony of erecting the Djed Pillar. This very elaborate and complicated ceremony is here confined to its two chief episodes: The erection and the adornment. Here also the emblem is considered as the God himself and is referred to as "Osiris the August Djed Pillar." Could it be just a pure coincidence that "The King" in the earliest chess game pieces took the exact form of a Djed Pillar?

The first episode shows Isis and the King setting the pillar upright upon its pedestal. The small statuette of the King, which was intended to support the Djed, is here shown helping to push it upright (Fig. 10-5).

In the second episode the Djed is upright. Its lower part clad in a long red garment bound by a wide white girdle, and the King is presenting it with two more strips of linen (Fig. 10-6).

In the sixth scene,

Fig. 10-3. Temple of Sety I. Osiris Hall (Western wall). Sety offers incense to Thot in the form of an ibis.

Fig. 10-4. Osiris Hall (western wall). Sety offers to Thot in the form of a Kherp baton. The offering table is below the baton. Temple of Sety I.

Sety is carrying offerings to two Gods standing in a golden shrine. Both are naked except for a narrow girdle. The first God, whose flesh is colored red, is named Ark-sep-ef. His companion, who is colored green, is named Wenti.

Next the King perfumes Osiris, again shown as a living being, with Isis standing behind him. Curiously enough, neither deity wears a headdress, which is most unusual, and they can only be identified by the inscriptions.

The eighth scene is very strange indeed. Sety offers bunches of flowers to the Nile God Hapi who is accompanied by the Goddess Maat and stands in a shrine. But the figure of the God is very unusual. Instead of his usual form of a stout man with female breasts, he here has a normal male body; his humam head is replaced by two heads of geese, one looking forward and one looking backward. There is a similar representation of him (but better preserved) in the upper register of the eastern wall.

The inscription in both scenes identifies this strange figure as Hapi, and on the western wall he says to the King, "I give to thee the Nile in its greatness, like Ra, every day." So far as we are aware, these are the only known representations of the Nile God in this form. Perhaps he is supposed to be the Nile at the apex of the Inundation, "the Nile in its greatness"?

Fig. 10-5. The Temple of Sety I. Sety and Isis erecting the Djed Pillar (detail). The Osiris Hall. Western wall.

Only the lower part of the last two scenes remain.

The Southern Wall.

Most of the western half of the southern wall is entirely destroyed. The center is occupied by a doorway leading to the Statue Hall by the western jamb of which are two crocodile-headed beings seated in a golden shrine. The jambs of this doorway are badly damaged.

On the eastern half of the wall is the lower part of a scene showing the King kneeling in front of the standard of Abydos behind

Fig. 10-6. *Sety decorates the Djed Pillar. The Osiris Hall, western wall. The Temple of Sety I.*

a falcon-headed man.

The third scene shows the King offering two round pots of wine to the Goddess Hekat who, in the form of a large green frog, squats in a portable golden shrine (We always thought that frogs were strictly teetotalers!).

In the fourth scene is the strange goose-headed form of Hapi who has already appeared on the western wall. But here he is accompanied by Nepthys in place of Maat, and the King is opening the door of the shrine in which they stand.

Next, Sety burns incense for Anubis, a jackal-headed man, naked but for his narrow white girdle.

In the sixth scene he performs the same service for Osiris and Isis.

The seventh scene shows the King, wearing the Crown of Lower Egypt, and offering flowers to a god, whose face and name have been destroyed, after which he offers perfume to Osiris and Isis.

In the ninth scene, the King burns incense to Horus who is in the form of a falcon wearing the Double crown and perched upon a green papyrus column.

In the last scene in this register, the King offers a conical loaf of white bread to Wepwawat a recumbent jackal lying in a portable golden shrine.

The southernmost scene in the lower register is very interesting. It shows Sety kneeling in front of a shrine and offering a nemset jar to Osiris. Behind the God, and drawn on the same scale, is seated a kingly figure wearing the

which stands Isis.

The Eastern Wall.

Although the upper part of this wall is destroyed, most of the scenes are intact except for the same mutilations made by the early Christians who must have gone to a lot of trouble to

reach and disfigure them. Real deep-rooted and jaunting fear of these abandoned gods must have been behind all this abominable destruction.

Scenes in the upper register show Sety kneeling in front of a shrine containing statues of Osiris and Isis and offering to Horus in his usual form of

125

Fig. 10-7. Temple of Sety I. The Osiris Hall. Eastern wall. The deified King Sety seated behind Osiris. In front of the King's crown is his prenomen or throne or temple name Men-maat-Ra, followed by "the Great God."

crown of Upper Egypt and a tunic with a single shoulder strap like those worn by the kings of the Archaic Period. His flesh is colored red, and he holds the Key of Life in his right hand. Behind him is inscribed: "Men-maat-Ra, the Great God"; the prenomen being written without a cartouche. This figure then represents the dead and deified Sety, and is apparently the only scene in which he is shown both living and dead. It is characteristic of him to have had this figure modestly tucked away in a rather obscure, dark corner of the hall (Fig. 10-7).

In the second scene, the King burns incense to the Goddess Shentayet, Patroness of Weavers. She is shown in the form of a red cow, a disk between her long horns, and she lies in a golden shrine (Fig. 10-8).

Next the King opens

the door of a shrine in which stands a god who resembles the usual form of Osiris. But the accompanying inscription identifies him as "Min-Horus, the son of Isis"; he then offers bouquets of lotus flowers to Geb and Nut.

In the fifth scene, Sety kneels to offer a conical loaf of white bread to Osiris whose face, by some lucky chance, escaped mutilation. Behind him stands Isis who clasps him in her arms.

Now the ox-headed God Merhy receives the gift of two golden libation jars from the King. Merhy was an ancient Memphite deity identified with Horus; hence he is here accompanied by Isis.

Next, Sety burns incense for Osiris-Andjty.

In the eighth scene he opens the door of a golden shrine containing Horus in the form of a

crowned falcon.

The king then offers pots of wine to a mummiform God whose face has also escaped disfigurement. His name is recorded as Ir-ren-ef-djes-ef (He Who Made his Name Himself). He seems to be a form of Min.

Finally Sety offers the symbolic image of Maat to Horus. The God is shown as a regal-looking falcon wearing the Double crown and standing in a golden shrine set upon a wooden sledge.

The Statue Hall.

The Statue Hall had been almost totally destroyed, but in recent years it has been accurately restored by the Egyptian Antiquities Department.

All that remains of the original structure are the lower parts of three "tree trunk" columns and the northern wall, the basement of the western wall and the basement and two niches of the eastern wall and the lower parts of the southern wall.

The Northern Wall of the Statue Hall.

On the eastern half of the northern wall is the lower part of a scene in colored bas-relief which shows Sety kneeling before a shrine containing statues of Osiris and Isis. As originally designed, the poles of the shrine were undecorated, but some officious artist later inscribed them in red paint with the titles and names of Ramesses II! This does little or no credit either to the artist or to whomsoever gave him instructions to do so.

The Eastern Wall of the Statue Hall.

Most of the niches are badly damaged, and only three scenes from their walls remain; these show Sety offering to Isis and Osiris.
All of the niches in the western wall are restorations.

The Southern Inner Chapels.

All the walls of these chapels are very badly damaged. Once they were adorned with beautifully carved and colored scenes in bas-relief; the remains of which make us regret all the more, the loss of the rest.
On the eastern and western walls of the easternmost chapel, the King is shown in front of a sacred boat.
All that remains on the southern wall are the feet of the King, the pedestal of a throne, and the slender feet of a goddess.

The Central Chapel.

It is unfortunate that the walls of this chapel have fared so badly as they bore some very interesting reliefs.
On the western wall is the lower part of a representation of the conception of Horus; a theme which is repeated but with less naturalism in the Chapel of Soker-Osiris. At the northern end the

Fig. 10-8. Eastern wall. The Weaver Goddess, Shentayet in the form of a cow. The Temple of Sety I.

King is kneeling on the ground, and in front of him Isis also kneels wailing for her dead husband. Next come the legs of two male figures, one of whom was wearing the royal kilt. They stand beside a golden bed in the form of an elongated lion on which lies the naked form of Osiris. The Goddess Isis, now in the form of a falcon, hovers over the erect phallus of the God and receives from him the divine seed with which she will conceive their son Horus.
At the head of the bed the Goddess Nepthys kneels mourning for her dead brother. Her grief-stricken expression is most unusual in Egyptian art and is carved with such delicate artistic feeling that touching her cheek, one almost expects to find it wet with tears (Fig. 10-9). There is something pitiful and tragic in this scene that cannot fail to move the observer, and judging

from scanty remains, it was repeated on the eastern wall of the chapel.
On the southern wall only the feet of Sety and a goddess remain.

The Western Chapel.

The southern wall is fairly well-preserved, and here Sety anoints the crown of Osiris with perfumed ointment. Isis stands behind her husband laying her hands upon his shoulders.
On the western wall, Sety kneels in front of the God and presents a portable golden chest to Osiris. On the side of the chest are two small figures of cows to which miniature royal figures are offering pots of wine. This was probably a clothes chest and the cows may be the bovine form of the Weaver Goddess, Shentayet.

The Three Northern Chapels of the Osiris Hall.

As mentioned above,

Fig. 10-9. *The Goddess Nepthys weeping for her dead brother Osiris (the central chapel of the Statue Hall, western wall). The Temple of Sety I.*

three small but beautifully decorated chapels lead out of the northern end of the Osiris Hall. By a happy chance, the scenes on their walls have suffered little from smoke blackening and escaped entirely the wanton damage to the faces of the figures which is so distressing to see in the Cult Chapel of Osiris and the Osiris Hall. Perhaps at the end of the Roman Period when the importance of Abydos was declining, the temple was understaffed, and all chapels not essential to the daily cult were blocked off by bricking up their doorways. This is probably the miracle by which this "Chef d'Oeuvre" of Egyptian art escaped destruction.

The Northern Chapel of Horus.

This is the easternmost of the three. Like the other two, its entrance was originally closed by a single-leaf wooden door; the upper and lower socket holes of which remain.

The Eastern Wall of the Chapel of Horus.

On all the walls of these chapels the scenes are supposed to be taking place inside a large golden shrine with a doorway at each end.

The depicted sides of the doorways bear incised inscriptions exactly like those of the real entrance to the chapel; a minute but realistic detail characteristic of the work in

this temple.

First we see Sety burning incense in front of Horus and pouring a libation from a golden vase shaped like the Key of Life (Fig. 10-10). The water falls upon a charming fan-shaped arrangement of lotus flowers and buds.

Horus sits facing the King and wears the Double crown encircled by a wreath of golden uraei.

Next the King presents perfumed ointment to Osiris. The two vases with the cones of perfume are held by a small figure of the King; a charming ornament for the divine toilet table.

Lastly Sety presents a golden collar to Horus.

The Northern Wall of the Northern Chapel of Horus.

Originally an offering bench built of masonry stood at the base of this wall. It has long since disappeared, but one can still see traces of its former presence on the wall and floor. A similar bench also existed in this place in the other two chapels.

The entire northern wall is occupied by a single scene in which Isis introduces the King to her son Horus. She places her hands on Sety's shoulders and gently urges him forward.

The figure of the King, as graceful and dignified as usual, wears the blue war helmet and the military kilt. By the skillful use of pink and white paint, the artist has given a wonderfully true effect of a transparent garment of fine linen. The King raises his hand to receive from Horus the royal emblems of crook and flail (Fig. 10-11).

The Western Wall of the Northern Chapel of Horus.

The scene to the north shows Sety, dressed as a priest, busily washing a golden offering table with his own hands, in front of Horus. Describing this scene, the inscription says: "Washing the offering table by the King himself."

It seems intended to show that the Great Pharaoh was not too proud to do menial work for his God (and was perhaps a delicate reminder to the priests not to shirk their duty--Fig. 10-12).

In the middle scene Sety burns incense and pours a libation before Osiris (Fig. 10-13) and Isis (Fig. 10-14). The face of the Goddess wears a particularly sweet expression, and the faint smile on her lips seems to be reflected in her eyes.

In the southern scene Sety skillfully flips round pellets of incense into a censer in front of Horus. The fine details of the King's costumes and ornaments are minutely carved.

The Northern Chapel of Osiris.

This is the central chapel, and although it is dedicated to Osiris, whose

Fig. 10-10. Sety burns incense and pours a libation to Horus. Note the libation vase shaped like the Key of Life. The Inner Chapel of Horus, northern wall.

figure appears on the important northern wall, it was also shared by the King who here cheerfully anticipated his own death.

It was the custom in ancient Egypt to identify all dead persons with Osiris, and when speaking of the deceased, they would refer to "the Osiris So-and-So," just as today we say, "the late So-and-So." And thus, the "Osiris-Sety" takes his place on the walls of this chapel though yielding the place of honor above the offering bench to the greater God.

The Eastern Wall of the Northern Chapel of Osiris.

First we see Horus performing the purification rite on the "Osiris-

Sety." This group is yet another example of the high artistic skill of the men who decorated this temple. The scene is overloaded with a mass of symbolic detail which could easily have obscured the whole composition, yet this has been skillfully avoided. The broad planes of the figures and the well proportioned blank spaces of the background counterbalance the areas of what otherwise might have been merely fussy superfluous details (Fig. 10-15).

Horus sprinkles a lustration of natron and water from three conjoined golden vases. From them issue six streams of water of which three fall in front of the King and three behind him. The two outer streams

Fig. 10-11. *Horus presents the crook and flail to the King. The Inner Chapel of Horus, northern wall.*

are drawn, as usual, as zigzag lines, but the middle streams are a chain of the emblems of Life and Prosperity (Fig. 10-16)).

In front of the King is a rectangular stand which forms the name of the temple "House of Men-maat-Ra." On it stands the Four Sons of Horus in the forms of small mummiform human figures (Fig. 10-17).

Sety is shown in the form and pose of Osiris and carries the crook and flail. He wears a most

Fig. 10-12. *(Right) The northern Chapel of Horus (western wall). King Sety, dresses as a Ritualist Priest, washes a golden offering table with his own hands. The complete inscription between the king and the offering table reads, "Washing the offering table by the king himself."*

Fig. 10-13. *(Page 131) The God Osiris, northern Chapel of Horus (inner) western wall. Temple of Sety I.*

130

Fig. 10-14. The Goddess Isis behind Osiris. The northern (inner) Chapel of Horus.
Western wall. Temple of Sety I or the "House of Men-maat-Ra" (see page 130).

remarkable headdress; the
basis of which is the flat-
topped crown of Amon-Ra
from which the ram's horn
of that God project and
curl around the King's
ear. On the flat top of
the crown, a pair of bull's
horns support a solar

disk from which spring
two tall plumes (Fig. 10-
18). Two pairs of uraei
also crowned with disks
and plumes rear up from
the horizontal horns while
two similar pairs wearing
only disks on their heads
hang below. It seems im-

possible that such a fan-
tastic headdress could
really have existed and
been worn. More likely
it is an artistic device
for showing that the de-
ceased King was given the
attributes of Amon-Ra as
well as those of Osiris.

Fig. 10-15. Horus purifies the mummy of Osiris-Sety. Note the very complicated crown on the head of the latter. The Inner Chapel of Osiris-Sety, eastern wall.

Next the ibis-headed God Thot, wearing the white robe of a Ritualist priest, holds out the Key of Life to the nose of the deceased King (Fig. 10-19). In his other hand he holds the lily and papyrus wands of Upper and Lower Egypt around which are twined uraei each wearing the appropriate crown of South and North.

Behind the King is a small falcon perched on a Serekh which encloses one of the King's names. The regal dignity of this small crowned bird is really awe-inspiring (Fig. 10-20). In front of it is an emblem of the King's Ka (two up-raised arms) and between them the hieroglyph meaning "King."

In the final scene Sety is seated on the sign for "feast." In front of him is an offering table supporting a single libation jar of water. Under the table stand two jars of beer invitingly decorated with entwined lotus buds.

Facing the King, and represented on the same scale, is the Iwn-mut-ef priest wearing his traditional costume of a leopard skin tunic (Fig. 10-21). The face of this man bears a close resemblance to Sety's son Ramesses, and it is doubtlessly intended to represent him acting as Mortuary priest for his dead father. Had he been an ordinary priest, he would not have been shown in the same size as the King according to the Royal Protocol in those times.

The Northern Wall.

On the northern wall of this chapel, Horus clasps the King's hand in a brotherly way and leads him

into the presence of Osiris who grasps Sety's arm to draw him closer. Isis stands behind her husband. Unfortunately this lovely scene is one of those which is slightly marred by smoke.

The Western Wall.

The northernmost scene on this wall is somewhat similar to that opposite to it on the eastern wall; here the King extends his head to a table laden with conventionalized slices of bread, and instead of the Iwn-mut-ef priest, it is the God Thot who recites the offering formula. However, the former appears again in the middle scene where he is flipping round pellets of incense into a censer in front of the deceased Sety (Fig. 10-22). Isis stands behind the priest shaking the sacred sistrum (Fig. 10-23).
Next the God Wepwawat presents the crook and

flail to the King (Fig. 10-24). Here again, the God's jackal-head is a masterpiece of modeling and has a mysteriously uncanny but captivating expression, half human and half canine.

The Inner Chapel of Isis.

This is perhaps the most beautiful of the three inner chapels and is certainly the best preserved. Happily, its walls are almost entirely unstained by smoke and are dominated by the gracious and lovely figures of the Goddess and her royally dignified worshiper. We can safely say that this chapel is a study in elegance.

The Eastern Wall.

It is typical of Isis,

Fig. 10-17. Inner Chapel of Osiris (eastern wall). The Four Sons of Horus stand on a table which gives the name of the Temple of Sety "Hwt-men-maat-Ra."

Fig. 10-16. Inner Chapel of Osiris (eastern wall). Horus purifies the mummy of Sety. The Temple of Sety I.

one of whose attributes
is that of the "perfect
wife," that she should
yield pride of place to
her husband, and so the
first scene on the east-
ern and western wall of
her chapel shows Osiris
receiving the King's hom-
age. Sety is burning
incense before Osiris,
but Isis lovingly rests
her hands upon his shoul-
ders, a tender expression
on her beautiful face.
She says to Osiris, "My
two arms are around thee,
and I embrace thy beauty."
(Fig. 10-25).
　　She then addresses
the King saying, "O my son,
Lord of the Two Lands, Men-
maat-Ra, my heart is con-
tent with what thou hast
done; I rejoice when I
see thy monuments, and

Fig. 10-18. Inner Chapel of Osiris (eastern wall).
Details of the crown of the deceased King Sety.

I give to thee all might."
　　In the next scene Sety
is "making incense and libations for Isis, the

Fig. 10-19. The God Thot, holding the wands of Upper
and Lower Egypt, presents the Key of Life to the mummy
of King Sety. Temple of Sety I.

Fig. 10-20. Horus as a
falcon on the "Serekh" (the
Inner Chapel of Osiris-
Sety, eastern wall). In
front of the falcon is the
standard of the King's Ka.

Fig. 10-21. Inner Chapel of Osiris (eastern wall). The Iwn-mut-ef priest offers water and beer to the dead King. Note the garment of leopard skin.

Fig. 10-22. Inner Chapel of Osiris (western wall). The Iwn-mut-ef priest throws incense in the firepot for the dead King Sety. The Temple of Sety I.

Mother of God." The goddess wears her hair in the fashionable XIXth dynasty style (Fig. 10-26).

In the last scene, the King carries a tray of offerings to Isis. It is a well-balanced meal of bread, meat, poultry and fruit garnished with the green salad "gargeer" still loved by the modern Egyptians (Fig. 10-27).

Here the Goddess is seated upright and very dignified but somewhat aloof (Fig. 10-28). In the first scene she is the loving wife; here she is the immortal Goddess receiving the homage of her worshiper. The scene is repeated on the western wall.

Fig. 10-23. Inner Chapel of Osiris (western wall). Isis with the sistrum, and the Iwn-mut-ef priest throwing incense in the firepot. The Temple of Sety I.

The Northern Wall.

Sety is standing in the presence of Isis who hands to him the emblems of the Heb-sed and "Mil-

136

Fig. 10-24. Inner Chapel of Osiris (western wall). Wepwawat (details).

Fig. 10-26. The head of Isis (detail). The Inner Chapel of Isis, eastern wall.

Fig. 10-25. The northern Chapel of Isis (eastern wall). The Goddess Isis embracing Osiris. The complete inscription in front of Isis reads, "My arms are around you, I embrace thy beauty."

lions of Years." Horus stands behind his mother embracing her and looks on approvingly at her gifts to the King.

The Western Wall.

In the middle scene, the King is "giving wine to Isis, the mother of God, that she may give him life like Ra" (Fig. 10-29). According to the Egyptian traditions, Isis was the inventor of wine, and Osiris was the inventor of beer.

In the southern scene Sety presents perfume to Osiris and Isis.

One last remark before closing this account of the inner chapels. We have always admired the wonderful fidelity with which the artists have reproduced the noble, humane and dignified features of Sety; and at first, one is inclined to ask, "But how could they have drawn the faces of the gods and goddesses with such breathtaking beauty?" But a closer scrutiny shows that the human faces of the gods are really idealized versions of the King's own features while the goddesses lovely faces are based on that of his mother Queen Sat-Ra whom he very closely resembled and who was certainly a woman of great beauty.

Fig. 10-27. Temple of Sety I, Abydos. Inner Chapel of Isis, eastern wall. King Sety presents a tray of food to Isis.

Fig. 10-28. Temple of Sety I. Abydos. Inner Chapel of Isis, eastern wall. The Goddess Isis. Sety is deified in the process completed here.

Fig. 10-29. The Inner Chapel of Isis, western wall. Sety offers two pots of wine to Isis. Temple of Sety I.

CHAPTER ELEVEN

THE BEWILDERING HALL OF SOKER AND ITS TWO CHAPELS

The Hall of Soker.

This hall (see page 156) was dedicated to Soker the Memphite God of the Dead who was identified with Osiris. Apparently kings (like women!) are entitled to change their minds, because this fine hall has undergone a drastic change of construction. Originally it was planned to be larger and to have had two rows of "tree trunk" columns supporting its roof (three columns to each row) and three chapels with vaulted roofs leading out of its western wall.

The building of the hall was completed according to this plan but was not yet decorated when it was suddenly realized, probably by the King himself, that there was no access to or from the temple from the western part of the Temenos. The nearest way for leaving or entering the temple would have been through the Slaughter Court, at the southern end of the Corridor of Kings, an inconvenient and often unpleasant route! Therefore, the southern quarter of the Hall of Soker was turned into a passage running westward from a doorway in the Corridor of Kings (see page 156).

This passage was accomplished by flattening the shafts of the columns in the southern row and then incorporating them into a new limestone wall built in between them. They can still be seen clearly on close examination. The original southern wall of the hall now became the southern wall of the passage. Also, the southernmost of the three vaulted chapels, which probably had been intended for the Goddess Sekhmet, was incorporated into the new plan. As the ground to the west of the temple is higher than the level of the pavement of the Hall of Soker, a flight of limestone steps had to be built most of which is in this erstwhile chapel.

That this alteration was made during the reign of Sety is proven by the decoration of the walls of the hall including that on the "new" southern wall.

The entrance to the Hall of Soker is in the extreme southwestern corner of the Second Hypostyle Hall. Its outer jambs each bear three scenes showing the King adoring Soker and Nefer-tem while the lower scene depicts Thot writing an inscription. He is accompanied by the Goddess Seshat. On both inner jambs are two elongated cartouches containing the King's titles and names in a strange enigmatic writing; the groups of signs are very artistically arranged and beautifully sculptured.

The entrance was closed by a single-leaf door opening against the eastern side which bears seven vertical lines of

Fig. 11-1. The King presents offerings to the sacred Henu-boat of Soker (the Hall of Soker, northern wall). The Temple of Sety I.

dedication texts in incised sculpture. On the western side is a fine scene in bas-relief. Sety wearing the war helmet and carrying a censer is, as the inscription says, "Entering to the Temple of Soker to adore the God." Soker is shown as though coming out to meet the King, to whose face he holds the emblems of Life and Endurance. The God is falcon-headed and wears the crown of Upper Egypt flanked by feathers, the traditional headdress of Osiris.

The scenes in this hall were never colored, and the figures are carved in a higher relief than elsewhere in the temple as though in imitation of the Memphite School of Sculpture of which such wonderful examples still exist in the tombs of Sakkara.

Each of the northern,

Fig. 11-2. Sety pours water into a vase of lotus flowers (the Hall of Soker, northern wall). Temple of Sety I.

southern and eastern walls had two registers of scenes, but the western wall is almost entirely occupied by the doorways of the two remaining vaulted Chapels of Soker-Osiris and Nefer-tem.

By good fortune, this hall, with the exception of the Chapel of Nefer-tem and a few places on the eastern wall, had escaped smoke blackening when the temple was burned.

One can spend quite some time admiring the vigor and individuality of the artists responsible for the masterful execution of the sculpture of this outstanding hall.

The Northern Wall.

The upper register, which is somewhat damaged, is mostly occupied by a long list of offerings and the titles of the God Soker. At the eastern end is a figure of the King reciting the offering formula, and at the western end he presents offerings to the sacred Henu-boat of Soker (Fig. 11-1).

In the first scene in the lower register, Sety offers a conical loaf of bread and a jar of milk. One would imagine that bread and milk is a rather unsuitable gift to offer to a falcon-headed deity, but we have already mentioned offerings of wine made to cows and to a frog! These apparently absurd offerings seem to prove that although the gods had these animal or hybrid forms, these were merely the forms which, by permission of the Creator, they had chosen to be known to mankind. It seems more logical that the animal forms were symbolic of deeper meanings.

An unusual scene shows Sety pouring water into vases containing lotus flowers (Fig. 11-2). Above the flower vases is a list of six different kinds of wine and below are a slaughtered and decapitated ox and oryx while choice pieces of meat: The head, heart, forelegs and cutlets, are laid out on a reed mat in front of Soker (Fig. 11-3).

Lastly the King dedicates a number of lamps to Soker. These are simple bowls (containing oil and salt) in which float three wicks. They stand on pedestals, and above them are the names of the places where they were to be lit and below, the number of lamps required. For example, the first entry in the lowest register says, "Temple of Sekhmet: Thirteen (lamps)" (Fig. 11-4).

The Western Wall.

The northern part of this wall is occupied by the doorway of the Chapel of Soker-Osiris; the outer jambs of which show the King adoring the Gods of Memphis in the three upper scenes, but in the bottom scene, Anubis, in the form of a jackal, lies on top of a tomb.

On the short wall between this doorway and that of the Chapel of Nefer-tem is a fine representation of the Djed Pillar which is surmounted by the head of Osiris most unusually represented fullfaced and wearing the divine headdress of disk, horns and plumes (Fig. 11-5). The pillar is supported by two statues of the King and stands in a chapel with a

Fig. 11-3. The Hall of Soker (northern wall). Joints of meat. An offering to the God Soker. The inscription reads, "Entering the temple to place on the ground consecrated choice joints of meat in front of Soker, that he may give him life."

vaulted roof.

Each of the outer jambs of the doorway of the Chapel of Nefer-tem have three scenes showing the King offering to the God in his various forms. In the lower scene, Sety is shown as a sphinx with human arms, the hands holding the symbolic image of Maat.

The Southern Wall.

There are four offering niches in this wall similar to those in the western wall of the Second Hypostyle Hall, and like them, decorated with scenes in relief.

Fig. 11-4. (Right) King Sety dedicating lamps (the Hall of Soker, northern wall).

142

Fig. 11-5. The Djed Pillar again regarded as Osiris, and surmounted by the head of that God. The Hall of Soker, western wall. The Temple of Sety I. The pillar is like a Tree of Life.

Fig. 11-6. Temple of Sety I. Some of the mummiform gods ("Osiris in Hwt-ka-Ptah" and "Thot in Setepet."). Hall of Soker, southern wall.

Most of the upper register was destroyed when the limestone blocks were later taken elsewhere for building purposes; but on the flattened shafts of the sandstone columns which remain, one can faintly make out parts of an offering list.

The first scene in the lower register (from the west) is a narrow one and shows the King supporting the standard of Nefer-tem which is surmounted by a lotus flower from the midst of which rise two tall plumes.

The First Niche.

The lintel of all the niches are topped by the winged disk under which are two rows of inscriptions giving the titles and names of Sety. Two similar lines of inscriptions adorn the jambs. The sides are sculptured with scenes of the King worshiping the gods. Next to the first niche comes a scene showing Sety burning incense before Nefer-tem and Sekhmet. Between the third and fourth niches Sety makes offerings to some mummiform gods (Fig. 11-6).

The last scene on this wall shows the King addressing the God Soker, who is in the form of a falcon-headed mummy, and who in return presents the Key of Life to the King's face (Fig. 11-7). But there is a very strange thing about the figure of the King in this scene. The face is quite different from all the others. The features are coarse. The eye is rounder and the nose quite different from the fine aquiline nose of Sety, and yet, the sculpture is of the highest standard and the modeling of the face, body and limbs, natural and expressive.

Fig. 11-7. Sety I adoring the God Soker who in turn is presenting a Key of Life. Note the uncharacteristic and coarse features of the King's face (the Hall of Soker, southern wall).

Fig. 11-8. Sety I offering a shin of veal to Nefer-tem (the Hall of Soker, eastern wall). The Temple of Sety I.

This coarse and vulgar face with its rather disagreeable expression was not due to lack of skill on the part of the sculptor, but appears to be a deliberate distortion of the handsome features of Sety. But why was this done, and how it was allowed to pass unaltered is a mystery that we shall never solve! Was it due after all to a disagreeable mood of the sculptor whose skill otherwise is beyond reproach? It may be!

The Eastern Wall.

In the southern scene on the eastern wall, Sety kneels and presents to Nefer-tem a bowl containing a shin of veal (Fig. 11-8). Next, the King again kneeling offers two jars of red pottery to Soker. These are the red jars that were ceremonially broken in one of the rites of the Mortuary Cult. Strange as it may seem, today this ceremonial breaking of jars still remains as a rather crude and vulgar expression of wanting to see no more of an undesirable person or sometimes on leaving a place one does not desire to come back to. Here the King kneels humbly before the God.

In the final scene Sety, in a very deferential attitude, approaches the God Soker.

The Vaulted Chapel of Soker-Osiris.

The northernmost of the two chapels leading out of the western wall of the Hall of Soker was dedicated to Soker-Osiris, that is

Fig. 11-9. The vaulted Chapel of Soker-Osiris (northern wall). The God Ptah-Soker, and the Goddess Sekhmet.

Fig. 11-10. The vaulted Chapel of Soker-Osiris (northern wall). The falcon on the right represents Horus. That on the left represents Isis. The small figures are statues of King Sety. The inscriptions read, "Horus who is in his boat, he gives victory to the Lord of Diadems, Sety Mer-en-Ptah. Isis who is in his (Horus') boat, she gives all health."

Soker identified with Osiris.

On both of the inner jambs of its doorway are the same elongated cartouches containing the royal titles and names as on the doorway of the Hall of Soker.

The walls of this chapel originally had two registers of scenes, but the upper one on the northern wall is almost entirely destroyed as is also the vaulted roof. This wall is also somewhat marred by smoke. The sculpture is of a very high standard, especially the exquisite portraits of the King, but the relief is flatter than that in the Hall of Soker. Here is a detailed description of its walls.

The Northern Wall.

Immediately inside the doorway is an offering list of nine entries with their accompanying formulae all of which were copied from the Pyramid Texts. Then follows a figure of the King kneeling and presenting two jars of red pottery to Ptah-Soker; these

same jars being the last item mentioned in the foregoing offering list. The God is seated upon a throne with Sekhmet, "The beloved of Ptah " behind him.

In the second scene, Sety kneels before Soker to whom he burns incense.

In the third scene, the King offers two nemset

jars to two large falcons each of which has a small royal statuette standing in front of it (Fig. 11-10). They stand in an ornamental shrine which seems to have been intended to be a cabin-shrine on a sacred boat as the inscriptions say that the falcons are "Horus who is in his boat,"

Fig. 11-11. Osiris being restored to life in order to beget his son Horus (the Chapel of Soker-Osiris, northern wall).

Fig. 11-12. *Dwa-mut-ef, a son of Horus, weeping for Osiris. The Chapel of Soker-Osiris. Northern wall. Temple of Sety I.*

wake up as though from sleep. One hand is languidly raised to his face, the other grasps his erect phallus. Isis tenderly helps him to raise his head and Horus, who is not yet even conceived, stands at the foot of the bed in an attitude of gentle concern.

Under the bed were figures of the Four Sons of Horus; each of which had a small figure of the King kneeling in front of him offering wine. The best preserved of these figures is Dwa-mut-ef who is represented as a boy naked, except for a girdle. He beats his breast with his clenched fists, and on his face is an expression of deep grief for the murdered God (Fig. 11-12).

All the figures in this scene are in a shrine, and the inscription says that it is "Soker-Osiris who is in his boat." Per-

and "Isis who is in his (Horus'?) boat."

The next scene illustrates the event in the story of Osiris where the dead God returns to life for one night in order to beget his son Horus (Fig. 11-11). Here Osiris lies on a bed which is in the usual form of an elongated lion. He is about to

Fig. 11-13. *(Right) A very rare representation of the Goddess Nut in the form of a pregnant hippopotamus. In front of her is a statuette of Sety offering wine. The Chapel of Soker-Osiris. Northern wall.*

Fig. 11-14. Nameless deities seated without chairs. Chapel of Soker-Osiris (southern wall, upper register). Temple of Sety I.

haps this and the preceding scene represent actual tableaux of statues which were once placed in a boat and carried in the processions of the God.

The last scene on this wall is a curious representation of the Goddess Nut in the form of a pregnant hippopotamus; she squats on her haunches and holds a large knife in her forepaws (Fig. 11-13). Most of her head is destroyed. In front of the Goddess is a small statuette of the King offering wine.

This is a very unusual form of Nut, and it is usually Ta-wer, the Protectoress of Women in Childbirth, who is shown as a pregnant hippopotamus. Moreover, this is an amazing coincidence; the pose of the Goddess is exactly the same as that adopted by the modern women of Abydos when in labor. They squat in exactly the same way and hold a large knife which they keep beside them for seven days after the child is born, "to keep away all the evil spirits."

It is sometimes amazing to see how many things tradition has left hanging over our every day life in this part of the world.

The Western Wall.

The surface of the western wall of the chapel is entirely destroyed by the action of salt in the stone coming out after torrential rains which occur only very infrequently.

The Southern Wall.

Here the upper register as well as the spring of the vault is perfectly observed.

In the first scene (from the west) are three gods one of whom has the head of a ram. They are all in a seated posture, but there are no chairs under them. This omission is intentional, and not an oversight (Fig. 11-14). Each deity holds a small snake and a lizard in his hands. Next comes the Goddess Nekhbet wearing the crown of Upper Egypt, then Anubis and Osiris. In front of each deity is a kneeling statuette of the King offering wine (Fig. 11-15).

The remainder of the register is occupied by a

Fig. 11-15. Anubis (Left) Nekhbet in human form. Chapel of Soker-Osiris, southern wall, upper register. Temple of Sety I.

list mentioning a number of gods who were worshiped in the Memphite district and at the end, a figure of Sety kneeling. He burns incense and recites the offering formula on behalf of the gods mentioned in

Fig. 11-16. Chapel of Soker-Osiris (southern wall). The mystic conception of Horus. The Temple of Sety I.

Fig. 11-17. *Chapel of Soker-Osiris (southern wall). The God Thot (Right) the Goddess Mut in the form of a uraeus.*

Fig. 11-18. *King Sety offering incense and libations to the God Soker. Temple of Sety I.*

the list.

In the lower register, the first scene from the west shows the mystic conception of Horus which has already appeared in the central chapel of the Statue Hall.

First comes a damaged figure of Anubis then Isis in human form approaches the bed on which lies Osiris. At the God's head and feet perch falcons which spread their wings in protection. the whole scene is full of bewildering, mystic symbolism, hard to understand at first glance.

Isis, now in the form of a falcon, hovers over the erect phallus of Osiris and conceives her son, and Horus, as though in a vision of the future (or the unborn spirit or Ka) is shown as a falcon-headed man leaning over the foot of the bed. The gestures of his arms and hands are very graceful and express loving concern (Fig. 11-16). The action takes place in a shrine, and the inscription says, "Osiris Wennefer, who dwells in the Temple of Soker, may he give life and prosperity to Men-maat-Ra."

Under the bed are seated Thot who says, "I make thy protection in thy temple," and two large cobras, one of which is called "Mut, who protects Osiris upon his great throne," (Fig.11-17) while the other is "Rennutet who protects Osiris." Lastly comes a monkey who is "Ifet, who protects Osiris in his temple."

The second scene is similar to that opposite to it on the northern wall.

149

Fig. 11-19. *King Sety presenting offerings to Geb (details). Chapel of Soker-Osiris (southern wall). Temple of Sety I.*

Sety pours a libation to two large falcons in a shrine, but here both birds represent Soker. The modeling of the King's face, expecially the lips and ears, is astonishing (Fig. 11-18).

In the next scene, which is entitled "Prospering the Garden of this God, with the Nemset Jar," the King is shown performing one of the rites in the mysteries of Osiris in front of Soker-Osiris. He is pouring water from a nemset jar into a rectangular trough called a "garden." In such a trough

was placed a golden mold in the form of the God Osiris which was filled with earth and barley. The trough and its contents were kept in this very chapel and watered daily until the seeds germinated. The living green shoots rising from the dried grain symbolized the resurrection of Osiris from death, and was a promise of renewed life in the Hereafter for all who believed in him. An inscription behind the King refers to this rite and to the presentation of libations to Ptah-Soker.

In the last scene, the King kneels and presents a tray of offerings to the God Geb. Of all the good portraits of the King in this temple, this is surely the most perfect. Not only has the artist reproduced the King's features with feeling and precision but has caught the intent expression of concentration as Sety fixes his gaze on the rather overladen tray (Fig. 11-19).

The Vaulted Chapel of Nefertem.

The walls of this

chapel are rather badly damaged by fire and the action of salt; nevertheless it has retained its original roof. It also contains a number of very interesting and unusual scenes as well as some inscriptions taken from the Pyramid Texts.

On the inner jambs of the doorway are again the elongated cartouches with the enigmatic writing as in the Chapel of Soker-Osiris (Fig. 11-20).

The Northern Wall.

Immediately inside the doorway, Sety is burning incense and pouring a libation for Nefer-tem. Between the King and the God is an offering list of eight entries again taken from the Pyramid Texts.

Next follows a long inscription giving an address by the King to Nefer-tem and a figure of him presenting offerings to that God. The face of the King and his hands holding the censer and raised to recite the of-

Fig. 11-20. (Right) Cartouche of Sety I in enigmatic writing, on the northern inner jamb of the doorway of the Chapel of Nefer-tem.

fering formula are very expressive.

The God Nefer-tem is in a most unusual form. He is shown as a lion-headed man holding the Eye of Horus; on his head is perched a falcon crowned with a lotus flower (Fig. 11-21).

Next comes the God "Nun, the Father of the Gods," kneeling upon a rectangular pedestal. He is followed by the God "Kheperi" in the form of a man with a large scarab upon his head. In front of him, a small royal statuette offers wine. A similar statuette kneels

Fig. 11-21. (Right) Vaulted Chapel of Nefer-tem (northern wall). An unusual form of the God Nefer-tem, in the form of a lion-headed man, carries the sacred Eye of Horus. In front of him is inscribed, "Nefer-tem, Protector of the Two Lands, Lord of Kas, Horus En-hap(?); he gives victory to Men-maat-Ra." Behind Nefer-tem is Nun, God of the Primeval Ocean, who is inscribed, "Nun, father of the Gods, who dwells in the House of Men-maat-Ra."

Fig. 11-22. *Amon-Ra, with a solar disk in place of his head, and Osiris, whose head is replaced by a Djed Pillar. The Chapel of Nefer-tem, southern wall, upper register.*

in front of the God Thot. Lastly come two goddesses, but their figures are damaged beyond recognition.

In the upper register (eastern end) Sety kneels before Ra-Hor-akhty who is in a shrine. There is another offering list between them.

In the second scene,

the King again waters the "garden" of Soker-Osiris after which he makes offerings to Soker, Nefer-tem, in his lion-headed form, and Thot. Lastly is shown a large lotus flower emblem of Nefer-tem and a statue of Sety in the form of a sphinx with human arms offering

a vase to Nefer-tem.

The Western Wall.

As in the Chapel of Soker-Osiris, the surface of the western wall is entirely destroyed.

The Southern Wall.

In the upper register of the southern wall (from the west), Sety offers to the God Thetnent behind whom kneels a very strange figure of Amon-Ra whose human head is disconcertingly replaced by a solar disk (Fig. 11-22). Next comes a kneeling figure of Osiris Wennefer whose head is replaced by a Djed Pillar. These uncanny-looking figures are followed by another statue of Sety in the form of a sphinx offering a "Henty" to Sekhmet (Fig. 11-23). All this adds to the bewilderment one feels as soon as he gets into the Soker Hall.

The second scene is badly damaged but shows the King kneeling in front of Soker.

The third scene resembles that opposite to it on the northern wall.

In the lower register, the first scene from the west shows the King kneeling before a number of deities; the first of whom is Nefer-tem. He is shown as a lion-headed mummy, and again has a lotus-crowned falcon perched on his head (Fig.11-24). He is followed by Ptah-Osiris, Shu, and "Horus Who is Over His Papyrus Column." The

Fig. 11-23. *Sety in the form of a sphinx presents the "Henty" to Sekhmet. The Chapel of Nefer-tem. Southern wall, upper register. The Temple of Sety I.*

Fig. 11-24. (Left) Chapel of Nefer-tem (southern wall). Sety adoring the lion-headed Nefer-tem.

Nefer-tem who is said to "protect the Two Lands, and make to live the common people of Egypt and their children."

Finally, Sety is shown offering to Min-Ra, a God in human form crowned with a solar disk (Fig. 11-26).

One can now see that there is quite a number of composite deities in these two chapels which do not seem to appear in any other temple in Egypt. This is one of many factors that make this temple u- nique, fascinating and hard to forget. The Hall of Soker is a temple with- in a temple.

latter is shown as a large falcon standing on a papy- rus column as we have already seen him in the great Osiris Hall. Next come Isis and Nekhbet and finally a most unusual form of Hathor. She is shown as a falcon with the head of a woman and crowned with the disk and cow's horns. The human-headed falcon was the symbol of the soul, and in the Pyramid Texts Hathor is called "Hathor, the Symbol of the Female Soul." But so far as we are aware, this is the only known representation of her in this particular form (Fig. 11-25).

Next follows another long inscription, the text of a beautiful hymn to

Fig. 11-25. Hathor as a human-headed falcon (Chapel of Nefer-tem, southern wall). Temple of Sety I.

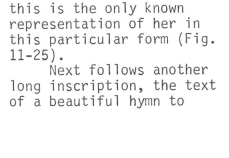

Fig. 11-26. The God Min- Ra, "King of the Gods." The Chapel of Nefer-tem, southern wall, lower register. The Temple of Sety I

CHAPTER TWELVE

A ROYAL PASSAGE WITH ROYAL NAMES

The Corridor of Kings.

This passage now known as the "Corridor of Kings," on account of the very famous list of royal names on its western wall, leads out of the southwestern end of the Second Hypostyle Hall. It gives access to the Western Corridor often called the Corridor of the Bull, the Hall of the Sacred Boats, and the Slaughter Court (see page 156).

The passage was originally closed at its northern end by a single-leaf wooden door which opened against its eastern side. Here are six vertical lines of incised inscriptions giving the titles and names of the King, and adding that he is beloved of Amon-Ra, Ra-Hor-akhty, Ptah, Lord of Truth, Osiris, Horus and Isis, namely the deities to whom the six Cult Chapels are dedicated.

The western side of the doorway bore a scene in relief, but of this, only the feet of the King and those of a mummiform god remain.

The Western Wall.

The first scene on the western wall shows Sety accompanied by his son the little Prince Ramesses in the presence of the God Soker. The latter is seated in a shrine with his mother the Goddess Sekhmet seated behind him.

The face of the King is of great beauty but bears an expression of gentle melancholy, one might even say of spiritual weariness. He holds a libation vase and censer and leans slightly over his little son who, standing upright with the confidence of boyhood, proudly recites the offering formula over a large pile of offerings standing between him and the two deities (Fig. 12-1).

Ramesses is dressed as a priest but wears the plaited sidelock of youth common to little children of all classes. He appears to be not more than ten years of age which would accord with his own statement in the dedication inscription on the facade of the temple in which he says that his father made him co-regent while he was still a little child.

The List of Kings.

Next comes the famous and extremely important document known as "The List of Kings." It extends from the northern jamb of the doorway of the Western Corridor to the scene just described. At the southern end, Sety, holding an incense burner, is reciting a prayer for offerings on behalf of his predecessors whose names appear in the list. In front of him little Prince Ramesses, again in priestly costume, is reading from

Fig. 12-1. *King Sety and Prince Ramesses adoring the God Soker. Ramesses is reciting the offering formula (the Corridor of Kings, western wall). Temple of Sety 1.*

a roll of papyrus (Fig. 12-2). This figure of the Prince is perhaps the best rendering of "childhood's innocence" that ancient Egypt ever produced. Here is a real little boy not a miniature man. The body and limbs though strong and healthy looking, are softly rounded and have an immature grace. It is in short, the portrait of a handsome, lively little boy already showing the charm for which the adult King Ramesses was famous.

The actual list of royal names commences at the southern end of the upper register with the name of Mena the first king of the Ist dynasty,

and ends at the northern end of the lower register with the name of Sety himself. In all there are seventy-six names, but although these are in chronological order they do not include all the rulers of Egypt. Unimportant kings or those whom Sety personally disliked are not included. These omissions are legitimate as this is not an intentionally distorted historical document but was meant to be merely a list of offering endowments by Sety in their behalf. It is temple work for the dead. As we may expect, the name of Akhen-Aton and those of his successors,

Semenkh-ka-Ra, Tut-ankh-Amon and Ay are all left out and ignored in ill-concealed disdain; and Hor-em-heb is placed immediately after Amon-Hotep III.[1]

Sety seems also to have disapproved of women pharaohs, for Khent-kawes of the IVth dynasty, Neit-Ikeret of the VIth dynasty, Sobek-neferu of the XIIth dynasty, and the great Hatshepsut of the XVIIIth dynasty, all of whom ruled Egypt in their own right, are neglected here!

A very interesting point is that the obscure King Djed-ef-Ra of the IVth dynasty is correctly placed between Khufu and Khafra; Most historians from Herodotus onwards say that Khafra was the direct successor of Khufu, and only fairly recently the late Dr. Reisner suspected that Djed-ef-Ra had ruled briefly between these two kings. He also suspected Djed-ef-Ra of having murdered his elder brother Kawab in order to supplant him! The discovery in 1953 by Mr. Kamal Mallakh of the great wooden boat in a rock-cut pit to the south of the Great Pyramid at Giza proved conclusively that Djed-ef-Ra had actually succeeded Khufu, and completed his burial arrangements as his name is written in red paint on the undersides of the stone slabs that covered the boat pit.

....
[1]After the end of the names of the Vth dynasty kings, the prenomens and not the personal names are given in this list.

Fig. 12-2. King Sety, Prince Ramesses and part of the famous "List of Kings." The King is reciting the prayer for offerings on behalf of his predecessors. Ramesses reads from a roll of papyrus. The first cartouche in the upper register of the list is that of Mena, of the Ist dynasty (the Corridor of Kings, western wall).

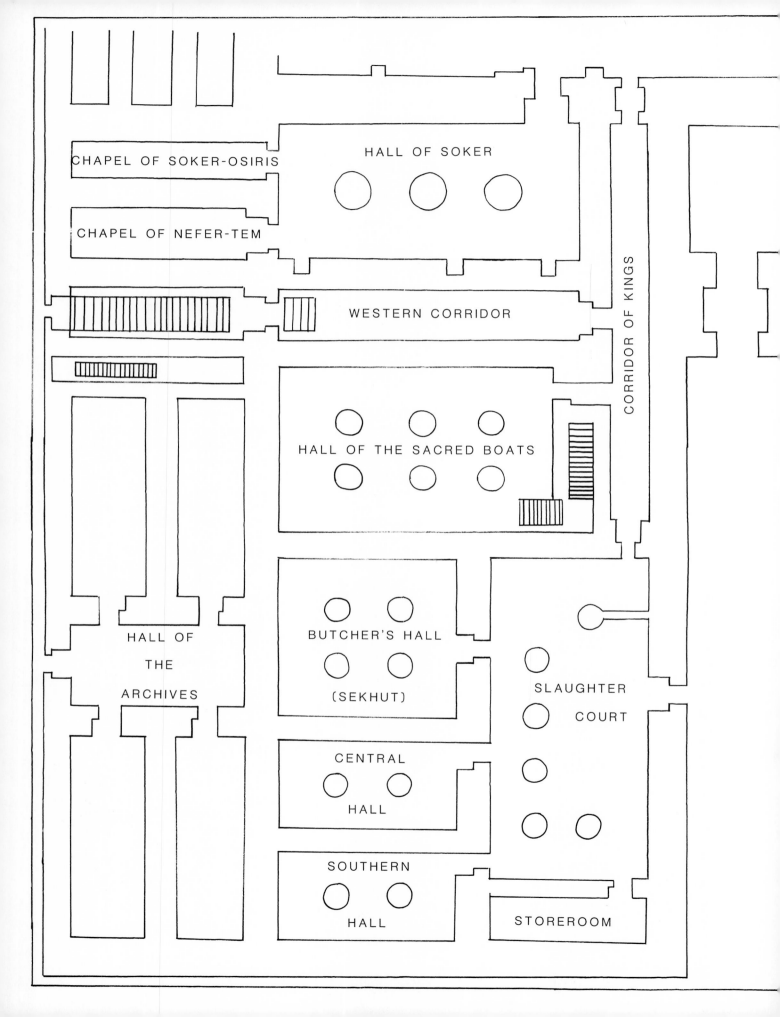

The point of this is that it proves that there must have been historical records from the earliest times still existing during the XIXth dynasty from which such lists could be correctly drawn up. Yet many people still wrongly believe that the ancient Egyptians had no written histories or historical records!

The third register of the list contains alternate inscriptions saying that the offerings are "given as a gift by the King Men-maat-Ra" and "given as a gift by the son of Ra, Sety Mer-en-Ptah."

Next comes the doorway leading into the Western Corridor; both jambs of which bear figures of the King. On the southern one is the warning inscription, "All who enter the temple must be purified."

Such warnings were later to be found in the first Israelite temples started by Solomon in Jerusalem. This does not mean that Sety's temple was the original, but his could have copied earlier forms.

On a short wall between this doorway and that of the Hall of the Sacred Boats, Sety wearing the Itef crown, is said to be "making a fourfold purification with the nemset jars for his father Ptah, Lord of Truth, that he may be given life." The King holds the four jars on a tray, and from them four streams of water flow out converging into two streams and falling in front of and behind a statue of Ptah.

The jambs of the doorway of the Hall of the Sacred Boats also bear figures of Sety to which Ramesses had added his own incised cartouches. In front of the King's figure on the southern jamb, someone had incised a carefully drawn human ear (Fig. 12-3). This was often done in or near sacred places, and the ear was supposed to represent the ear of a god "listening" to the complaint of the worshiper. The latter made his prayer into it, and the petition remained "filed for reference" until the god saw fit to attend to it once he had heard it.

At this part of the passage the roof ends, and so the remainder of the wall was left undecorated. The southern end of the passage was left unroofed.

Fig. 12-3. *Corridor of Kings. Western wall. "The Ear of the God." Temple of Sety 1.*

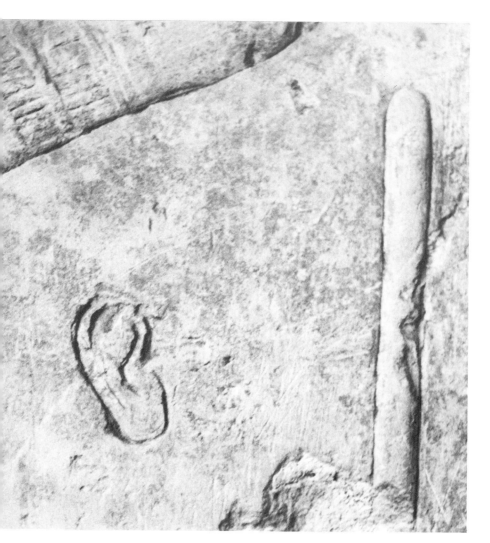

Fig. 12-4A+B. Greek and Coptic graffiti at the southern end of the Corridor of Kings.

because it ends at the Slaughter Court where the sacrificial animals were killed. Had the roof been continued to the end, untoward sounds (to say nothing of smells) would have entered the temple.

Many Greek and Coptic graffiti are scratched on the wall here or daubed in red paint (Fig. 12-4A and 4B). These include a large "Star of David." Many of the Greek graffiti are thank offerings for cures effected by means of prophetic dreams. It appears that at this late period, sick people were allowed to pass the night in this part of the corridor and in the Slaughter Court. If the gods so willed, they sent dreams to the ailing showing them the remedy for their sickness. In gratitude, those who were cured sometimes returned to record their thanks in simple, pathetically grateful words. However, one nasty fellow wiled away his time by enumerating the charms of an apparently well known lady of the town (even in those remote times, "vital statistics" seemed to count!). Below and in another handwriting, someone else added, "Yes, she is all that you say but to my taste she is too short." The whole thing seems so out of place and time!

The doorway leading into the Slaughter Court was closed by a single-leaf door opening on the eastern side. On the western side was a figure of Sety in the presence of the God Min. This scene was executed in colors but in paint only, and has almost disappeared.

The Eastern Wall of the Corridor of Kings.

The first scene on the eastern wall of this corridor shows Sety and little Prince Ramesses offering to Osiris and Isis. Next comes a long list of one hundred and thirty entries giving the names of various gods and their places of worship. The purpose of this is the same as that of the List of Kings, to record an offering endowment made by Sety on behalf of the deities mentioned. At the beginning of the list (southern end) Sety is shown reciting the prayer for offerings while Ramesses pours a libation on a bunch of herbs lying on an offering table.

In the next scene to the south, the King makes offerings to Ra-Hor-akhty, and in the last scene he offers to Amon-Ra. The text accompanying this scene is of great interest (Fig. 12-5). It is a magic spell designed to protect the God's offering endowment and has been taken from the Pyramid Texts of the Old Kingdom where it was originally used to protect the Pyramid Complex.

On the undecorated end of this wall are some more Greek graffiti, and someone, with a very apparent sense of humor, has scratched a figure of the God Anubis wearing the typical costume of a Roman soldier, but they made his kilt so full that it looks like a ballet dancer's tutu (Fig. 12-6). In front is a fairly well drawn lion and below a dog with a long body, short legs, curled tail and prick ears (Fig. 12-7). This breed of dog still exists in the near-by town of Sohag. Someone else had tried (and failed) to copy the first figure of the lion. There is also a well drawn, life-sized human leg and a small figure of Min, apparently copied from the side of the doorway to the Slaughter Court.

The Ceiling of the Corridor of Kings.

The original ceiling of the corridor, of massive slabs of brown Nubian sandstone, is still intact. It is decorated with five-pointed stars among which are the cartouches of Sety and the Heb-sed emblems. Down the center is a long vertical inscription beginning at the southern end, and the interesting part of which reads, "he the King, made it as his monument for his fathers, the Company of Gods, Lord of Heaven and Earth, who dwell in the 'House of Men-maat-Ra' making for them their noble chapels at the gateway of the Lord of the Sacred Land,[2] constructed

[2] The chapels are the Cult Chapels of the temple; the gateway of the Lord of the "Sacred Land" is Pega-the-Gap which was regarded as the gateway leading direct-ly to the Kingdom of Osiris.

Fig. 12-5. Corridor of Kings, eastern wall. Sety offering to Amon-Ra. The accompanying text is from the Pyramid Texts of the Vth dynasty. The shadowing is from sunlight through bars.

of stone, decorated with gold as a work for the ends of Eternity, creating divine statues, modeling their bodies, granting their offerings and presents from the food placed by him every morning for them."

In spite of the fact that the southern end of the corridor was never roofed, it was apparently considered to be too dark, and so a small skylight

was cut in the ceiling near the northwestern end just before the doorway. Here stood a priest whose duty was to inspect the offerings brought in from the Slaughter Court, and consecrate them by tapping them with the special scepter called the "Kherp." Are we to suppose that on one occasion, and being unable to see properly in the gloom, he inadvertently passes in a joint of meat not quite up

Fig. 12-6. (Left) Late graffiti of Anubis in the costume of a Roman soldier. From the southern end of the Corridor of Kings.

to standard? And maybe, in order to prevent a repetition of such an untoward incident, the skylight was cut even though it interfered with the already existing decoration of the ceiling.

In short, we can say that the Corridor of Kings contains one of the most valuable documents of Egyptian history. A meticulous and exacting pharaoh like Sety is not likely to have accepted any "messing about" with the names of his predecessors, and so the List of Kings remains a most reliable source for our knowledge of ancient chronology in Egypt.

Fig. 12-7. (Below) Late graffiti of a lion and a dog. From the southern end of the Corridor of Kings.

CHAPTER THIRTEEN

THE WESTERN CORRIDOR, A
SURPRISE TO ANY COWBOY

Rodeo is Not an American
Invention.

Sometimes called the
"Corridor of the Bull," on
account of its most striking relief, the Western
Corridor is formed from
the alteration to the
plan of the Hall of Soker
(see page 156). It opens
out of the Corridor
of Kings immediately to
the south of the list of
royal names.

The walls of the
corridor originally had
two registers of scenes,
but the upper register on
both walls is almost totally destroyed. The sculp-
ture, which is in incised
relief, dates from the
reign of Ramesses II, but
it is very possible that
the scenes were already
drawn upon the walls while
Sety was still living, and
that Ramesses made, shall
we say, some of his famous
"minor changes," and had
them sculptured.

On the northern side
of the doorway are four
lines of inscription of
Ramesses, and on the
southern side a scene
showing him embracing
Osiris.

The first scene in
the lower register of this
wall is another master-
piece in composition and
drawing. It is also the
answer to those critics
who claim that Egyptian
art is lifeless, conven-
tional and static! Here
a king and a prince,

Fig. 13-1. Western Corridor (northern wall). "Lassoing the long-horned bull of Upper Egypt."

(originally Sety and
Ramesses?) are performing
a ceremony that took place
in the temple court. A
wild bull was let loose,
and the king was supposed
to lasso it, throw it down
and cut its throat as a
sacrifice. In this case
the "long-horned bull of
Upper Egypt" runs at full
gallop, its tongue lolling
out, and its eyes round
and staring with terror.
Already the skillful, agile
king has thrown a noose
over its horns, and (cow-
boy's style) has twisted
the rope around its right
hind leg. He holds the
slack of the rope looped
in his right hand, and with
the left one is about to
throw another noose, the
slipknot of which is accurately shown. The king
wears the Red Crown of
Lower Egypt, and the short,
royal shendyt kilt. The
young prince runs behind
the bull, grasping it by
the tail! Above the bull
is inscribed, "Lassoing
the long-horned bull of

Upper Egypt by the King."
The rite is performed in
the presence of Wepwawat
and Osiris (Fig. 13-1).
Naturally, one is inclined
to believe that the whole
ceremony must have had
some important religious
significance such as animal
sacrifice.

The whole composition
is magnificent, so vibrant
with life that it sometimes
looks as if it were about
to move. With admirable
skill the sculptor has
portrayed the wild-eyed
terror of the frenzied bull,
the powerful muscles of its
shoulders, and its swift
gallop.

The human figures are
not less well done. The
striding legs of the father
and son, their feet scarcely
touching the ground, the
postures of their arms,
and the streamers of the
king's crown flying out
behind him, all convey an
impression of speed, grace
and power (Fig. 13-2).

The next scene, most
of which is destroyed,

Fig. 13-2. The Western Corridor. Northern wall. Lassoing the "long-horned bull of Upper Egypt" (detail). Note the slipknot on the noose held in the king's raised hand.

showed the king sacrificing an animal, perhaps an oryx, or possibly a gazelle, in front of a god and goddess. The animal lies bound upon an offering table, and the king was apparently grasping it by its now missing horns and thrusts a long knife into its throat. The expression on the face of the dying animal is pathetically resigned and helpless. As the king bends forward, the muscles of his body and limbs are brought into play and are shown with great accuracy and vividness under his thin clothing. He stands well away from the animal as though to avoid getting splashed with its blood (Fig. 13-3).

The third scene shows the king performing the ceremony of dragging the sacred Henu-boat of Soker on its wooden sledge (Fig. 13-4). The king, again wearing the Lower Egyptian crown and the shendyt kilt, grasps a rope attached to the sledge under the boat and turns forward towards the God Thot and the deceased King Sety. The figure of the latter may originally have been that of another deity but altered by Ramesses to represent his father. The

Henu-boat is a very curious-looking vessel and resembles the boats in predynastic vase paintings. The hull is shaped like a crescent, and the prow is surmounted by the head of an oryx looking backwards. Below it hangs the head of an ox, with a stream of blood flowing from its mouth. Down the curve of the hull behind the prow, are a bulty fish and six small falcons, and below them, and projecting outwards, are twenty-two oars attached by a rope to a scaffolding amidships. This scaffolding holds in place a rectangular sarcophagus surmounted by a mummified falcon, a form of the God Soker (Fig. 13-5). Another scaffolding attaches the boat to its sledge.

The stern of the boat is destroyed, and with it the head of a smaller figure of a prince or a priest, who carries a long-

Fig. 13-3. The king cutting the throat of a sacrificial animal (gazelle). The Western Corridor, northern wall. The Temple of Sety I.

handled feather fan.

The last scene on this part of the wall shows the king burning incense and reciting the offering formula before Ptah who sits in front of a well-laden offering table with the Goddess Sekhmet behind him (Fig. 13-6).

We have now reached what was originally the doorway of the third chapel of the Hall of Soker (see page 156) to which a short flight of four steps ascends. Both outer jambs bear the incised inscriptions of Ramesses, but on the inner jambs are the elongated cartouches in bas-relief with the enigmatically written titles and names of Ramesses. These were however, undoubtedly carved during the reign of Sety and seem to be further proof of the co-regency between father

and son.

The sides of the doorway are inscribed in bas-relief with the titles and names of Sety only, but Ramesses has added an incised inscription underneath them claiming that he had "renewed" the monuments of his father.

Immediately to the west of the doorway there is a further flight of twenty-two steps leading up to the western door of the temple. The roof of this part of the corridor is vaulted being, as already mentioned, the erstwhile third chapel of the Hall of Soker. Here the walls are all decorated in bas-relief and date from the reign of Sety.

The Goddess Seshat Praises the King.

The first scene on the northern wall shows

Fig. 13-5. The sarcophagus in the sacred Henu-boat of the God Soker (the Western Corridor, northern wall).

the Goddess Seshat, seated and raising her hand in the ancient gesture of one speaking. Her speech, which is in praise of the King, is recorded in the long

Fig. 13-4. Western Corridor (northern wall). The king drags the Henu-boat of Soker (detail). The Temple of Sety I.

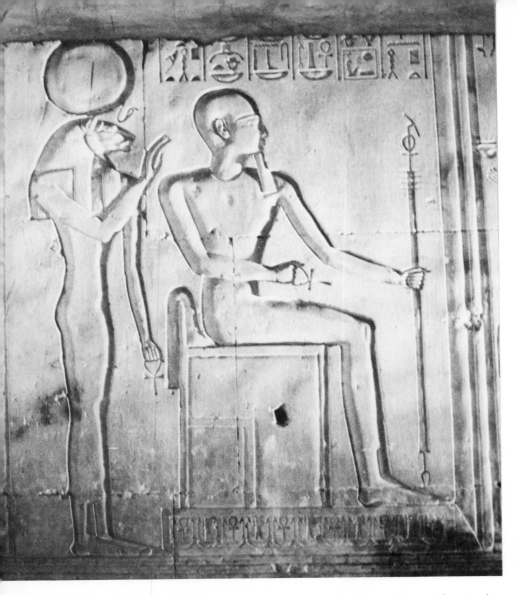

Fig. 13-6. Western Corridor. Northern wall. The God Ptah and the Goddess Sekhmet. Temple of Sety I.

inscription in front of her. She says, "O my son, my beloved, Lord of the Two Lands, Men-maat-Ra, the son of Ra, Sety Mer-en-Ptah, thou hast set up completely excellent monuments for those who are in thy noble temple in exultation and satisfaction. Every god is thy protector."

She then refers to the building of the temple, "in western desert of Abydos, which was measured by me...Ta-tanen measured out its ground."

She then refers to

the King digging the foundations (see page 74). "Thy two hands hold the pick; its (the temple's) four corners are well established like the foundations of Heaven; words of magic are made for its protection by Neit and Serket. Thou has completed it as a work of eternity, the outer walls of the chapels thereof; its columns come truly; all its doors are of bronze; food is in it, through the provisions of Sia (Understanding). Every god rests in its interior, possessing a

chapel through thee, together with Osiris...[1]

"His divine statue is hidden in thy temple. Horus and Isis, their place is there protecting them. Ptah-Soker is joyful, modeled in the divine boat. Nefer-tem is at their side; Geb is at the head of it, together with his children, and the ennead of the gods of his father. Shu and Tefnut rest within their chapels which thou hast made in their names. All of the gods and goddesses are fashioned by thee in thy temple; the images and the secret images are upon their standards which are in the divine boats; every one of the chapels is erected upon its base. Thine excellence creates the horizon of Heaven. Those who are in the solar disk to the Underworld of Osiris support thy sculptures for millions of years. Thou are protected upon the throne of Ra as the balance.[2] Thou art the mooring post of thy time.[3] Thou art excellent, one is aware of thy goodness; Heaven is pregnant with these thy beauties. The mysterious Underworld rejoices concerning thy plans; thou art vigilant as he who is active; thou givest light to those in

....
[1] The Goddess now mentions the gods who are adored in the temple.
[2] The King was supposed to maintain the balance of the realm.
[3] The King is the firm mooring post of the "Ship of State."

164

darkness. Tired-heart (Osiris) is joyful; the dead in their tombs raise their faces because thou hast pronounced their names and remembered them in order to set up their affairs and in order to place for them offerings in thy temple twice daily. For thee the Sacred Land is inundated to the level of thy temple; the gods rejoice in thy time. How Abydos rejoices because of thy name, throughout eternity. 'Thy plans are splendid, thy monuments are permanent' so say the patricians and the plebeians, everyone praising thee together. Thou art an adviser because of thy righteousness. The gods come to thy side, thou art one among them; thou art like Ra in Heaven, like Wennefer (Osiris) in the Underworld, like the majesty of Amon in Thebes, like Geb in this land. All life to thy nose! Thou art King in every respect. Thy temple exists eternally; thou appearest in the land like Sah (Orion in his season."

Very simple, sometimes rather curiously fervent. Nevertheless it is quite a speech.

The People Trust in Sety.

"The people come to thee for counsel because thy name is established in their mouth (i.e. thou art famous) as thou art profitable to the gods. Thou art a nurse to the common people.

"I support thy goodness in writing according to

Fig. 13-7. Part of the inscription on the northern wall of the staircase. Note the figure of the pregnant woman in the second line of text from the left. The Western Corridor. The Temple of Sety I.

the order of Ra; my power is thy protection; my hand writes for thee of these thy benefits like my brother Thot. Atum spoke to us, he said, 'Yes, my affairs are under thy will; thou hast united Upper and Lower Egypt under thy sandals. It is thou who revealest thyself in glory upon thy portable throne of the Heb-sed Jubilee, like Ra,[4] in the beginning of the seasonal festival. There come for thee the rays of the sun disk brightening the side of thy temple, O King of Upper and Lower Egypt, Men-maat-Ra, the son of Ra, Sety Mer-en-Ptah, given life."

The hieroglyphs of the inscription are beautifully carved, and some of them are very unusual and interesting as for example,

....
[4]See the scene on the southern wall (lower register) on the vaulted Chapel of Sety (page 118).

the determinative of the name of Sahu (Orion) which shows the Warrior God armed with a spear and standing in a boat. And the determinative of the word "pregnant," a daintly little lady wearing the costume and hairdo of the XIXth dynasty and obviously in "an interesting condition" (Fig. 13-7).

Following this inscription is a scene showing Ramesses II as an adult king offering to his father Sety behind whom is seated the Goddess Isis and the ennead of the nine gods. This seems to suggest that Sety again anticipated his death. He is depicted among the gods,[5] and is honored by his successor and erstwhile co-regent, Ramesses.

....
[5]This reminds us of the Mormon doctrine which states, "As man is God once was and as God is man may become."

165

Fig. 13-8. The Western Corridor, southern wall. A New Year's Day ceremony. The King drives four calves around the city walls for prosperity in the coming year. Note the King's stick which ends in a serpent's head. The God Khonsu, wearing on his head the full and crescent moons, stands to the right. Temple of Sety I.

The Southern Wall of the Western Corridor.

The first scene shows a ceremony that was performed on New Year's Day.[6] The King, wearing the Itef crown, drives four calves around the city wall to insure prosperity through the coming year. The colors of the calves were fixed by tradition, two white, one red and one black. A cord terminating in a Key of Life is attached to a hind leg of each animal and is held by the King. He also carries a stick terminating in the head of a snake reminding us of the staff of Moses which was said to have turned into a serpent! The ceremony is supposed to be performed in front of the God Khonsu and the deceased King Sety, but the latter's figure was probably originally that of another deity (Fig. 13-8).

Next comes a figure of the King running towards a mummiform god of whom only the legs remain.

The legs of a goddess, turned to the west, seem to belong to the next scene which shows the King assisted by four gods catching ducks with a clapnet (Fig. 13-9).

The net is spread in a pool of water full of ducks and surrounded by

[6] New Year rites were common in many ancient lands and had religious significance. H. Nibley, An Approach to the Book of Mormon. Deseret Book Company, Salt Lake City Utah. 1958

papyrus reeds. The royal and divine fowlers have hauled on the rope shutting the trap, and they run to pull their catch ashore. By analogy with a similar scene at Edfu Temple we understand that these are not supposed to be real ducks but are in reality the enemies of the gods shown in the form of ducks to render them magically harmless.[7] In the scene

[7] We must never forget that the Egyptians believed that all the figures in these reliefs had a mysterious and magical life of their own. This might explain the abominable mutilations to which the sculptures of gods and goddesses were particularly subjected during the early days of Christianity in Egypt. The Egyptians, being pious by nature,

at Edfu, human enemies, their arms prudently bound behind them, appear among the birds in the net.

The gods whose identifying inscriptions are destroyed have the heads of a jackal, a falcon, a ram, and another jackal; they are led by the King.

The last scene on this part of the wall shows the King and his son (here called Amon-Ra-khopesh-ef) offering live birds to Amon-Ra and Mut (Fig. 13-10).

The Speech of Thot.

The first scene on the southern wall of the staircase is similar to that in the same place on the northern wall, but instead of

seemed to find in this systematic destruction a confirmation of their newly adopted faith.

Fig. 13-9. (Left) Western Corridor. Southern wall. Ducks, symbolizing enemies of the gods, caught in a clapnet. Note grooves in the sandstone blocks of the wall.

Seshat, it is the wise Thot who praises the King, and he says, "All beings rejoice for thee. Established is thine office, thy kinship; thy name is placed at the forefront of the starry sky;[8] thy sculptures exist for millions of years. The All Lord himself made firm thy temple like Heaven. I inform thee; established in writing at the side of Ra, written with ochre, engraved with chisels, testifying to thy goodness. Thou art pleased by my making it in writing. All the gods are satisfied by thee; their offering tables are provisioned by thee; doubled are their baskets of loaves in hundreds of thousands in excess of their daily offerings."

[8] On the ceiling of the Corridor of Kings, the cartouches of Sety are shown among the stars (see page 159).

Fig. 13-10. (Left) Western Corridor. Southern wall. The God Amon-Ra and the Goddess Mut. In front of Amon-Ra is inscribed, "Amon-Ra, King of the Gods, Lord of Heaven, Ruler of Thebes, who dwells in the House of Men-maat-Ra; he gives all life, all gladness of heart." Mut is inscribed, "Mut, Mistress of Heaven."

Fig. 13-11. Part of inscription on southern wall of staircase. Note the winged man in the middle line of text. Western Corridor.

Sety Protects Egypt and Her Common People.

Thot then continues in a very significant passage, "Egypt is strengthened by thee, her Lord; thou spreadest thyself in protection over her common people; thou art for her as a rampart of iron, its roof of flint, thy fortress upon it of bronze. Thou bringest up the young man; it is thou who knoweth what they need doing the work of the gods. Every god and every goddess rejoices at thy coming; it is pleasant to all."

The God Thot then continues by recording all the good deeds that Sety has done on behalf of Osiris, and he continues, "To thee belongs the goodly inheritance. Eternity comes, it is in exultation for thee forever. Thy temple was founded, its (columns?) of sandstone; thou art like Ra in its interior; it rightly belongs to thee with all its possessions. (The other monuments) of thy establishing, like (those of) Heliopolis and Memphis, excellent temples, existing like Ra when he traverses the sky. The ennead of the gods (speak) from mouth to mouth remembering thee forever; thou art placed on earth as King of Upper Egypt, as King of Lower Egypt. Thy name is well-known to the people; they make for thee incense on the fire, as for Ra, to beg petitions, never forgetting thee and thy goodness, O King of Upper and Lower Egypt, Men-maat-Ra, the son of Ra, Sety Mer-en-Ptah, given life."

In this inscription also, the signs are of exquisite beauty, and especially pleasing is the small winged figure determining the word "Pesh" meaning "to spread over in protection" (Fig. 13-11). The bird and animal signs are also charming and are true to nature.

The final scene is the same as that opposite to it on the northern wall but is very badly damaged.

The Western Doorway.

On the northern inner jamb of the western doorway is a figure of Sety in bas-relief. He wears the crown of Lower Egypt and warns all comers that "All who enter the temple must be purified." The southern inner jamb was undecorated.

On the northern side of the doorway was a relief showing the King adoring a god, but the heads of both figures are lost. Here, as in the Inner Chapel of Isis, the sculptor has given the King five toes instead of the conventional great toe!

Below the scene on the plain part of the wall, someone has engraved a charming little figure of a prince. This was certainly done in ancient times perhaps by a priestly doorkeeper wiling away an idle hour in the shade of the doorway. The southern side of the doorway is undecorated.

CHAPTER FOURTEEN

THE HALL OF THE SACRED BOATS

The entrance to this fine, large hall opens out of the western wall of the Corridor of Kings (see page 156). On both sides of the doorway are scenes carved in incised relief by Ramesses II showing him making offerings to Osiris and his dead father, Sety.

The roof of the hall is supported on two rows of "tree trunk" columns, three to each row, and along the base of the northern, western and southern walls is a wide bench formed of massive sandstone blocks. Here stood the beautiful sacred boats of the gods on those days when their presence was not needed in the ceremonies. They must have made a splendid sight glittering under the shafts of sunbeams that fell upon them like searchlights from the rectangular openings in the roof and the large window high up in the eastern wall.

Along the edge of the bench is a long inscription describing the boats. This, like the scene on the walls, was originally meant to be colored painting only, but Ramesses decided that it would be better if sculptured in incised relief. However, he did not complete the job, and so part of the decoration remains in paint only and part in sculpture!

The inscription commences from the eastern end of the southern bench, and after enumerating the royal titles, reads, "The good God who pacifies (the gods), who fashioned their divine statues which rest upon their seats in the beautiful craftmanship of Ptah and the Bearer of the Beauty[1] of the Lords; their cabin-shrines gilded with fine gold; their divine boats are overlaid with silver[2] of one finger thickness; the oars are of engraved gold. Those who are in the divine boats exist as august statues with their correct forms and names." The remainder of the text recounts the King's generosity in the matter of offerings.

The beginning of the inscription on the northern bench is destroyed, and the preserved part starts with the names of some deities. Among them is the Moon God Iah. Some of the most renowned and serious Old Testament archaeologists argue that Iah was the forerunner of Iaweh, the Israelite God mentioned in the Jehwiste versions of the Bible. After the list of divine names, the inscription reads, "A sanctuary is made for them, and divine offerings to gladden every face are offered to them in excess of everything upon their pure offering tables in the interior of their secret places... Their divine boats are protected for bearing their beauties which were made to equip them..."

In the southeastern corner of the hall a flight of stairs leads up to a terrace at the northern end of which is a large window opening upon the entrance passage mentioned above.

The scenes on the walls of the hall all show the King offering to the divine boats and are similar to those in the western half of the vaulted chapels except that here the King is represented as wearing sandals. This shows that the ceremony is supposed to be taking place in the courtyard of the temple.

Needless to say, when the original paintings were changed to sculpture, the cartouches of Sety were replaced by those of Ramesses!

The best preserved boats, those of Osiris, Isis, Horus and Sety, are on the southern wall. The western and eastern walls are also in fairly good condition.[3] But on the latter, the boat which is that of Sety himself is partly painted and partly sculptured. Most of the northern wall is destroyed, but at its western end one can see the boat of Ptah with the Djed

[1] A name for the sacred boats.
[2] Here it implies that the boats were of silver, but in all the colored scenes they are painted yellow indicating that they were made of gold. Perhaps they were of silver gilt?

[3] The boats on the western wall are those of Ra-Horakhty (north) and Amon-Ra.

Pillars on the prow.

Although there is plenty of room on the walls for two registers of scenes, only one register was made, and this is placed high up so as to leave a wide blank space above the level of the benches. Had there been two registers of scenes, the lower one could have been hidden by the boats standing upon the benches.

On the whole, one can say that what remains of this once splendid Hall of the Sacred Boats bears little resemblance to the stupendous, breath-taking grandeur of what was once perhaps the richest and most fabulously precious hall of all Egyptian temples.

Temple of Ramesses II,
First Hypostyle Hall.

Temple of Ramesses II,
Chapel of Horus, north-
ern wall. Hekat in
human form (see page
228).

Temple of Ramesses II,
First Hypostyle Hall.
Procession of Nile Gods
and cultivated lands
(see page 217).

Right: The God Khonsu as a falcon-headed man. Temple of Sety I, the Second Hypotsyle Hall, the western wall (see page 93).

Bottom: Temple of Sety I, Second Hypostyle Hall, western wall. Sety and the God Khonsu (see page 93).

Corner: Temple of Sety I, eastern wall of the Inner Chapel of Osiris. The Iwn-mut-ef priest (see page 134).

Left: Temple of Sety I, the second Portico, pillar number six. Ramesses is about to enter the temple (see page 66).

Bottom: Temple of Sety I, the Second Hypostyle Hall, western wall. Sety kneels beside the Tree of Life (see page 94).

Corner: Temple of Sety I, the Inner Chapel of Horus. The Goddess Isis behind the God Osiris (see page 129).

Temple of Sety I, Cult Chapel of Osiris, southern wall. Sety offers incense to the standard of Abydos (see page 102).

Temple of Sety I, Inner Chapel of Osiris. The God Thot holding the lily and papyrus wands of Upper and Lower Egypt presents the Key of Life to Sety (see page 133).

Temple of Sety I, Inner Chapel of Osiris. Here Horus purifies the mummy of Sety (see page 129).

Temple of Sety I, Inner
Chapel of Horus. Sety
burns incense and pours
libations to Horus (see
page 128).

Temple of Sety I, Inner
Chapel of Osiris. The
Four Sons of Horus in
the form of mummiform
human figures (see
page 130).

Temple of Sety I, Inner
Chapel of Osiris. Isis
with the sistrum.

Temple of Sety I, the Cult Chapel of Amon-Ra. The sacred boat of Amon-Ra (see page 107).

Temple of Ramesses II, the Cult Chapel of Thot. Ramesses offers wine to Ra-Hor-akhty (see page 220).

Temple of Ramesses II, the Clothing Room. Priests carrying the clothing chest (see page 229).

Khonsu in human form
(see page 258).

Temple of Sety I, Cult
Chapel of Amon-Ra,
southern wall. Sety
burns incense before
the sacred boat of
Amon-Ra (see page 107).

Temple of Sety I, Inner
Chapel of Horus. Sety
presents a golden col-
lar to Horus (see page
128).

Top: Temple of Ramesses
II, the Chapel of Osiris
eastern wall. The Heb-
sed symbols (see page
223).

Right: Temple of
Ramesses II, Chapel of
Osiris Khenty-Amentiu,
southern wall. Thot
and the Iwn-mut-ef
priest (see page 212).

Corner: Temple of
Ramesses II, southern
Statue Hall, western
wall. The winged Djed
Pillar with Ramesses and
Osiris in front of it
(see page 231).

CHAPTER FIFTEEN

THE SLAUGHTER COURT AND ITS ROOMS

The Northern Wall of the Slaughter Court.

As mentioned above, the Slaughter Court (page 156), where the sacrificial animals were killed, may be entered from the passage outside the temple or from the doorway at the southern end of the Corridor of Kings.

The court was surrounded on three sides by a colonnade supported on seven "tree trunk" columns, five along the western side, and one at each of the southern and northern ends. The latter is attached to a short screen-wall between it and the eastern wall of the court. This prevented unpleasant scenes in the court from being visible in the temple when the door of the Corridor of Kings stood open.

The columns bear many Greek and Coptic graffiti similar to those in the Corridor of Kings.

The edge of the roof of the colonnade is very peculiar; instead of the usual palmetto cornice, it ends in a bevelled edge sloping downwards.

Originally the walls of this court, and of the rooms leading out of it, were decorated with colored paintings as in the Hall of the Sacred Boats, but Ramesses had some of them sculptured in incised relief over the original paintings.

The best preserved scenes are those on the northern wall and the northern end of the western wall. On the former, in its upper register, Sety offers some sacrificial victims to Osiris, Isis, Horus and Wepwawat while below and on the adjoining western wall, butchers lead more victims, and are shown busy at their gory tasks. The scenes are vivid and lively; both human and animal figures looking lifelike and expressive.

Just to the north of the eastern entrance to the court are three very large earthenware jars embedded in a low bench of burned brick and mortar. They appear to have been storage jars for water, but are from the Roman Period or even later.

The Western Wall of the Slaughter Court.

Apart from the butchery just referred to, almost nothing remains of the decoration of the western wall, but in it open the doorways of three large halls which lie to the west. The first of these is the Butcher's Hall, or as it was called in Ancient Egypt, the Sekhut.

Sekhut or "Meat a la Francaise."

In this hall the dismembered joints of meat from the sacrificial cattle were trimmed and made presentable before being carried into the temple. The roof is supported on four "tree trunk" columns and, in addition to the rectangular skylights, there are two large windows high up in the northern and southern walls. The floor and the first course of the masonry of the walls are of sandstone. This is because the hall must have been washed down daily to remove the blood that would have dripped upon it, and sandstone is less affected by water than limestone.

Most of the paintings that once adorned the walls have disappeared; some having been deliberately washed off to make room for some Coptic daubings, for it is certain that the southern wing of the temple was inhabited by some early Christians at some late period perhaps before the building of the near-by Deir Sitt Damiana, early in the seventh century A.D.

The Western Wall of the Sekhut.

A double dedication inscription commences in the center of the western wall of the Sekhut, continues on the northern (and southern) wall, and terminates on the eastern wall. The part on the western wall consists of an enumeration of the titles and names of Sety. Above this there are some apparently unfinished paintings; one of which represents a wooden press perhaps used to extract oil from the fat of the animals. Another scene shows some priests carrying a large vat.

The Northern Wall of the Sekhut.

The interesting part of the dedication inscription begins on the western end of this wall and reads, "He (Sety) made it as his monument for his father Amon-Ra, King of the Gods, Ra-Hor-akhty, Ptah south of his wall, Lord of Ankh-Tawi (a quarter of Memphis), Osiris Khenty-Amentiu, Lord of Abydos, the gods and goddesses who dwell in the 'House of Men-maat-Ra,' making for them a pure Sekhut of beautiful white stone of Ayan,[1] its roof of sandstone, the walls are...the doors of cedar wood of Lebanon bound with Asiatic copper; inscribed on them is the great name of the Lord of the Two Lands, Men-maat-Ra who offers pure offerings for his fathers the Lords who are in..." (Here follows a break about one meter--3.3 feet-- of the text having been washed off to make room for a Coptic inscription). But the original text con-

[1]Actually, Ayan is the ancient name of the modern Tura near Cairo where fine white limestone is still quarried. But any good quality limestone was called "of Ayan" which as today we refer to Portland cement; little of which is really made in Portland. In reality, the Temple of Sety is built of local limestone.

tinues on the eastern wall (still referring to the King's generosity in the matter of offerings)"... everyday, and on special days for them, of cattle, young cattle, long-horned cattle, gazelles, ibex and oryx, established for their every feast day in the 'House of Men-maat-Ra" in Abydos. Life, strength and health to the son of Ra, Sety Mer-en-Ptah, like Ra."

All that remains here of the original painted scenes is a representation of a winepress.

The Eastern Wall of the Sekhut.

Apart from the end of the above quoted dedication inscription, there are faint traces of vertical texts on each side of the doorway.

The Southern Wall of the Sekhut.

In the upper register of this wall are the remains of a scene showing the sacrifice of animals in the presence of the King.

In the lower register, butchers supervised by priests, are slaughtering and dismembering oxen. One man who is assisting in the dismembering is called the temple scribe.

The Central Hall.

Immediately to the

south of the Sekhut is a large hall with two "tree trunk" columns. It is also lit by large windows as well as by rectangular sky-lights. Its exact purpose is not stated, but from the religious tone of what remains of its painted scenes, it would appear to have been a priestly administrative office.

The walls have suffered badly from smoke blackening, but one can still distinguish some figure of the gracious Isis and stately Sety appearing wraith-like amid the gloom.

The Southern Hall.

This is almost the same as the Central Hall, but has fared worse in the matter of its decoration. At some later time, probably when the place was inhabited by Copts, a door was cut high up in the southern end of the western wall, and a flight of roughly built steps led up to it. It gave access to the south-western room of the archives (see page 38).

The remaining room in this group is a small one. It was apparently undeco-rated and leads out of the southern end of the Slaughter Court. It originally had no connection with the Southern Hall, but a door was later forced through its western wall into the latter hall. This small room was probably a storeroom where the butchers kept their implements.

CHAPTER SIXTEEN

THE ARCHIVES OF THE TEMPLE

Time Reveals Everything.

In the southwestern end of the southern wing of the temple is a group of five small rooms, situated at a height of about three meters (10 feet) above the level of the eastern half of the southern wing. As originally planned, they had no direct connection with any other part of the temple, but were entered from the western Temenos, through a door in the wall of the temple. But there seems to be something rather unusual about this doorway which appears to have been made fairly late in the reign of Ramesses II. It has a sandstone lintel, but the decoration on its outer side is clearly an interruption in the decoration on the western wall of the temple, a series of groups in incised relief showing Ramesses in the presence of various deities.

In the case of the part now occupied by this doorway, Ramesses stands and addresses his dead father Sety who was also standing and holding a long staff in his extended hand (The top of this staff can still be seen in the center of the lintel.). There was probably an offering table between the two kings. But when the doorway was opened, it became necessary to change the pose of Sety's

figure. The left arm was recut to bend at the elbow, and the clenched hand holding the crook was placed on the chest. The point of the kilt was narrowed and the left leg drawn back somewhat. As the carving is all in incised relief, the alterations were all disguised by filling them with plaster. This has long since fallen out, and we now have a rather startling representation of Sety with three arms and three legs.

Judging by the sandstone lintel, there should have been a doorway here during the reign of Sety. This was apparently blocked up by order of Ramesses, and then later, after the decoration of the outer wall was completed, he had it reopened. Why, we cannot say. With Ramesses, anything is possible!!!

There was also another small doorway in the western wall of the temple immediately to the south of the western entrance. This opened on to a staircase leading to the roof of the temple, but it was also blocked up by Ramesses, and the decoration of the wall was continued over it.

But to return to the first mentioned entrance. It opens into a hall measuring about 10.5X4.25 meters (34.4X13.9 feet) from which open four long, narrow rooms, two on the south and two on the north. All the walls of this hall were originally decorated with colored paintings from the time of Sety, but only faint traces of these now

remain. However, the eastern wall and the lintels and jambs of the four doorways were sculptured in incised relief by Ramesses' son and successor Mer-en-Ptah.

The Eastern Wall of the Hall of the Archives.

The entire eastern wall is occupied by a double scene showing Mer-en-Ptah adoring Osiris. Behind the King stands Thot, but he is facing in the opposite direction. However, the rest of the scene was never finished, and even the scepter of Prosperity carried by Thot remains in paint only. At some later period, a door was forced through the southern end of this wall, into the Sekhut Hall which lies behind and below it.

The walls of the four side-rooms that open out of the central hall were all decorated with finely detailed colored paintings of a most unusual subject namely, a number of decorated chests; the originals of which were probably housed in these rooms (see page 156). These are neither shrines nor treasure chests as beside each one was an inscription describing its contents and these include objects which could not possibly have been contained in a chest. For example, we have mentions of a "great gateway," some object probably a shrine with "copper doors," a granite shrine with "copper doors inlaid with figures of gold." What these chests contained were rolls of papyrus some of which were inscribed with specifications of the objects referred to. There is also mention of "the King's annals, recorded in writing."[1] How we wish that these had survived! They would have told us a handsome lot!

Thus, we are safe in saying that these rooms were the archives of the temple. Further proof for this is, as we shall see, the prominence given to the God Thot who was always associated with writing and recording.

The Southwestern Room of the Archives, the Northern Wall.

Most of this wall was occupied by the doorway on the lintel of which was a double scene showing a god (on one side Amon-Ra) seated in front of an offering table. On the left of the lintel, and continuing onto the jamb, is an inscription which reads, "...his beloved, the son of Ra, Sety Mer-en-Ptah, given life. Everything which enters the Double Treasury of the Temple of Millions of Years, of the King of Upper and Lower Egypt, Men-maat-Ra, of gold, silver, lapis-lazuli which he has given you, things of every precious and august stone belonging to every land, belonging to the God's land (Punt, or Somaliland)..." The re-

....
[1] On the first chest on the eastern wall of the southeastern room.

mainder is much effaced but refers to "products from every foreign land."

The mention of the Double Treasury in this inscription is very interesting and will be discussed later.

The Western Wall.

Only part of the paintings are preserved. Most of the western wall was occupied by a large scene showing Sety and the God Thot (at the northern end) inspecting a number of golden objects which include musical instruments, offering tables, vases (some having lids in the form of falcons' heads), collars and other ornaments. After these is another large male figure, but it is too badly effaced to be identified.

Nothing is preserved of the scenes on the southern wall.

The Eastern Wall.

At the northern end of the eastern wall are the remains of large figures of the King and Thot, but both are badly effaced. Next come representations of five chests the first being of wood with a rectangular golden panel in its side. Its top is surmounted by the figures of two sphinxes lying face to face with a bowl between them. The inscription describing its contents is effaced.

The fourth chest was of gold its sides being divided into twelve square panels each bearing a

minute scene of the King adoring some deity. Among those we can identify are Min, Mut, Khonsu and Monthu. It contained the specifications for some object probably a shrine of "Khes-stone with doors of copper decorated with inlaid figures of gold."

The Southeastern Room of the Archives, the Northern Wall.

On the lintel of the doorway is a figure of a sphinx, and another inscription referring to "the great treasury of the Temple of Millions of Years of the King of Upper and Lower Egypt, Men-maat-Ra, of gold, silver, every august stone brought from every foreign land reckoned in millions, hundreds of thousands, tens of thousands, thousands, hundreds and tens, by Thot, Lord of Khemenu, who dwells in the 'House of Men-maat-Ra.'"

The Western Wall.

At the northern end of the western wall is a scene resembling that in the same place in the southwestern room. Again nothing is preserved on the southern wall.

The Eastern Wall.

At the northern end of the wall are traces of a large scene, but it is too badly effaced to show any details. Next come three decorated chests the first of which contained "The annals (of the King) recorded in writing."

The Northwestern Room of the Archives, the Southern Wall.

On the left-hand side of the lintel of the doorway, Osiris is represented seated with Isis behind him. There was a similar scene to the right.

To the left of the doorway is a large figure of Sety holding a Kherp-baton and the scepter of Prosperity.

The Eastern Wall.

At the southern end of the eastern wall is another large figure of Sety after which are the representations of seven chests. The first chest is decorated with a Djed Pillar flanked by two figures of sphinxes facing each other with a bowl between them.

The Northern Wall.

No scenes are preserved on the northern wall, but a small doorway in its western end leads to a narrow staircase to the roof.

The Western Wall.

All that remains on the western wall is part of a scene showing the King and Thot inspecting some golden objects including musical instruments.

The Northeastern Room of the Archives, the Southern Wall.

To the east of the doorway are the remains of a figure of the King. There was a similar figure on the western side of the doorway and above it the royal titles.

The Eastern Wall.

At the southern end of the wall is a scene of the King, followed by Thot, standing in front of two golden offering tables on which are spouted libation jars. Next come two red chests, apparently made of wood, the first of which contained specifications of something (perhaps a doorway) named "Men-maat-Ra is the Life of the Two Lands, of... stone, its door-leaves of copper, fashioned with ..."

There are no scenes preserved on the northern wall.

The Western Wall.

At the northern end of the wall is the lower part of a figure of Sety facing north in front of a seated god. Next was a figure of a goddess seated on an elaborately decorated throne, but only her legs remain. In front of her was a golden offering table.

Those Early Christians Again.

In the year 1960, Dr. Abdel Hamid Zayed, who was then Chief Inspector of Antiquities for the area, had some of the paving stones of this room removed to see what lay beneath in view of the difference in height between it and the pavement of the eastern half of the southern wing of the temple.

Immediately below one of the paving stones was a very large jar of late Roman or Coptic date. Inside it was a similar but smaller jar in which was found a round basket of red and natural palm leaves. It had a flat lid and is exactly the same as those made here at the present day. It measured about twenty-five centimeters (10 inches) in diameter and contained a small ebony stick of the kind used for applying kohl (black eye paint), a wooden spindle with a limestone whorl, and a broken wooden comb. All these were clearly the property of some woman who lived in this room during the early Coptic times.

A Great Find is Missed.

Near the large jar was a smaller and older one. To our horror it contained a completely destroyed papyrus! It had been inscribed in hieratic but had been eaten by insects, and not a fragment larger than one centimeter square (1/6 sq. inch) remained; the remainder was merely dust. One could not help feeling a certain sense of great loss.

The mystery is how did these jars come to be under the pavement? To put them there must have entailed a great deal of very hard work which the value of their contents does not seem to have warranted. We tried to persuade Dr. Zayed to investigate further, but he refused, and the paving stones were replaced. Maybe a great archeological discovery lies in waiting for further investigators.

The Question of the Treasury of the Temple.

The mention of the treasury of the temple in some of the rooms of the archives and the representations of precious objects in some of the scenes may lead one to suppose that the archives and treasury were combined here. But this can hardly have been the case for security reasons. One thing is evident, those rooms could easily be entered from the western Temenos. Also, there is reason to believe that the central hall was open to the sky, and it is very easy to climb up to the roof of the side-rooms from the southern wall of the temple, and from there slip down into the hall. And furthermore the archives must have been a fairly busy place with plenty of coming and going of priests and temple scribes as well as tenants of the temple estates wishing to consult documents relating to their properties. Being apart from the purely religious quarters of the buildings, layfolk had the right to enter here.

Regarding the golden objects represented in the scenes, these may have been things needed often in the religious services, and like the sacred boats, were housed in a place from which they could easily be fetched when wanted. On the other hand, they may be merely illustrations of some of the precious contents of the treasury, records of which were certainly kept in the archives. So where is the treasury?

Wherever it is we personally believe that it is still intact. Had it been discovered and robbed, it would be standing open and its place known as in the case of the famous crypts at the Dendera Temple.

An Unusual Experience of Omm Sety.

For what it is worth, I will relate a strange experience that happened to me in 1958. At that time I was working in the Hall of the Sacred Boats cataloging and fitting together about 3000 pieces of inscribed stone that had once formed the doorways, columns and window-grills of the magazines and Audience Hall of the temple (see page 50). At that time, work was also in progress in roofing the temple, and although I had the key to all the doors,[2] it was

2..................
[2]The Main Entrance to the temple, both doors of the Corridor of Kings, both doors of the Western Corridor, and that of the Hall of the Sacred Boats

easier to get in and out of the building by going up the stairs to the roof, walking along the top of the southern wall of the unroofed Western Corridor and down the scaffolding at the west of the temple. We then had an epidemic of Asiatic flu in the neighborhood, and I caught it. One morning I was feeling rather bad, and as a couple of aspirins and a short rest had no effect, I decided to call it a day and go home. I went up the stairs and started walking along the top of the wall when I suddenly became very dizzy and fell twisting my right ankle and hurting my left shoulder. I remember hearing a loud grating sound like that of a grindstone at work, and I rolled down a fairly steep slope; the grating sound was renewed, and I found myself in darkness.

After a while, the dizziness passed off enough to allow me to stand up and grope for a wall. I touched some smooth limestone blocks and stood there wondering what to do next. Presently I sensed very faint threads of light filtering down from above as though through cracks in the roof, and as my eyes became accustomed to the gloom, I found that I was standing in a narrow passage less than three meters (10 feet) wide. A narrow
....
are fitted with iron gates that are always kept locked.

path, perhaps about fifty centimeters (20 inches) wide, ran along the base of the wall, but the remainder of the width of the passage appeared to be completely filled with boxes, offering tables, vases, bales of linen; and everywhere was the gleam of gold. Feeling my way along the wall, I limped along. The passage seemed to be endless and to my left, crowded with objects.

The Encounter With "Horus"!

I stumbled and fell, and, on trying to rise, saw what I took to be the God Horus himself bending over me, his hands raised as though in astonishment. From his waist down, he was standing upright, but from the waist upwards was bending over, his fierce falcon's face peering down at me, and his Double Crown sticking out at right angles without any visible means of support. There I squatted meekly, thoroughly embarrassed, and trying to think of how one should address a god under such circumstances. Then I suddenly realized that "Horus" was only a painted wooden statue, life-sized, and originally standing upright with the arms bent at the elbows and the hands raised. Insects had eaten away part of the front of the body, causing the upper part to lean over. Scrambling to my feet, I noticed similar life-sized statues of Osiris and Isis leaning against the far wall and apparently uninjured.

Near where I stood was a golden vase about twenty-five centimeters (10 inches) high. It had an oval body, a long neck and a trumpet-shaped mouth and stood in a wooden ring stand. By the faint light I could see a cartouche engraved on its body, but it was too dark to read it. But by the length of the frame I knew that it was not the cartouche of Sety but one of the later kings perhaps from the XXVIth dynasty. I picked it up. It was very heavy, and at first I thought I would take it as evidence of what I had discovered by accident; but finally decided against it, and put it down in its place.

I began to feel very ill again but continued to limp along, half unconscious. Suddenly, I found myself out in the open air almost blinded by the sunlight. I was standing beside the well in the Second Court of the temple, and approaching me was a young man, a stranger. He stared at me in frank astonishment and asked if I knew where the architect in charge of the restorations was. I told him, and still staring in a surprise, he thanked me and left. I went to enter the temple by the main door only to find that the keys were not with me. I went around to the back of the temple in order to re-enter the Hall of the Sacred Boats by the way I had left it when I met two of the gaffers.

They cried out, "Where have you been? You are all dirt and cobwebs!" And so I was; no wonder the young man had stared at me so hard!

I replied that I had fallen down and hurt my ankle and had forgotten my keys. But I did not tell them anymore. I managed to crawl back to the Hall of the Sacred Boats, and there were the keys just as I had left them on the table.

Did It Really Happen?

Two days later the Chief Inspector of Antiquities for this area came here, and I told him about this experience. He was very astonished and interested, but neither of us could decide if it had really happened, or if it was just a hallucination caused by the fever; and to this day, I do not know for certain. All that I am sure of is that I really fell, my ankle was swollen and painful for a week, and I had a big bruise on my shoulder. Also I was really covered with dust and cobwebs, and having left the keys behind, there is no way in which I could have reached the front part of the temple except by going around from the outside, where the gaffers would have seen me and where, moreover, I would not have collected any dust or cobwebs all over my clothes. If this really did happen, then there is only one possible explanation! I must have hit a stone with my shoulder as I fell which turned on a pivot and opened into a sloping passage. This would account for the grating sound. But how did I get out again? All that I can suggest is that a deserted hyena's lair in the side of the well may have communicated with the "Treasure Passage." Later, the lair caved in, but its place remains still clearly visible. The Chief Inspector got interested and told me to try and find the supposed pivot-stone, which I did, in every possible place in the temple including the "Blind Rooms." But no results, except some more bruises!

There is one significant point however. The paving stones of some of the aisles in the hypostyle halls are large, single slabs resembling those in the upper "Blind Room." These could well be roofing subterranean passages. But in all other places the paving stones are smaller and irregularly shaped. One thing I am certain of, the Temple of Sety still holds some secrets, as a matter of fact lots of them. One day a patient archaelogist may come to Abydos to investigate all its unknown and fascinating possibilities. Maybe he will stir the enthusiasm and admiration of the entire world maybe with something bigger and more important than Lord Carnavon's discovery of Tut-ankh-Amon's mortuary treasures in 1922.

Fig. 17-1. The upper "Blind Room." Looking south, and showing part of the lower room. Temple of Sety I.

Fig. 17-2. The lower "Blind Room." Showing the abnormally short and thick pillar. Temple of Sety I.

CHAPTER SEVENTEEN

MYSTERIOUS ROOMS AND
TANTALIZING GRAFFITO

The "Blind Rooms" and the
Roof.

Situated in the north-
western corner of the
temple immediately be-
hind the Inner Chapels
of the Osiris Complex
are two rooms each meas-
uring about 10.5 meters
(34.4 feet) long and
40 meters (131 feet) wide
and about 3.0 meters (9.8
feet) high. They are
situated one above the
other. Neither room had
any doorway or windows
though the upper one may
have had skylights in
its roof which are now
missing. Furthermore,
there is now no visible
communication between
either of these rooms
and the rest of the
temple. There is just
one word that could

describe both rooms,
"intriguing."

The Lower Room.

The limestone walls
are neatly smoothed but
bear no traces of deco-
ration. The roof, which
forms the floor of the
upper room, is supported
on two very massive
square pillars of sand-
stone far too large
and thick for their
height; in fact, they
are almost square. They
stand on circular bases
that look very much like
the half-buried capitals
of papyrus bud columns
(Fig. 17-1). These
pillars support massive
sandstone architraves
out of all proportion
to the comparatively
light (60 centimeters--
2 feet--thick) limestone
slabs that they carry.
Some of these slabs
have been broken away
at the western end thus

revealing the presence of
this room which might
otherwise have been un-
suspected (Fig. 17-2).
Its purpose is a complete
mystery.

As some of the inscrip-
tions on the columns in
the Osiris Complex state
that Sety had built the
western end of the temple
on the site of an older,
ruined temple, perhaps
this room is part of the
original building incorporated into the new one. It
was the custom in ancient
Egypt to reuse stones
from older temples in the
foundations of new ones
not for reasons of economy,
but for the sake of tra-
ditional continuity.

On the other hand,
this subterranean room
might have at one time communicated with the Osirion
which lies very near it
though at a lower level.
However, this room has
never been seriously ex-
amined in a scientific
manner, and it may well
go down far deeper than
its present floor level
indicates.

I have spent many
hours pushing and butting
against the walls of this
room (as mentioned before)
hoping to find a movable
stone that turned on a
pivot and that might
open into a passage lead-
ing to who knows where or
what. But all was in vain.
This is real life; had we
been in Hollywood, someone
would have written a better
script!

During the early
1950's the Antiquities
Department was consolidat-
ing the western wall of

the temple which was, and still is, leaning to the west, and was then in danger of collapsing altogether. To prevent this happening, twenty-two steel and concrete pillars were sunk in the ground at the back of the building between it and the eastern Transverse Room of the Osirion. The pillars extended from ground level down to below the level of the floor of the Transverse Room, and the pit containing them was filled in solid with concrete. The pavements of the temple were then repaired, and while this was in progress, it was found that at some time a narrow pit had been opened in the floor of the Inner Chapel of Isis in its southwestern corner. Investigation showed that this pit ended in a narrow passage built of limestone blocks and sloping down towards the south. After a few meters, the burial of an adult was discovered. The body, a mere skeleton, lay on its back, and near it was a jar of rough red pottery. It certainly dated from a very late period. Unfortunately, no further investigations were made, and the concrete reinforcements mentioned above prevent any further work being done in this place. But it is a pity that the passage was not investigated towards the north to see where it led to, and where its original entrance was. As the pit in the floor of the Inner Chapel of Isis is now filled in with concrete, this is another mystery that must remain unsolved!

The Upper "Blind Room."

This is almost the same as the lower room except that the sandstone pillars are better proportioned, not nearly so massive, and stand upon rectangular bases. The upper parts of all the walls are damaged, but enough remains to show definitely that there was no doorway in any of them. It has been suggested that this room may have been a serdab[1] containing statues of the gods to whom the three Inner Chapels were dedicated. But this cannot be so because although the so-called serdabs are doorless, windowless chambers for statues, they always have a small opening or slot in their front walls through which the spirits residing in the statues may look out and through which the living may peer in. Also, so far as I am aware, serdabs are confined to tomb chapels.

It has also been suggested that these two rooms may have been the lost treasury of the temple. But again, this is unlikely, for although the treasury should be in a secure place, it should also be easy of access to the priests in charge of it. Neither of these two rooms ever could have been easily

....
[1]Serdab is an Arabic word meaning a narrow, underground passage. Egyptologists use it to designate a doorless statue chamber.

accessible to priests.

A Tantalizing Graffito.

Like the lower room, the upper one is entirely undecorated, but on the western wall at a height of about thirty centimeters (one foot) from the floor level is a most tantalizing graffito. It is in well-formed hieroglyphs deeply scratched into the stone and reads, "Travel to the north for three hundred and three paces and take to thyself the Eye of Horus."

Now the term, "Eye of Horus" was often used idiomatically for anything good and desirable; it could mean an offering, a gift or a treasure. But did the priestly writer mean true geographical north or the local conventional north? Was he serious or was he pulling our leg? Above all, how in all the world did he get into this room to write the graffito? At what period and for what real purpose? Priests of ancient Egypt were a descrete, taciturn lot and did not go about giving signs and indications of possible treasure caches. The whole thing will remain a mystery until further investigation is carried out.

The Roof of the Temple.

In the ancient days, the roof of the temple could be easily reached from the stairs in the Hall of the Sacred Boats, or those in the northwest-

Fig. 17-3. Hollows for drink-jars on the roof of the temple. Temple of Sety I.

Fig. 17-4. "Seega" gaming board and hollow for drink-jar on the roof of the temple. Temple of Sety I.

ern room of the archives. Every night, certain priests would go up to the roof and spend the time until the dawn observing the movements of the stars. As the dry air of Abydos can be bitterly cold at night, even in the height of summer, one wonders how fared these men in their linen robes. Perhaps some of the offering wine served to ward off chills? When not observing the stars, they apparently played a game of skill which, under the name of "Seega" is still played by the peasants and workers of modern Egypt. This game can be played anywhere; the "board" is simply two rows of shallow hollows or chalked rings marked on any fair-

ly flat surface. The playing pieces may be two sets of light and dark colored pebbles. Numerous "Seega" boards are hollowed out in the sandstone roofing blocks of the temple (Fig. 17-3), and beside some of them are larger hollows just the right size to accomodate a drink-jar (Fig. 17-4)! Cold beer or warming wine and "Seega" were the real "Passe-Temps" on the roof.

The Footprints of Pilgrims.

All over the roof of the temple are scratched outlines of bare and sandalled feet (Fig. 17-5, 17-6, 17-7). Some are large and wide while others are obviously those of

small children. Some have the great toe widely separated from its fellows showing that the owner had habitually worn toe-thong sandals. Some of these footprints have the name of their owners inscribed in Greek or hieratic inside their outlines.

Who made these footprints? They were made by the later pilgrims to Abydos who desired to leave a permanent record of their presence in the Holy City. These footprints seem to say, "See, ye of the generations to come, I have actually stood here having reached my goal, the Sacred City of Osiris!"

Looking at them, one can imagine the deep feel-

Fig. 17-5. *Scratched and inscribed footprints of pilgrims on the roof of the temple. Temple of Sety I.*

ing of religious fervor and personal satisfaction of the people who made them and saw the record of their pilgrimage graven forever on the roof of the Temple of Millions of Years.

This temple is the House of Men-maat-Ra (Sety). A temple is the House of God, so Sety has become a god; this was the purpose of the temple.

Fig. 17-6. *(Above) and* Fig. 17-7. *(Right) show scratched and inscribed footprints of pilgrims on the roof of the temple.*

182

CHAPTER EIGHTEEN

OTHER MONUMENTS OF SETY AT ABYDOS

The Temple for Ramesses I.

As the reign of Ramesses I was too brief for him to have undertaken any major building works, his temple at Abydos, the mutilated, desecrated remains of which lie among the houses of the modern village, was built after his death by his son, Sety I.

In its day, it must have been of great beauty, and those wall scenes that have survived show the same high standard of workmanship as those in Sety's own temple and were probably carved by the same school of sculptors.

Unfortunately, the temple was discovered by some local villagers some time ago and has since almost completely disappeared. Some of the decorated blocks fell into the hands of an antiquity dealer in Cairo who in turn sold some of them to a collector in Paris. Others crossed the Atlantic, and eventually the authorities of the Metropolitan Museum of Art, in New York, became interested in them and obtained permission from the Antiquities Department of Egypt to excavate the spot in which they had been found. The expedition, under the direction of Prof. Winlock, found some more blocks and also bought up those which were still in the market. One of the blocks dis-

covered by the Americans is the lower part of a white limestone dedication stela on which Sety tells how he came to build this temple. He says, addressing the spirit of Ramesses I, "Come in peace, O good God! Mayest thou occupy the seat which I have made for thee, and behold thy Mortuary Temple at the side of Wennefer. I establish for thee offerings within it and daily libations. O King of Upper and Lower Egypt, Men-pheti-Ra (Ramesses I), I am thy son Men-maat-Ra. I did those things which were beneficial to thee when I built for thee a temple to thy Ka to the north of my great temple. I excavated its pool, planted it with every kind of tree, and made it blazing with flowers, and I caused that thy statue should rest within it; food, drink and every kind of offering being established for it every day as is done for all gods.

"I am thy true son of thy heart; I did that which was required of me, because thou didst love me. I exalt thy name to Heaven, I elevate thine arm, and I establish thy name upon earth as Horus did for his father Osiris."

Then the spirit of Ramesses I is supposed to break the silence of the tomb, and speak to Sety, "Thou art my true son of my heart who hast done that which was required. May the gods increase thy years upon earth, multiplying thy jubilees because thou

hast done those things which were beneficial to me. I am thy true father."[1]

One of the finest scenes from this temple (now in the Metropolitan Museum), shows Ramesses I and Queen Sat-Ra followed by three men and three women. These people are inscribed, "The brother and sisters of the god (i.e. Ramesses I)." Therefore they are the paternal uncles and aunts of Sety I. The men all bear the title "Judge" which at this period had become the equivalent of the modern "Esquire" and just as meaningless. It was applied to any educated man. The ladies all bear the title "Mistress of the House" common to all married women. This is another sidelight on the character of Sety I. He was not ashamed to portray his non-royal relatives as they really were. A lesser man would have given them some fancy, high sounding honorable titles.

A headless statue of black granite representing Ramesses I, said to have come from this temple,[2] somehow found its way to the shop of an antiquity dealer in the near-by town of El Balyana. This also had been made for him by Sety I who in the inscriptions on it says that "he made his (Ramesses')

....
[1]This stela now stands in the First Hypostyle Hall of the Temple of Sety I.
[2]Perhaps the very one mentioned in the inscription quoted above.

Fig. 18-1. *Baboons in high relief and added cartouches of Ramesses II. In the foreground is a fragment of an Osiride statue in red granite. The southern side of the entrance. The limestone colonnade. Kom el Sultan (see page xxii).*

name to live in the Thinite nome; he caused him to be installed in his tomb. He made it as his monument for his father, the son of Ra, Ramesses, the Justified. He made the name of his father stable and flourishing in the nome of Abydos for eternity and everlastingness. Here is that which His Majesty made for his father Men-pheti-Ra, the Justified. Here he is in his quality of King of Upper and Lower Egypt, Lord of the Two Lands."[3]

Sety also made some

. . . .
[3]This statue was sold more than thirty years ago, and its present whereabouts is unknown.

additions to the old traditional Temple of Osiris at Kom el Sultan, but all that remains of this is part of a wall of finely polished red granite bearing his name. This wall has a rounded upper edge suggesting that it must have been either a screen-wall or the edge of the coping of a terrace. A similar block, also bearing the name of Sety, was later reused as a threshold to the western entrance to the great enclosure wall of Kom el Sultan.

The Limestone Colonnade.

Immediately to the

west of the western entrance to Kom el Sultan stands a colonnade of white limestone. The huge columns of which only the lower parts remain were of the papyrus type, but they bear the incised cartouches of Ramesses II. However, the sides of the entrance bear figures of apes adoring the Sun God carved in high relief which is not at all characteristic of the work of Ramesses II (Fig. 18-1). These, and a sandstone roofing block, with the cartouche of Sety in high relief, make one suspect that this was one of the unfinished buildings in the cemetery begun by Sety and completed

184

by Ramesses as the latter mentioned in his inscription on the face of the great temple (see page 64).

Petrie dubbed the colonnade "a monumental gateway leading to the necropolis." Later archaelogists seem to have accepted this statement[4] in spite of the fact that the Egyptians were not in the habit of erecting free standing portals after the manner of the Arc de Triomphe or the Grandenburg Gate in Paris and Berlin respectively.

Recently the Pennsylvania-Yale Expedition partly cleared this monument (in the winter of 1969) and proved that it is indeed a temple, but unfortunately, almost totally destroyed. Many sculptured blocks came to light bearing the name of Ramesses II, and others, of much finer work, of Sety I. There seems to be quite a lot of work to be done yet on the site.

The pavement of the temple runs over a number of small, ruined structures of mud-brick perhaps ruined and abandoned cenotaphs from an earlier (Middle Kingdom?) period. This has yet to be proven beyond any lingering doubt.

At the time of writing, these excavations are unfinished, but some interesting results may be expected when the digging is resumed in this important site (Fig. 18-2, 18-3).

....

[4] It is sometimes called "The Limestone Portal of Ramesses II."

Fig. 18-2. Kom el Sultan. The pool marks the site of the original temple.

Fig. 18-3. Kom el Sultan. The site of the recent excavations.

CHAPTER NINETEEN

RAMESSES II, THE MAN, THE BUILDER, AND THE KING

Ramesses II and His Monuments.

Ramesses II is perhaps the most famous of all pharaohs and is often referred to as Ramesses the Great. Actually there were other rulers of Egypt, including his own father Sety I, who better deserved the epithet of "Great," yet Ramesses earned it for himself by sheer force of personality which is felt as much in the world today as it was in his own time.

Ramesses the Man.

Ramesses is a very controversial figure, and Egyptologists are often at loggerheads with each other whenever an analysis of his character is under discussion. To some, he was an arrogant, overbearing tyrant, a thief, and the world's champion liar.[1] His character was further blackened by an early and quite unfounded identification of his person with the "Pharaoh of the Oppression" a role in which, in recent years, he was also cast by Mr. Cecil B. De Mille in his epic film "The Ten Commandments."

[1] In the district of Abydos at the present day, any overbearing man who insists on things being always done for his benefit is nicknamed "Ramesses."

However, contemporary evidence from the monuments tell quite another story although we must admit that he was certainly a "show-off" and had a decidedly too good opinion of himself!

Ramesses was the son of Sety I and his second wife Queen Tuy (who seems to have spoiled her eldest son!). At the early age of ten, Sety had the handsome and lively boy crowned as co-regent with himself. Sety also appointed him Commander in the army where he certainly became a prime favorite with the soldiers (Probably the officers held other opinions!).

Sety died while Ramesses was still a teenager, and deprived of the sober far-sightedness and wise influence of his father, it is a miracle that the young King's character was not entirely ruined by a doting mother and a palace full of toadying officials all trying to flatter the lad to gain their own ends. But Ramesses came of good military stock; what he lacked in mature wisdom he made up for in sound common sense and indomitable courage. Nobody can really deny him this.

Early in his reign he proved himself to be a brave, determined fighter (though a bad general) and was clever enough to turn a near disaster in the Battle of Kadesh into an apparent victory.

Like most of the greatest of Egyptian pharaohs, he had a keen, if sarcastic, sense of humor as we can tell by the tongue-lashing he gave to his runaway troops after the Battle of Kadesh (see page 242) which, by the way, was the only punishment they seem to have received.

Ramesses was also fond of animals and never forgot his two brave chariot horses Nakht-em-Wast and Mut-Hotep who brought him safely through the fierce Battle of Kadesh. He also kept pet lions which not only prowled about the palace but accompanied him into battle and lay like watchdogs outside his tent when in camp. His troops adored him and took the liberty of referring to him as "King Sisi"; a nickname which he probably gained as a child. He was equally popular with his subjects in general.

Ramesses married many women including his sister Hent-mi-Ra who died young. But his lifelong favorite was the beautiful Queen Nefertari (whose name means "The Beautiful Companion"). She was the mother of twenty-two (yes twenty-two) of his many children. Judging by this imposing number of children, we believe that her name was fully deserved!

"I Want it Built Now!"

Ramesses was a great and tireless builder, and apparently his first monument was his temple at

Abydos which he commenced while he was still co-regent with his father, and which he claims to have designed himself. Of course, his most spectacular work still existing is his great rock-cut temple at Abu Simbel, in Nubia; but its sculpture is much inferior to that in his Abydos temple. The temple at Abu Simbel was transferred recently to the top of the mountain overlooking its original site in one of the most gigantic monument-saving operations ever to be undertaken in modern times. It still attracts a great number of tourists in its new site some miles south of the High Dam. A regular airline service flies daily to a new, near-by airfield.

But the trouble with Ramesses was that he demanded more work than his architects could cope with, and also when he wanted a monument, he wanted it NOW! The result was that the standard of work declined, and with few exceptions, his later buildings were flamboyant and showy but shoddy in workmanship.

Ramesses is also notorious for usurping the works of his predecessors. In his dedication inscription on the facade of Sety's temple, he frankly and shamelessly states that when completing the work in this building, he put his own name on it as well as his father's. Apparently with the passing of time, this habit grew, and like a drug addiciton, became worse. But we can

not be sure whether all the usurpations were made with his knowledge, or if his hard pressed architects were partly responsible for them. Perhaps they merely altered the inscriptions on already existing monuments in order to save time and so escape the biting, acid remarks of their impatient monarch.

However, if Ramesses was a hard taskmaster to his architects, he was certainly not a tyrant. It was his custom when a monument was completed to throw a great banquet to which all the workmen were invited, and Ramesses set down and ate and drank with them. After one such occasion, the men clubbed together and made a stela recording the event. They ended the inscription on it by saying "the wine and beer flowed like the Nile in its inundation and the men thanked God for it! "This does not sound quite like the Pharaoh of the Oppression," does it? One is sometimes inclined to imagine that his workmen must have been singing an Egyptian version of "For He is a Jolly Good Fellow" on such gay occasions!

In person, Ramesses was a very handsome man, tall[2] and strong and having a most charming smile. In all of his portraits, his face radiates a very un-

....
[2]His mummy measures just over 188 centimeters (74 inches); in life, he would have been a little taller.

assuming confidence and cheerfulness which seem to have been the keynotes of his character.

The perfectly preserved mummy of Ramesses was found along with many other bodies in a pit near the Temple of Deir-el Bahari where they had been hidden to preserve them from the gangs of tomb robbers who were breaking into the royal tombs at the end of the XXth dynasty. He was a very old man at the time of his death but still remarkably handsome and imposing. Even in death, his face retains its famous cheery smile. Doctors have examined his body and pronounced him to have been in excellent physical condition in spite of his advanced years though, like his father Sety, he suffered from arthritis in some of his fingers!

When the body of Ramesses was laid out for burial, the forearms were crossed over the breast, and the hands closed upon a crook and flail (stolen by the ancient tomb robbers?). Nowadays one hand remains in this position, but the other is raised and the forefinger pointing, and there is a strange but true story attached to this.

A Mummy Comes to Life.

At the time when the royal mummies were brought to the Cairo Museum, the great Egyptologist Professor Maspero was Director General of the Antiquities Department. He decided to have the mummies unwrapped and examined by his European colleagues and some medical experts. It happened that when they had gotten the mummy of Ramesses stripped to the waist, an attendant came and announced that lunch had been served in Professor Maspero's office. The distinguished company retired to refresh themselves leaving the attendant with instructions not to leave the mummy or let anyone come near it. But while they were eating, this man suddenly burst in upon them, his eyes staring in rank terror and cried, "The King has come to life! He moved." Before anyone could reply, the attendant fled for his life.

Maspero and his guests rushed to the room where Ramesses lay, and to their astonishment and sure enough, the King *had* moved! The hand that they had all seen quietly closed upon his breast was now raised, and the forefinger pointed at them! And so it remains to this day. The unfortunate attendant was later found on the grounds of the museum where he had fallen dead from shock.

Doctors have suggested that the movement of the King's hand was caused by the warmth of the sun acting upon the perfectly preserved muscles causing them to contract. Whatever was the real reason, one thing is very certain, even after three thousand years of death, Ramesses is still capable of causing a sensation.

Incidentally, the day when the royal mummies were transferred by boat from Luxor to Cairo was a never-to-be-forgotten occasion. As the boat sailed away from the quay, the townsfolk of Luxor began to mourn, the men firing off their guns, and the women wailing as though at the funeral of some great personage. The same thing happened at every town and village that the boat passed on its journey northwards. There was no radio in those days and very little telephonic communications, so how did the people know that the boat carried the bodies of the ancient kings? And even more strange, what provoked these sentiments of very real grief and respect from the people who at that time were largely illiterate and who normally showed no regard for the mummies of their ancestors whom they classed as "benighted heathens"? But those who had watched the scene were stirred by the sincere emotional reaction of the crowds on both banks of the river. Theirs was a very genuine grief as if someone very dear to them was going away. It was much like an Old Greek melodrama played in an Egyptian setting.

CHAPTER TWENTY

THE TEMPLE OF RAMESSES II, OUTSIDE

The Approach.

The Temple of Ramesses II lies in a wadi on the eastern edge of the desert a little less than one kilometer (0.6 mile) to the north of the Temple of Sety I. Compared with the latter, this temple is badly ruined; in fact, seen from the top of the wadi, it looks as though its upper half had been sliced off with a gigantic knife. Its walls nowhere exceed the height of four meters (13 feet).

Local tradition says that before it came under the care of the Antiquities Department, a wealthy family living in the near-by town of El Balyana had used it as a quarry years ago and had built a large house from its stones! Its modern name is Malaab el Benat which means "Playground of Girls," and before the outer walls were restored and an iron gate fitted to its entrance, the little girls of the neighborhood used to go there to play. Did they unconsciously sense the gay and happy-go-lucky personality of Ramesses himself the father of so many beautiful little girls?

In spite of the vicissitudes which this temple has undergone, wanton damage and over one hundred years of exposure to the elements, the remaining reliefs are wonderfully well-preserved, and many of them retain their original brilliant colors. These reliefs are of a very high standard of workmanship and are interesting in subject. It is amusing to notice the marked difference in style and subject matter between the scenes on the exterior walls and the inner walls of the court and those in the interior of the temple. The former, which were intended to be seen by the populace, are lively and natural and often display an unmistakable print of the age-old Egyptian sense of humor. The latter, which were to be seen only by the gods and their priests, are very formal and dignified.

The ancient name of the temple was "House of Ramesses Mery-Amon Who Enriches the Abydos Nome." It was of course dedicated to Osiris but included chapels for other deities as well as for the Mortuary Cult of Sety I and Ramesses himself.

The building is mainly composed of local white limestone, but much black and red granite, red quartzite sandstone, Nubian sandstone and alabaster were also lavishly used. These materials are mentioned in an inscription on the southern outer wall where it says, "(He made it as his monument for his father...) making for him (Osiris) a beautiful and august temple fashioned excellently for eternity of beautiful white stone of Ayan, two great pylons of excellent workmanship, doorways of granite, door-leaves made of copper wrought with inlaid figures of real electrum, a sanctuary of pure alabaster roofed with granite."

The temple is rectangular in plan and originally consisted of a pylon, court (surrounded by a colonnade), a portico, two hypostyle halls, and thirteen small chapels. Many years later, when Ramesses celebrated his first Heb-sed Jubilee, he added an outer pylon and court as well as a small pavilion to the east of the original facade. These additions were partly excavated in 1905, but the greater part of this additional court is still encumbered with mud-brick ruins of the Roman and Coptic times.

The walls of this additional court and even the towers of the pylon were built of mud-brick, and only the central doorway and the small pavilion were of limestone.

Two colossal statues of Ramesses must have stood in front of the pylon, but only their sandstone bases now remain, and these are decorated with figures of bound foreign prisoners of war, and on one of them is inscribed, "The Great Ones (Chieftains) belonging to the Asiatics are under the feet of the good God User-maat-Ra Setep-en-Ra given life."

Fragments of a red granite colossus of Ramesses are scattered about in front of the temple, but this would have been too large for the sandstone bases and must have stood in front of the original pylon. It would be very worthwhile to see

how much of this colossus
could be restored.

The Limestone Pavilion.

This small building
(it measures only about
fourteen meters--46 feet--
from south to north) is
badly ruined. It consists
of a narrow room fronted
by a portico upheld by four
square pillars and ap-
proached by a short flight
of steps. It seems to be
too small for an Audience
Hall and was probably
connected with some cere-
mony in the Heb-sed.

On each of its pillars
is inscribed, "The first
time of performing very many
Heb-seds, like Ra." The
lower part of the walls of
the portico were decorated
with figures of Nile Gods.
There was also an upper
register of scenes, but
these are nearly all de-
stroyed.

The Pylon.

Only the lower part of
the pylon remains, but it is
enough to show what an imposing monument it was.
In the outer face of each
tower are two grooves for
masts, and its Central
Gateway was a magnificent
portal of red granite.

The Southern Tower.

On the southern tower
is a frieze of crenelated
ovals each surmounted by
the bust of a Nubian prisoner with his arms bound
behind his back. Each oval
contains the name of a
southern state or district
conquered by Ramesses. Below, the Goddess Seshat,
or as she is called here
Sefekh-abui, is seated on
a throne, and above her is
an inscription referring
to the Southern Lands.

Further to the north,
the King is seated in a
pavilion, and in front
of him is a row of Nubian
prisoners bound together
by a rope passing round
the neck of each man.

There were similar
scenes on the northern
tower relating to the
Asiatic enemies of Egypt,
but these are very badly
damaged.

The Red Granite Gateway.

This magnificent door-
way once stood well over
six meters (20 feet) high,
and was composed of two
monolithic jambs, lintel
and threshold. Now the
upper parts of the jambs
are missing, but the re-
maining parts measure
4.29 meters (14.0 feet)
on the south, and the
lintel is broken into
several pieces.

Both outer jambs bore
scenes showing Ramesses
adoring the gods, and at
the bottom, Thot with
his assistant behind him,
writes a long vertical
dedication inscription
running down the edge of
the jamb. Above them is
inscribed "Words spoken
by Thot: 'I write for
thee millions of years,
hundreds of thousands of
Heb-sed; thy temple exists
which thou hast founded,
like Heaven, the divine
form of thy sacred boat
resting upon its water
eternally.'" At the base
of the jambs is a text
describing the gateway
as being of "granite stone,
its door-leaves of copper
with inlaid figures (named)
'The Great Doorway of User-
maat-Ra Setep-en-Ra Who
Establishes Monuments in
the Abydos Nome.'"

To this Mer-en-Ptah
has added a line giving his
own titles and name.

On both inner jambs
are an elongated cartouche
containing the titles and
names of Ramesses to which
Mer-en-Ptah could not resist
adding a line to his own
glory.

All the scenes and
inscriptions on this gateway are very deeply cut
(on an average of between
3.0 to 3.5 centimeters--
1.2 to 1.4 inches). But
despite the hard nature of
the material, the model-
ing of the figures and
the details of the hiero-
glyphs are wonderfully
well-executed, and the finish
of the stone is really excellent.

CHAPTER TWENTY-ONE

RAMESSES' TEMPLE, THE COURT

The Court of the Temple of Ramesses II.

The court of the Temple of Ramesses measures 32.7 meters (107 feet) wide (from north to south) and 24.2 meters (79 feet) long. Its Main Entrance, which faces east, is through the red granite doorway of the pylon, but like the First Court of the Temple of Sety I, it has a small doorway near the eastern end of its southern wall.

The southern eastern and northern sides of the court were protected by colonnades supported on rectangular sandstone pillars. The fronts of which were adorned with colossal Osiride statues of Ramesses. The western side of the court had no colonnade, but three flights of shallow steps led up to a portico. Originally, the whole court was paved with slabs of limestone.

The Eastern Wall of the Court.

The northern half of the eastern wall is so badly destroyed that none of its scenes remain. The southern half of the wall has fared better, but even here the upper register of scenes has vanished. At the top of the remaining part is the end of a long inscription that commences at the western end of the southern wall, and it records two speeches made by Ramesses, one of which is addressed to kings. For the sake of clarity we will give the whole text here. After enumerating the royal titles and names, Ramesses gets down to business and says, "I say unto the Lord of the Gods Osiris Khenty-Amentiu, the plans which were commanded by the Inheritor of the Two Lands for the gods and goddesses by the excellent Heir under Heaven... (Here comes a long break in the text)...together with the Company of Gods who are with thee, who rest upon their seats in my august temple which was newly built for their statues, fashioned by Ptah according to the writings of Thot for themselves and revised from the Great Book which is in the House of the Archives.[1] I settled for them (the statues) excellent divine offerings as established (permanent) offerings; grant thou that it (the decree) exists like thy temple. (Here the text continues on the eastern wall)...food renewed every day, my statues conducting my divine boat, accompanying it to rest in my great temple. Grant thou to me existence like thou art. Thou hast protected it (the temple)

. . . .
[1]Of the Temple of Sety I? So far, no archives have been found in the Temple of Ramesses. The Great Book could be of much interest also.

for their coming. Like that of the Lord of Eternity as King of Upper and Lower Egypt in thy time,[2] thou doest exist forever in thy majesty as King of Upper and Lower Egypt, O King of Upper and Lower Egypt, Osiris."

Words spoken by the son of Ra, Ramesses Mery-Amon, "O ye kings of Upper and Lower Egypt who shall come afterwards, who shall be united to the Double crown upon the throne of Horus, who shall desire the place of the Abydos nome, the District of Eternity; may your Kas exist for you without ceasing.[3] May your time be happy like my time; may the Nile come for you in fullness at his season. May you have courage without flinching like the victories of my battle-ax in every foreign land. May you capture those who rebel against Egypt. May you give your captives from among them to my august temple.

"Behold! As for the King, he is of the divine seed when he is in the highland tomb as when he was upon earth.[4] He makes

. . . .
[2]Ramesses is recalling to Osiris that he was and still is King of Upper and Lower Egypt. Like King Arthur of Britain, he is the "once and future King."
[3]This phrase really means, "May you always be in good spirits."
[4]Ramesses reminds posterity that although he is dead and buried, he is still a king of the divine royal blood and is to be re-

transformations that please
him like the Moon God Iah.
Establish the offering
bread which is in my Temple
of Osiris whose august,
divine image rests within
it, the Company of the Gods
who are his followers at
his side. Then shall
favors be requested from
their hands making sound
your limbs. A good reward
shall be given to him who
does it if you protect my
temple for its goodly
Company of Gods and hearken
to the good God User-maat-
Ra Setep-en-Ra, given life."

Here we have another
reference to the statues
of the gods being fashioned
in accordance with tradi-
tional specifications as
we have previously seen on
the stela of King Nefer-
Hotep (see page 30).
But perhaps this rule
referred only to statues
in the round as at least
two reliefs in this temple
and several in that of
Sety are decidedly unusual
and certainly do not seem
to be "according to the
Great Book which is in
the House of the Archives."

The lower scene on
the eastern wall of the
court shows part of a
festival in which the
army was participating.
Maybe it was a feast of
victory. Commencing from
the northern end, we see
some men bringing offer-
ings. First comes a very
fat ox led by a man (Fig.
21-1). The animal is
brightly decorated; his
horns are tipped with
....

spected and obeyed as
though he were still
living.

Fig. 21-1. The decorated sacrificial ox and offering-bearers. The eastern wall of the court. The Temple of Ramesses II.

papyrus umbels, and an
arrangement of cloth and
feathers is stretched be-
tween the horns and tied
in place with ribbons. A
wide strip of cloth is
tied around its neck. A
man walking beside the
ox carries some conical
loaves of white bread,
and over his shoulder is
a bundle of papyrus reeds.
The next man carries
papyrus reeds, lotus
flowers and two live
pigeons. His companion

Fig. 21-2. Priests welcoming the offering-bearers, (Right) a soldier blows a trumpet. The eastern wall of the court. The Temple of Ramesses II.

Fig. 21-3. The trumpeter frightens the King's chariot horses. Below, part of the "king-sized" inscription of Ramesses IV. The eastern wall of the court.

an attempt to soothe them while the charioteer, holding the reins, turns to a group of officers, raising his hand to warn them not to start shouting and frighten the horses still more (Fig. 21-3)! The charioteer is a cautious fellow. He has taken off his sandals but has slung them by their straps on his upper arm. Obviously he had lost a previous pair and did not intend to leave these lying about!

The potential noise-makers are officers and military scribes, and behind them are some Libyan soldiers each of whom wears two feathers in his hair and then some Egyptian soldiers marching two by two. The latter are armed with spears and shields and two types of battle-axes. Next come some Nubian soldiers armed with clubs and accompanied by their drum major who carries his instrument slung over his shoulder (Fig. 21-4). Finally, two Egyptian officers conduct a group of six Asiatics, all of whom wear their national costumes. They are not prisoners and are described as "Chiefs of all the foreign lands" (Fig. 21-5).

is really heavily laden. He carries a large amphora of wine upon his shoulder and a trayful of pomegranates decorated with lotus flowers. A tame oryx walks beside him; its neck is decorated with ribbons, flowers and live pigeons.

Fig. 21-4. Eastern wall of the court. The Nubian drum major.

The man who leads the oryx has his work cut out as he also leads a gazelle decorated like the oryx and at the same time carries bouquets of flowers and papyrus in each hand.

The offerers are met by four priests with shaven heads and ungirt robes. They are smiling broadly and clapping their hands (Fig. 21-2). They are followed by four men who carry brooms and bow humbly.

The next scene shows the King's empty chariot awaiting the convenience of its royal owner. In front of it are four fan-bearers and a military trumpeter; the latter is blowing his trumpet and has scared the two chariot horses who have become restive, tossing their heads and fidgeting about in a most natural manner. A groom has grabbed at their headstalls and is stroking their faces in

Below the scenes, the wall was originally left blank, but at the northern end Mer-en-Ptah put a short inscription in his own honor. But later, Ramesses IV made the inscription to end all inscriptions! He filled

Fig. 21-5. Eastern wall of the court. Asiatic envoys. The Temple of Ramesses II.

the remainder of this wall and all the blank space on the southern wall with an inscription in such large and deeply cut signs that no future king could erase them or find space to add his own text (Fig. 21-6)!

The Southern Wall of the Court.

On this wall also the upper register of scenes is destroyed, and the lower register under the horizontal inscription quoted above shows two processions of offering-bearers. Each group is being led by a priest carrying a statue of Ramesses upon his shoulder. All the offering-bearers are shown walking from east to west as though they were bringing their burdens to the portico where they are met by priests who consecrate the offerings and temple scribes who note down their kind and quantity.

Commencing from the western end of the wall, the scene shows the reception of the offering-bearers.

At the top of the stairs where the wall of the court merges into that of the portico stands a shaven-headed priest; he is a stately-looking man clad in a long robe of white linen over which is draped a leopard skin, the insignia of his office. He stretches out the Kherp-baton to consecrate the offerings before they are taken into the temple. He is the High Priest, and although his name is not given (the inscription concerning him is unfinished), we know from contemporary monuments that he is the famous Wennefer. This is the man who filled the old Temple of Osiris at Kom el Sultan with statues of himself (but so far as we know, with none of Osiris). We also know that when he wanted to erect a stela in honor of his brother, the Vizier Monmes, he had a block taken from some older temple and reused.

In front of the High

Fig. 21-6. The added inscriptions of Mer-en-Ptah, Ramesses III, and Ramesses IV on the basement of the wall. The eastern wall of the court (southern side). The Temple of Ramesses II.

Priest stands one of the temple scribes busy with pen and papyrus. He is inscribed: "The scribe of the divine offerings totaling the 'Divine Offerings'."

The procession is met by a priest carrying an incense burner. He is a ritualist and burns incense to purify the offerings.

Now comes the procession of men bearing offerings headed by a man carrying the statue of Ramesses. This figure is not one of the offerings but acts as a "Deputy" for the King who by this means was able to conduct the divine offerings into the temple on every sacred occasion. A feat which of course he would not have been able to do personally in every temple in the land!

The men are carrying flat stands laden with

Fig. 21-7. Offering-bearers from the Department of Honey-cakes (Right), followed by colleagues from the Department of Per-sen Bread. The southern wall of the court. Temple of Ramesses II.

wedge shaped objects, probably cakes, and they come from the Department of Honey-cakes (Fig. 21-7). Other men coming from The Department of Per-sen Bread carry different kinds of bread, and another man carries a load of meat. Next come five men carrying large rectangular offering tables laden with jars of beer followed by a companion who carries a libation vase and a nemset jar. He is inscribed: "Doubly good wine in nemset jar for the Wen-her Feast."[5]

Apparently a Near Accident!

The next man is in serious difficulties! He is carrying a large and obviously heavy amphora of wine. He tries to take some of its ill-balanced weight upon his shoulder, but it threatens to slip, and he clutches it desperately with both arms to try to save the precious burden from crashing to the ground (Fig. 21-8).

....
[5]A feast in which the statue of the God was revealed to the worshipers.

Fig. 21-8. A near accident! The center man who is carrying "wine for the Wen-her Feast," seems about to let his amphora slip. The southern wall of the court. Temple of Ramesses II.

Fig. 21-9. *The chief Wab priest halts the procession of offering-bearers (Left); a priest carries a statue of Ramesses; a policeman sweeps the ground; a priest burns incense; the temple scribe registers the offerings. The southern wall of the court. Temple of Ramesses II.*

Two men carry trays of poultry on their heads while others bring "sweet green things for the Wen-her Feast."

This ends the first procession; separating it from the second is a vertical text reading:

"Consecrating the divine offerings of the regular offerings of every day from the magazines belonging to the rear of the 'House of Ramesses Mery-Amon Who Enriches the Abydos Nome.'"

Next follows the group

Fig. 21-10. *Offering-bearers carrying beer and wine. The southern wall of the court. Temple of Ramesses II.*

of priests and temple scribes and the man carrying a statue of Ramesses as we have already seen, at the head of the first procession. But here a policeman carrying a broom bends double to pass under the arm of the statue-bearer presumably to sweep the ground in front of him (Fig. 21-9). Behind the statue-bearer, the "chief Wab priest" looks backward over his shoulder and raises his hand signalling to the offering-bearers to halt.

Next come twelve men all carrying heavy trays of offerings on their heads. They steady their loads by holding on to hanging cords. How skillfully the artist has relieved the monotony of such a scene by varying the positions of the men's arms which are shown in very natural attitudes (Fig. 21-10).

They are followed by some men who are coming from the Department of Beer.

Eight more men are carrying a long pole on which are suspended four heavy sacks of linen. One man has allowed his sack to swing and hit the leg of the fellow in front of him. The latter turns his head to swear at him, but the offender politely puts out his hand to stop the bag from swinging again (Fig. 21-11).

The last group is carrying bread, but they come from the Department of Beer,[6] and the Depart-

....

[6]In ancient Egypt certain

ment of Sweet Drinks.

Now comes the small doorway on the outer jambs of which are figures of Ramesses and the warning that "All who enter the temple must be purified twice."

The remainder of the southern wall to the east of the small doorway bears a continuation of the scenes of offering-bearers.

The first man carries four ducks in his left hand and has a large goose tucked under his right arm. He is inscribed: "Geese and ducks to fill the Wen-her Feast from the Department of Divine Offerings." He is followed by another fellow who carries "many pigeons for the divine offerings."

Another man carries a tray laden with slices of melon. His companion carries a tray of vegetables and two bunches of papyrus reeds. The next man carries a bundle of vegetables on his head and with a very natural gesture steadies the load with his right hand. He also carries bunches of papyrus reeds.

Next comes a man leading a very fat ox, and he turns his head as though to speak to (or probably swear at?) the animal (Fig. 21-12). Above the back of the ox is inscribed: "An ox for the day of the feast, a divine offering." The animal must have been stall-fed for some long

....

types of beer were made from soaked and fermented barley bread.

Fig. 21-11. A slight argument! The second man from the left has let his bag swing and hit the leg of the man in front who turns to swear at him! The southern wall of the court. Temple of Ramesses II.

time as its hooves have grown long from lack of friction by exercise, and they are awkwardly turned up in front like Turkish slippers.

The last man is bringing a calf which is clearly causing him some trouble as he has to push it along from behind. The unwilling victim is inscribed: "A calf for the regular offering" (Fig. 21-12).

The once plain dado of the entire wall is occupied by the "king-sized" inscription of Ramesses IV. Being only a wearisome display of his titles and names, it is really only of interest to his august person. So we will just leave it where it is.

Fig. 21-12. The stall-fed ox and the reluctant calf. The southern interior wall of the court. The Temple of Ramesses II.

The Northern Wall of the Court.

Again the upper register of scenes has been destroyed, and as on the southern wall, the remaining decoration starts with a long horizontal inscription; the end of which is unfortunately missing. After the recital of some of the titles and names of Ramesses who is "beloved of Osiris Khenty-Amentiu and Wepwawat, Lord of the Sacred Land," it reads, "He (Ramesses) became a vigilant king, a beloved protector of Osiris calculating in his heart how to fashion excellently for him like Ptah settling the land from the beginning. Lo, His Majesty was still a youth, young but with a powerful arm; his splendor on earth pervading everyone like the Moon God Iah; his child of the offspring of his heart reckoning like the Lord of Khemenu (Thot), guiding his heart towards Truth. He commanded work according to his own desire on the Serekh Chapel within his palace; he pondered upon plans seeking what was beneficial for guilding his Temple of Nif-wer (Abydos) to the Glorious Place of Truth..."

It seems from this, that Ramesses designed the temple himself, and as it follows a simple form of a traditional New Kingdom temple, there seems to be no reason to doubt him

....
[7] Ramesses claims to have been good at arithmetic.

Fig. 21-13. The priestly Reception Committee. (Right) the temple scribe, the Priest of Osiris, the High Priest, the Ritualist. The northern wall of the court.

especially as he also says that he was "good at math"![7]

The scenes in the lower register on this wall are rather unsavory for any vegetarian. They show the arrival of sacrificial animals at the temple, butchered meat offerings, and the slaughter and dismemberment of oxen with full anatomical details. As in the scenes on the southern and eastern walls, the style is free and lively. In fact, some of the butchers

Fig. 21-14. A fat ox brought to the temple for sacrifice. Note the temple scribe on the left registering the offerings. The northern wall of the court.

Fig. 21-15. An ox whose belly measures "four palms" from the ground. The northern wall of the court.

are drawn in a perfectly natural and almost "modern" way. The figures of the men who are bringing meat offerings are full of movement and vigor as they rush from the Slaughter Court to the temple. Their exuberance contrasts with the grave dignity of the priests and temple scribes.

The animals too are excellently rendered. The artist has caught the ponderous gait of the fattened oxen, the nervous tread of the half tamed oryx, and the dainty mincing steps of the gazelles. The grouping of the figures is also artistic and natural.

Fig. 21-16. A fine oryx is brought to the temple. The northern wall of the court. Temple of Ramesses II.

Some of the men walk on the off or near side of an animal, and many turn their heads to speak to their companions or to the animals they lead, thus linking the figures into groups. The Amarna spirit[8] still seems to pervade the sculpture in this court. But the artists of Ramesses had employed all that was best of that period, for example, its fresh naturalness, and avoidance of the morbid distortions that marred most of the early Amarna work, and made it so distasteful to the common taste of a very conservative people.

At the western end of the wall is a group of priests and a temple scribe similar to those on the southern wall (Fig. 21-13).

The Fattened Oxen and a Strange "Fattening Index."

Now come the offering-bringers headed by a man who leads an enormously fat ox with long curling horns. The man is the "Controller of the purification of the cattle of the pure Slaughter Court[9] of the cattle-stalls of the 'House of Ramesses, Mery-Amon Who Enriches Abydos.'" An inscription over the back of the ox gave its length, but it is too damaged to be read (Fig. 21-14).

The next man also leads a fat, long-horned ox of which he seems to be fond

. . . .
[8]From the Akhen-Aton Period.
[9]So far, the Slaughter Court of this temple has not been discovered.

199

Fig. 21-17. A fat ox, its belly is only "Five palms, two fingers" from the ground. A man carries a young gazelle. Note the graffito drawing of In-hert on the basement of the wall (under the ox). The northern wall of the court.

First comes the inevitable temple scribe carrying a roll of papyrus. The inscription in front of him says, "Usher in the choice pieces of meat." He is approached by a ritualist carrying an incense burner and a libation vase. Behind him, the offering-bearers come running (Fig. 21-19).

The first of these runners carries a large and heavy foreleg of beef; the second carries the head of an ox; and the third carries a tray laden with pieces of meat (Fig. 21-20). The upper part of the scene is destroyed, and most of the figures are headless.

Some more men bring live poultry; the first of them, who also runs at full speed, has a live crane tucked under his arm, and he wisely holds its beak shut. His companion car-

Fig. 21-18. Bringing gazelles, "a gift from His Majesty," and live ducks. The northern wall of the court.

as he turns to stroke it. Under the animal's belly is inscribed "four palms," meaning that it is so fat that its belly clears the ground by only four palms width (Fig. 21-15).

Now come two men and an oryx. The first man holds a rope attached to its halter, but this is not enough to control the lively, half-tamed animal, and a second man walks beside it grasping its long, pointed horns with both hands (Fig, 21-16). Then follows a man leading a fat, short-horned ox. He obligingly puts his hand on the rump of the oryx giving it a push in the right direction.

Next we have a man leading a fat ox which has long, bent horns. The inscription tells us that the animal came from Nubia. The height of its belly from the ground is "five palms and two fingers"

(Fig. 21-17).

He is followed by a man carrying a small gazelle over his shoulders holding its legs with both hands. He is "bringing gazelles from the pure Slaughter Court of the temple." Two men follow. One is leading a large gazelle, and the other is carrying a young one in his arms. The animals are described as gazelles, "a gift from His Majesty" (Fig. 21-18).

The last man in this part of the scene carries a bunch of pintailed ducks in each hand; the birds are being suspended by strings tied to their feet. He is "bringing ducks to the temple" (Fig. 21-18).

The Meat Offerings.

The second part of the scene shows the bringing of meat offerings.

200

Fig. 21-19. *Offering-bearers in a hurry! The northern wall of the court. The Temple of Ramesses II.*

ries a live duck, and a third man carries a pair of slaughtered and trussed geese.

The Butchers.

The next scene shows the slaughter and dismemberment of the sacrificial animals which take place under priestly supervision. First, are two priests clad in long robes. The first of them carries a roll of papyrus while the second had a libation vase in the shape of the Key of Life. They are watching two butchers dismembering an ox. The animal already has its head cut off, and the men are now severing one of the forelegs. One of them pulls the leg upright while the other severs the flesh with a large flint knife. Next comes a ritualist holding a papyrus. He is walking westward, but he turns his head and gestures to two men behind

him. They are slaughtering an ox which lies bound upon the ground. One man is bending down to cut the animal's throat. His figure is drawn according to modern rules of perspective. As he slashes the animal's throat, a priest pours a

purifying libation upon the wound (Fig. 21-21).

The next group is really a minor masterpiece and shows a powerful ox being thrown down for slaughter. It has been lassoed, the loop of the rope passing round the base of the horns while the slack has been tangled in the animal's legs thus tripping it up. One man hauls with all his might on the rope drawing the legs tighter together. A second man grasps the creature by its tail while a third grips the long horns. The ox bellows in fear and rage as it sinks to its knees (Fig. 21-22). The whole group is alive with vivid action, and the contrast between the agility of the comparatively puny men and the slow, ponderous strength of the ox is marvellously rendered.

Next comes another priest carrying a roll of

Fig. 21-20. *Severing the foreleg of an ox. Note the natural figures of the two butchers. Behind them are two priests. One carries a libation vase and the other carries a roll of papyrus. The northern wall of the court.*

papyrus and addressing a group of butchers who are slaughtering another ox. This animal lies bound and helpless on the ground, but no chances are being taken, and two men haul strongly upon ropes binding its legs while a third man cuts its throat. A priest burns incense to purify the victim.

All that remains of the last group is part of a figure of a man who was grasping an ox by one of its horns.

Amateur Talent.

The lower part of the northern wall is un-decorated, but some an-cient amateur artists, among whom were priests, have painted and scratched some interesting graffiti here. From the western end, the first is a figure of a gazelle partly in red paint and partly scratched. The next is the incised bust of a man done by someone with more ambition than talent. The third is a very well done figure of the God In-hert, (Fig. 21-23) and on each side of him, but in paint only, are two kneeling priests. The one in front of the God has a neatly incised inscription read-ing: "Djed-Iah, the Justi-fied, the Wab priest of Osiris. His companion is the Wab priest of Osiris Djedi-ankh-ef." Just be-yond them there is paint-ed another man who is kneeling. He is "Pay-ha, the Overseer of the fan-bearers."

Fig. 21-21. Cutting the throat of an ox. A priest puri-fies the wound. Note the natural figures of the butcher and the man at the extreme left. Also a graffito draw-ing of Osiris on the basement of the wall (left). The northern wall of the court.

The Western Wall of the Court.

This is a low wall only about 70 centimeters (28 inches) high and sur-mounted by a palmetto cor-nice. There was once a low screen-wall above the cornice, but of this, only a few blocks remain. On them is part of a scene showing Ramesses present-ing meat offerings to five deities. Three shallow staircases lead from the

Fig. 21-22. Throwing an ox. Note the natural figure of the man holding the animal's horns. The northern wall of the court. The Temple of Ramesses II.

202

Fig. 21-23. (Above) A *nicely carved graffito of the God In-hert. The northern wall of the court (basement).*

level of the court to the portico. One flight is in the middle of the court and one at each of the southern and northern sides.

The Pillars of the Court.

None of the pillars in this temple are preserved to their full height, and in the case of those in the court, the Osiris statues, on their fronts, all lack the heads, shoulders and breasts. On the three flat faces of these pillars were first a dado of panelling then a rectangle containing a kneeling figure representing gods, the blessed dead, the aristocracy and the common people of Egypt. The latter are usually shown in the form of birds (Fig. 21-24) sometimes with human arms raised in adoration as in the Temple of Sety.9 But on these pillars, the figures symbolizing the common people

Fig. 21-24. *The common people of Egypt represented by the "rekhyt" bird whose human arms are raised in adoration to the King's cartouche. The Second Hypostyle Hall. Column shaft. The Temple of Ramesses II.*

(called the "rekhyt") are sometimes shown as men with a bird's head (Fig. 21-25) or with a human head with only the bird's crest at the back (Fig. 21-26) or even in full human form (Fig. 21-27). This latter form may perhaps be an oversight on the part of the artist.

On the upper part of the flat faces of the pillars were large scenes showing the King and a deity, but few of these are preserved higher than the feet and ankles of the figures.

. . . .

9The head of the bird resembles that of a hoopoe which as it is always seen pecking the ground and digging in search of food is a good symbol of the Egyptian peasant. One cannot however fail to discern the underlying sarcasm that is so characteristic of the Egyptian character in both ancient and modern times. There is a local expression used for anyone who eats very scanty or simple fare. The expression that is used is, "He is eating dust," which is exactly what the hoopoe appears to be doing.

Fig. 21-25. (Top) The common people of Egypt represented by the head of the "rekhyt" bird and a human body. From a pillar in the court. Temple of Ramesses II.
Fig. 21-26. (Bottom) The common people of Egypt in human form but retaining the crest of the "rekhyt" bird. From a pillar in the court. The Temple of Ramesses II.

Fig. 21-27. (Left) The "rekhyt," the common people of Egypt represented in full human form. They are identified by the name "rekhyt" inscribed in front of them. From a pillar in the court.

CHAPTER TWENTY-TWO

THE PORTICO, GATEWAY AND CHAPELS

The Portico of the Temple of Ramesses II.

The portico at the western end of the court had its roof supported by sixteen rectangular pillars, eight to the north and eight to the south of the Central Gateway. Four beautifully decorated chapels open out of the western wall of the portico and at the eastern end of its southern and northern walls was a small doorway communicating with the Temenos. For some reason or other, the northern doorway was blocked up before the temple was completed and there is no trace of its existence on the outer side of the wall.

The Southern Wall of the Portico.

This wall originally bore a large scene showing Ramesses slaying a Nubian prisoner of war in the presence of Amon-Ra.[1] But all that remains are the feet and ankles of the God and the toe of the kneeling captive. Below is a horizontal inscription referring to "captives of every foreign country from among the stongholds

....

[1] The identification of the God as Amon-Ra is based on the blue color of his feet. See also a similar scene in the same place in the Temple of Sety I (see page 65).

of the negroes, rulers of the foreign lands of Nubia" (Fig. 22-1).

This is referring to the nine crenellated ovals below the inscription, each of which is surmounted by the bust of a negroid prisoner of war and containing the name of a southern people or state conquered by Ramesses. They are very similar to those on the southern tower of the pylon.

The Western Wall.

Except where it is interrupted by the jambs of doorways, the western wall bore one (or perhaps two?) register of scenes on a large scale below which was a horizontal inscription. On the lower part of the wall was a

Fig. 22-1. Ovals containing the names of southern states or peoples conquered by Ramesses. They are surmounted by Nubian prisoners of war. The portico. Southern wall.

Fig. 22-2. *Portico, western wall. The personified irrigation canals. The Temple of Ramesses II.*

The Black Granite Gateway.

The Central Gateway in the western wall (which gives access to the First Hypostyle Hall) is a magnificent monument. Of highly polished black granite, its monolithic jambs soar to a height of more than five meters (16 feet), and were surmounted by a massive lintel. The whole gateway was adorned with sculptured scenes and inscriptions. The signs and figures are very deeply incised and have a wealth of fine detail and beautiful modelling. The work is exquisitely finished; even the sides of the deeply cut reliefs are polished to the smoothness of glass. It seems more like the work of a lapidary (a cutter and polisher of precious stone) than that of a stonemason (Fig. 22-3).

The Lintel of the Black Granite Gateway.

The lintel had been overthrown and smashed to fragments, but many of these have been collected and restored. However, most of the northern half is still missing.

On the southern half is a scene showing the King performing the ancient ritual sprint in front of Osiris and Isis.

The Southern Jamb of the Black Granite Gateway.

The decoration of the jambs resemble those of the red granite gateway in the pylon. They bore three

dado of figures that look like Nile Gods. But by the signs carried on the head of each one, we know that they are personifications of the great irrigation canals (Fig. 22-2).

At the extreme southern end of the western wall is the doorway leading to a chapel dedicated to the Mortuary Cult of Sety I. On its jambs are figures of Ramesses and the familiar warning about purification.

On the short wall between this doorway and the next, very little remains except the figures of two personified canals. The jambs of the second doorway are similar to those of the Chapel of Sety and the decoration of the part of the wall which follows has almost entirely disappeared.

superposed scenes, the upper ones showing Ramesses adoring the gods. The lower scene shows Thot enthroned writing the vertical inscription that runs down the edge of the jamb. Behind the God stands his assistant holding a water-pot and ink palette. Only the lower half of the vertical inscription that Thot is supposed to be writing remains, but it appears to be the same as that on the northern jamb, and after giving the royal titles, reads: "He made it as his monument for his father Osiris who dwells in the 'House of Ramesses Mery-Amon Who Enriches the Abydos Nome,' making for him a doorway of black stone, its door-leaves sheathed with copper, gilded with electrum; I made it for him, (namely I) the son of Ra, Ramesses Mery-Amon, like Ra."

The northern outer jamb bears the same scenes and inscriptions, and on both inner jambs are elongated cartouches containing the titles and names of Ramesses in beautifully carved and detailed hieroglyphs.

All that remains of the upper scene on the wall to the north of the black granite gateway are four pairs of human feet colored red. Below them is part of the horizontal inscription which refers to the personified irrigation canals who are supposed to address the King thus, "We come near to thee, our arms bearing offering trays laden with food and provisions; our abundance is

Fig. 22-3. Details of the inscription on the northern jamb of the black granite gateway. The portico, western wall. The signs read: "Beloved of Amon." The Temple of Ramesses II.

for thee which was created by Nun, everything which grows upon the back of the earth we haul for thee, the (products) of the meadows of the Northland, the bird-swamps in which all birds alight, for the hall of thy Temple of Nif-wer." Below this are fourteen figures of the personified canals similar to those on the southern half of the wall.

Next come the jambs of the doorway of the chapel dedicated to the ancient kings of Egypt. Both outer jambs bear figures of Ramesses and the warning about purification. Beyond the northern jamb is the continuation of the horizontal inscription referring to bringing provisions to the temple, and below it two more personified canals. The jambs of

Fig. 22-4. Names of the Asiatic states conquered by Ramesses. The central name reads Isel or Iseru (the country of Isru). The ovals are surmounted by representations of Asiatic prisoners of war. The portico. Northern wall. The Temple of Ramesses II.

the northernmost chapel are similar to the others but are better preserved.

The Northern Wall of the Portico.

On the upper part of the northern wall of the portico is the lower part of a once fine, large scene which shows Ramesses slaying an Asiatic prisoner of war in the presence of a god. The upper parts of all figures are destroyed. Below, a horizontal inscription reads: "All lands, all foreign countries, the islands of the sea,[2] the distant marshlands, seat of the rebellious ones...all foreign lands, rebel lands to Thy Majesty, form the limits of darkness to the four supports of Heaven[3] are under the feet of this

. . . .
[2]The Aegean Isles.
[3]The Cardinal Points.

good god, the Lord of the Lands, beloved of Ra."

Below are nine crenellated ovals, each surmounted by the bust of an Asiatic prisoner of war (Fig. 22-4) and containing the names of countries conquered by Ramesses. Among these are Libya, Naharina, Crete, Mesopotamia, Armenia, Phoenicia, and a place called Isel (or Iseru) which Professor Gauthier identifies as a part of Palestine. Can this be a reference to Israel earlier than the one on the famous Victory Stela of Mer-en-Ptah?[4] It could be since it rep-

. . . .
[4]Gauthier, "Dictionnaire Geographique" Vol. 1 p. 105. This particular inscription is of great importance and deserves further investigation. It might lead to important conclusions concerning the Exodus.

represents half of the name of Israel (Iser-el) which in Hebrew means, "Slave of God."

The Chapels of the Portico.

Four small chapels open out of the western wall of the portico; they all measure about 8.5 meters (28.5 feet) long and 2.7 meters (8.9 feet) wide.

The Chapel of Sety I.

The southernmost chapel was dedicated by Ramesses to the Mortuary Cult of his father. On the southern side of the doorway are four lines of inscriptions, the first three of which give the titles and names of Ramesses. The fourth line related to Sety, but the beginning is lost, and the remainder reads, "...temple for his (Sety's) divine image protecting the followers of his father Osiris in my Temple of Millions of Years which is in Abydos."

The Southern Wall of the Chapel of Sety I.

The upper part of all the walls of this chapel are destroyed, but here there are the remains of two large scenes which still retain much of their original beautiful colors. The first scene from the east shows Ramesses offering in front of the sacred boat in which the statue of Sety would have been carried on feast days. Ramesses is followed by his Ka, a small male figure bearing a pair of upraised arms on his head.

In front of Ramesses is the lower end of an inscription in which he speaks to his father saying, "...O Men-maat-Ra, I am thy true son raising up thy name in my temple which is in Abydos."

The boat is colored yellow to show that it was made of gold; the stern terminates in a head of Sety, and a small kingly figure works the steering-oars. The boat and its carrying-poles rest upon a rectangular pedestal blue in color and having a golden panel in which are inscribed the titles and name of Sety.

The second scene shows Ramesses standing with both arms raised in the presence of Sety who is seated in a golden shrine. Of the latter only the legs and part of the throne remain. An inscription behind Ramesses gave his address to his father of which is preserved, "...thy beautiful face, O my father King Men-maat-Ra. I am thy son, thine heir upon earth on account of the excellent things which I have done for thee."

The Western Wall of the Chapel of Sety I.

This wall is entirely occupied by a scene which was left unfinished. It shows two persons (male) standing in the presence of Amon-Ra. The latter is seated in a shrine, the poles of which as well as the pedestal of the throne were never sculptured. In front of Amon-Ra are faint outlines of a figure of a king, but this was never completed. Behind can be seen the legs of another figure; perhaps they were intended to represent Sety and Ramesses.

In the Alabaster Sanctuary (see page 226) is a group of statues in black granite. They represent Sety and Ramesses seated with Osiris, Isis and Horus. They are not now in their proper place, but their dimensions suggest that they originally stood against the western wall of this chapel which for that reason was left unfinished, as the statues would have hidden most of its lower part.

The Northern Wall of the Chapel of Sety I.

At the extreme end of the wall is the lower part of the standard of Abydos which appears to have been housed in a shrine. Following this, Sety is seated in a golden shrine. In front of him is an offering table and two jars of beer. Standing in front of Sety were an Iwn-mut-ef priest and Ramesses, but only their legs remain.

To the east of this scene the wall is denuded down to the level of the horizontal border of stripes, and no scenes ramain.

The Chapel of Ramesses.

This is the second chapel leading out of the southern side of the portico. It is unfortunate that the fourth line of the inscription on the southern side of the doorway is damaged as this would have told us to whom it was dedicated, but from what remains of the inscriptions plus the scene on the western wall, we believe that we can safely say that it was dedicated to the Mortuary Cult of Ramesses himself.

The Southern Wall.

Only the lowest part of the scene on this wall is preserved. It showed Ramesses standing in front of a sacred boat which was apparently being carried by the Souls of Pe and Nekhen, but only their legs in front of and behind the boat are preserved.

The Western Wall.

The entire western wall was occupied by a scene showing Ramesses seated on a throne rather precariously balanced on the elongated upper bar of the symbol of Union. On each side is a god, almost certainly Horus and Thot, who are tieing the lily of Upper Egypt and the papyrus of Lower Egypt to the symbol of Union. The plants are correctly drawn in their proper places, the lily being on the southern side of the scene and the papyrus on the north. No inscriptions are preserved.

The Northern Wall.

At the western end of the wall is the lower part of a large figure of a goddess. She is standing behind a shrine in which some mummiform deities are seated. The heads of all these figures are missing.

The Wanderings of a Valuable Document!

The remainder of the northern wall was originally occupied by a list of royal names similar to that in the Corridor of Kings in the Temple of Sety. However, this list known as the Second Abydos List is now in the British Museum, London, having been purchased from the French Consul.[5] All that now remains of this list are a number of headless, squatting figures, the determinative figures of royal names.

At the eastern end of the wall a small doorway was cut giving access to the First Hypostyle Hall. This was clearly an afterthought as it was made after the decoration of both sides of the wall were completed. Probably its purpose was to give easy access to the inner parts of the temple without having to keep on opening and shutting the huge copper sheathed door-leaves of the black granite gateway.

The Chapel of the Gods of Abydos.

This is the first of the two chapels that open out of the northern side of the western wall of the
....

[5]No. 117 see, "Guide to the Egyptian Sculpture in the British Museum," (1909) p. 163.

portico. Happily its walls are very well preserved and are brightly colored. From the fourth line of the inscription on the southern side of the doorway we know that it was dedicated to the gods of Abydos. The text reads; "He (Ramesses) made it as his monument for his fathers,[6] the Company of the gods of Abydos, the followers of Khenty-Amentiu in all his Wag Feasts;[7] making for them a chapel in my temple which is in Abydos, that he may be given life."

The chapel may well have been dedicated to the gods of Abydos, but as we shall see, it is young Ramesses who dominates all the scenes and "steals the show!"

The Southern Wall.

The scene on the southern wall shows Ramesses accompanied by two gods presenting offerings to the sacred boat. The ceremony is supposed to be taking place in the court, as the King is wearing sandals. In front of him are four golden of-

....
[6]Doesn't this ring of Malachi 4:5 in the Old Testament?
[7]The Wag Feast was a kind of "All Saint's Day," and people used to go to the cemeteries carrying offerings of beer. There they sat by the tombs of their dead, pouring some of the beer as a libation and drinking some themselves in a kind of supernatural family reunion.

fering stands placed close together and bearing a large tray piled high with offerings. Next comes a god who carries a notched palm branch but he is headless and so remains anonymous.

The golden boat has its prow surmounted by a royal head. Its miniature crew resembles those of all the sacred boats in the Temple of Sety. Behind the boat stands another large figure of a god.

The Western Wall.

In the scene on this wall, Ramesses is being purified by two gods (Horus and Thot?). The upper part of the scene is destroyed but we can see that the King was kneeling on a pedestal, and the gods were pouring water over him. As in the purification scene in the First Hypostyle Hall of the Temple of Sety (see page 75) the water takes the form of the emblems of Life and Prosperity, and this is referred to in a vertical inscription which reads: "Making purifications with Life and Prosperity for the Lord of the Two Lands, User-maat-Ra, given life forever,"

The Northern Wall.

The whole of this wall is occupied by a fine large scene showing Ramesses seated in a sacred boat which is being towed by the Souls of Pe and Nekhen (Fig. 22-5). Ramesses is addressed by Thot who stands at the eastern end

of the scene. He carries a scribe's palette in his left hand and raises the right one as he says to the King, "...O User-maat-Ra, I come to thy temple to behold thy beautiful face in thy festival; thou appearest as king, resting in thy divine boat for bearing thy beauty...the followers of Horus, their hands are holding the tow-rope of more than one hundred cubits thrown overboard by the hand of the crew like Ra in the Primeval Ocean in the Night Boat of the Sun (Fig. 22-6).

This scene is a rare exception to the general rules of Egyptian art because here Ramesses is facing out of the chapel while the God Thot faces inwards. But perhaps the King is supposed to be dead and deified.

The Souls of Pe and Nekhen are arranged in two registers of three each. The ones in the upper row are headless, and the ones in the lower row are falcon-headed.

The boat has a golden hull with a blue panel amidships and is attached to a wooden sledge to which two towropes are fastened. Ramesses is seated in a large golden shrine, and a goddess (headless) stands behind him. In front of him stand the two little Mert goddesses stretching out their arms to him (Fig. 22-7). Above the prow of the boat is a damaged inscription praising Ramesses and recording the joy of the gods and of the entire

Fig. 22-5. The Souls of Pe and Nekhen tow the sacred boat. The Chapel of the God. Northern wall. The Temple of Ramesses II.

population of Egypt at his appearance in the festivals.

Except for some damage to the upper part, the scene is well preserved, and the colors are still brilliant.

Ramesses has an Afterthought.

A curious feature of this chapel is the fact that some scenes and inscriptions were added to the basement of the walls not by later kings but during the reign of Ramesses himself. These additions which are rather crudely incised in outline are versions of a religious work known as "The Litany of the Sun" and chapter CXLVIII of the Book of the Dead, a New Kingdom funerary work. All are accompanied by appropriate illustrations (Fig. 22-8).

Fig. 22-6. Thot addresses the King. The Chapel of the Gods. Northern wall. Temple of Ramesses II.

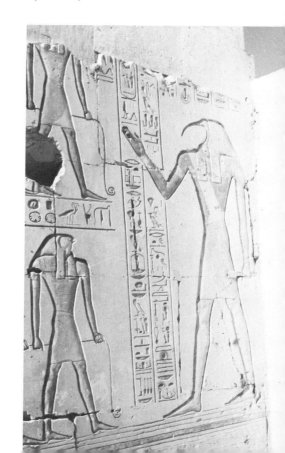

Fig. 22-7. *Ramesses in his sacred boat. The Chapel of the Gods. Northern wall. Temple of Ramesses II.*

Fig. 22-8. *Scenes and texts from "The Litany of the Sun" on the basement of the wall. The Chapel of the Gods. Northern wall. The Temple of Ramesses II.*

The Chapel of Osiris Khenty-Amentiu.

According to the fourth line of the inscription on the southern side of the doorway, Ramesses made this chapel "as his monument for his father Osiris Khenty-Amentiu, making for him a chapel, a place of repose for the kings of Upper and Lower Egypt who are the followers of Osiris, in his Temple of Millions of Years which is in Abydos."

The scenes on the walls are well preserved and retain most of their color.

The Southern Wall of the Chapel of Osiris Khenty-Amentiu.

This wall bears a single large scene showing a king seated on a throne in front of an offering table. The royal figure is headless but even without the confirmation of the inscription we can guess that it represents Ramesses!

In the middle of the scene is an offering list of which seven items of bread, onions and meat are preserved together with the formula for their presentation. These are all taken from the Pyramid Texts (Fig. 22-9).

At the eastern end of the scene are the figures of the Iwn-mut-ef priest and Thot who are reciting the offering formula on the King's behalf.

The Royal Names Personified.

At the extreme western end of the wall are two registers of male figures, three to each row, but the upper ones are all destroyed from the knees upwards. They look like figures of gods, all having the divine plaited beards and carrying the Key of Life and scepter of Prosperity. But from the inscriptions accompanying them we know that they are the personifications of the royal names.

When a prince was crowned as Pharaoh, he received four names which were carefully chosen for him and usually had a bearing on his policy or proposed course of action. As the Egyptians believed that the name of a person like the body, soul, Ka, Glorified Spirit, and Shadow was one of the integral elements of man, it is not inconsistent that the name like the other elements would be personified.

The Western Wall.

On the western wall of this chapel is a scene (upper part destroyed) showing two kings standing in the presence of a god. This is somewhat similar to that on the same wall in the Chapel of Sety.

The god's flesh is colored blue, and he sits in a golden shrine. In front of the god stands a king probably Ramesses as he holds in his hand the bird which symbolizes the common people of Egypt. Behind him stands a god-

Fig. 22-9. The offering list. The Chapel of Osiris Khenty-Amentiu. The southern wall. The Temple of Ramesses II.

dess and finally another king.

The Northern Wall.

This wall is occupied by an interesting and fairly well preserved scene showing Ramesses consecrating offerings to the Goddess Hathor who is shown in the form of a cow.

At the eastern end of the scene stands Ramesses. In his left hand he holds an incense burner; his right arm is outstretched, and his hand is holding

the Kherp-baton with which he consecrates the offering in front of him. His figure is a perfect study of youthful vigor and regal dignity. His handsome, cheerful face is clearly a portrait (Fig. 22-10). The inscription behind him says: "...King of Upper and Lower Egypt conducting the double portions (of offerings). He guides the Two Lands as Lord of the Living upon the throne of Horus, like Ra, forever."

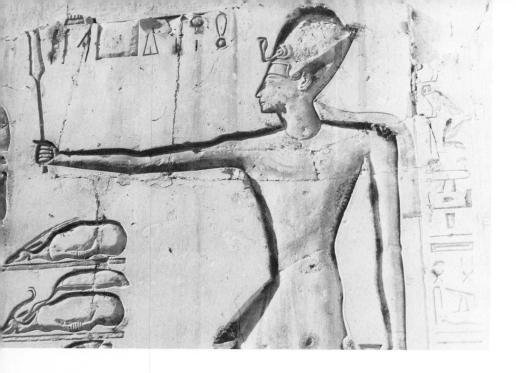

Fig. 22-10. (Above) Ramesses dedicates the offerings (detail). The Chapel of Osiris Khenty-Amentiu. Northern wall (see Fig. 22-11).

An Artist's Mistake or a Freak Ox?

In front of Ramesses are the carcasses of some sacrificial animals laid upon mats. These are an oryx, a gazelle with a goose laid on its back, and three decapitated oxen. Next comes a rectangular golden altar piled high with bread, meat, fruit and lotus flowers. Now we can perhaps catch the artist in an amusing mistake. Although there were only *three* decapitated oxen on the mat, there are *four* ox heads shown upon the altar (Fig. 22-11)! The Goddess Hathor stands in a golden boat which has a blue panel upon its hull and is attached to a sledge. She is in the form of a cow and wears a blue and gold

214

Fig. 22-12. The sacred boat. Hathor in the form of a cow suckles the King. The Chapel of Osiris Khenty-Amentiu. Northern wall. The Temple of Ramesses II.

menat necklace around her neck. Unfortunately only the lower part of her body is preserved. In front of her, his back against her chest, stands a figure of Ramesses. Ramesses is represented again, this time as a young child, under the belly of the cow. He eagerly presses the animal's udder to his upturned face in order to suck the divine milk (Fig. 22-12). The inscription behind him records the words of the Goddess who says, "Suck for yourself of my milk everyday; it is sweet. The milk enters thy belly with Life, Endurance and Prosperity!"

This group is almost the same as the famous statue of the cow from Deir el Bahari which is now in the Cairo Museum.

Behind the boat is a goddess. She is headless and rests her hand upon the boat. Probably the goddess is Hathor in her human form.

CHAPTER TWENTY-THREE

FIRST HYPOSTYLE HALL

The First Hypostyle Hall of the Temple of Ramesses II.

Passing through the black granite gateway, one enters the First Hypostyle Hall. The roof now missing was supported by eight rectangular pillars of sandstone, the decoration of which, with the exception of the Osirid statues, is the same as those in the court and portico. Although all the sculpture here is in incised relief like that of the pylon, court and portico, it was decorated while Ramesses was still co-regent. This is proved by his prenomen which has the simple form of User-maat-Ra. It was only after the death of his father that he added the epithet Setep-en-Ra ("Chosen of Ra").

The Eastern Wall.

The decoration on the southern half of the eastern wall has entirely disappeared except for the horizontal border of stripes.

On the upper part of the northern end of the wall is a fragmentary scene which showed Osiris enthroned in a golden shrine with Isis standing behind him. In front of them is a damaged version of chapter CXLI of the Book of the Dead which gives the many names and epithets of Osiris.[1]

Below the scene is a dado of kneeling figures alternately male and female. The former are Nile Gods and the latter are personifications of the cultivated lands. The figures of the Nile Gods are sometimes colored

....
[1]See also in the antechamber of the Osirion, page 16.

Fig. 23-1. The procession of the sacred standard of Abydos (eastern end). To the right are the legs of the King, then a group of priests, and the Souls of Pe and Nekhen who are carrying the standard. Below are figures of the Nile God and the cultivated lands. Temple of Ramesses II. Abydos. First Hypostyle Hall, northern wall.

red and sometimes green or blue. These are the colors to which the Nile water seems to change during the course of the year; red is during the inundation, blue is in winter and green is in summer.

The Northern Wall.

The upper part of the wall bore a single large scene showing the sacred standard of Abydos being carried in a procession, but only the lower part remains (Fig. 23-1). The procession is followed by the King who appears again at the western end of the scene to receive it. Below is another dado of Nile Gods and cultivated lands. All of which are brightly colored.

The Chapel of In-hert.

At the western end of the northern wall is the entrance to the Chapel of In-hert. The lintel and outer jambs are inscribed with the titles and names of Ramesses. The eastern side of the doorway is carved to represent a wooden door of vertical planks held together by horizontal strips of wood. Between each strip is again inscribed the royal titles and names. On the western side of the doorway are four vertical lines of royal inscription, the last of which is the dedication text and reads: "He made it as his monument for his father In-hert, Horus of the Powerful

Arm, making for him a great chapel for his august, divine form in the 'House of Ramesses Mery-Amon Who Enriches the Abydos Nome.'"

The Western Wall.

The upper parts of all the walls of this chapel are destroyed; consequently the figures in the scenes are headless and so are sometimes difficult to identify.
On the western wall where the color is almost perfectly preserved on the remaining parts of the scenes, we can detect Ramesses being introduced by In-hert to a god and goddess. Next comes an unidentifiable god, another representation of In-hert, this sequence being repeated a second time.

The Northern Wall.

Originally there was a stone offering bench standing against the lower part of the northern wall. It seems to have been removed in fairly recent times as the part of the wall which it covered is clean and light in color. Above this clean patch, the wall is stained by being repeatedly splashed with dirty water when the priests washed the upper surface of the offering bench as in the great Osiris Hall in the Temple of Sety I.
The scene on the northern wall is somewhat better preserved than that on the western wall, but much of its color has faded.

It shows the God In-hert seated in a golden shrine and holding a spear. His throne rests upon the sign of Union to which are tied the conventional plants of Upper and Lower Egypt. On each side of the base of the throne are small statuettes of Ramesses. The King himself stands in front of the shrine pouring a libation from a golden vase. Behind the shrine stands a goddess; the upper part of her head is destroyed, but her chin, which is that of a lion, remains and serves to identify her as Tefnut.

The Eastern Wall.

Again, all the figures on this wall are headless, but at the southern end a god and a goddess clasp Ramesses by the hands and lead him into the presence of In-hert. At each end of the scene stands a goddess holding a notched palm branch.
The second scene shows Ramesses adoring In-hert and a goddess both of whom are seated in a golden shrine. The colors on this wall are exceptionally well preserved.

The Western Wall of the First Hypostyle Hall.

To return again to the First Hypostyle Hall, the first scene on the northern end of the wall (in the upper part) showed Ramesses kneeling beside the Tree of Life of Heliopolis. In front of him was "Ptah, Lord of Truth," and another god

Fig. 23-2. The lower part of a procession of the sacred standard of Abydos. Below, Nile Gods and personified cultivated lands. The First Hypostyle Hall, southern wall. The Temple of Ramesses II.

who says, "I write thy cartouche with mine own fingers; thy name is inscribed anew in Heaven like that of Sah (Orion), in the Hau boat."

The god is of course writing the King's name on the leaves of the Tree of Life. But only the lower part of this magnificent scene has survived.

The next scene, of which again only the lower part remains, showed Ramesses (wearing sandals!) standing in the presence of a mummiform god.

Underneath these scenes is a well-preserved and brightly colored dado of kneeling Nile Gods.

In the center of the western wall is a large doorway opening into the Second Hypostyle Hall, but no inscriptions or scenes now remain on its sandstone jambs.

On the southern half of the western wall, only a mere fragment of the upper scene remains, but the dado of Nile Gods is preserved.

The Southern Wall of the First Hypostyle Hall.

The upper scene on the southern wall seems to have been of a procession like that on the northern wall. However, all that remains are the feet of a number of men.

Below is a dado of Nile Gods and the personifications of the cultivated lands. (Fig. 23-2).

The Staircase.

At the western end of the wall is a narrow staircase just over one meter (3 feet) wide which originally led up to the roof of the temple. Only twelve steps are preserved.

218

CHAPTER TWENTY-FOUR

RAMESSES BECOMES ONE OF THE GODS

The Second Hypostyle Hall of the Temple of Ramesses II.

The Second Hypostyle Hall, like the First, had its roof supported by eight sandstone pillars. Nine chapels open out of this hall, three in each of the southern, northern and western walls, and with the exception of the Alabaster Sanctuary, all their walls are decorated in colored bas-relief and bear the early prenomen of Ramesses, User-maat-Ra.

The Eastern Wall of the Second Hypostyle Hall.

The southern half of the eastern wall is very badly preserved, and all that remains on it are the feet and legs of Ramesses and some deities.

The northern half of the wall has fared little better, but on it is part of a scene which represented the divine creation of Ramesses to which he lays claim in the dedication text on the facade of the Temple of Sety and again on the southern wall of the First Hypostyle Hall of the same building (see page 18). At the northern end of the scene Ramesses as a small, naked boy, stands upon a rectangular pedestal. He has been modelled like a clay statue by the God Khnum who is seated behind him, and he is now being colored by another god who sits in front of him. A goddess wearing a red robe stands behind the latter.

Behind Khnum are the legs and feet of four goddesses almost certainly forms of Hathor waiting to receive the divine child. Like the "Fairy Godmothers" of western folk tales, each goddess bestows a blessing on the little Prince. The first gives him "all endurance and prosperity." The second bestows "all life, like Ra." The third gives "all gladness of heart," and the fourth gives the great blessing of "all health."

At the southern end of the scene are the feet of a woman who was seated upon a throne. This may have represented Tuy, the mother of Ramesses.

The Northern Wall of the Second Hypostyle Hall.

Most of this wall is occupied by the doorways of the chapels dedicated to Thot, Min and Osiris. All these doorways have their lintels and jambs inscribed with the titles and names of Ramesses. The eastern sides of the doorways, against which the single door-leaf opened, are incised to represent a wooden door as in the Chapel of In-hert with inscriptions between each crossbar. The western sides of the doorways all have four vertical rows of inscriptions of which the last is the dedication text. Each chapel measures about 5.5 meters (18 feet) long and 2.6 meters (8.5 feet) wide.

The Chapel of Thot.

This is the eastern-most of the three chapels. The dedication text on the western side of the doorway affirms its attribution to the God Thot.

The Western Wall of the Chapel of Thot.

At the southern end of the western wall is a fine and well-preserved scene showing Ramesses burning incense in front of the God Nun who was one of the important deities worshiped along with Thot at Khemenu which is the modern Ashmunein (Fig. 24-1). Behind Nun is his speech to Ramesses in which he says, "I am the father of thy fathers; behold, I am in the chapel, concerned with enlarging thy state more than that of the kings of Upper Egypt, the ancestors of former times. I grant to thee eternity as King, raising thee up even as thou hast made great the gods." The upper part of the second and third scenes is destroyed.

The Northern Wall of the Chapel of Thot.

A massive offering bench still stands at the base of the northern wall. It originally continued for about 2.5 meters (8.2 feet) along the western and eastern walls, but except for one block these projections have vanished. The scene on this

Fig. 24-1. The God Nun (detail). The Chapel of Thot. Western wall. The Temple of Ramesses II.

wall has lost its upper part. It showed Ramesses anointing Thot who, in the form of a mummy, sits in a golden shrine.

A goddess stands behind Thot. No inscriptions are preserved.

The Eastern Wall of the Chapel of Thot.

The northernmost scene on this wall shows Ramesses presenting the image of Maat to Osiris.

In the middle scene, Ramesses offers a conical loaf of white bread to Horus. The face, hands and right arm of the King have been wantonly effaced with some pointed tool.

The third scene shows the King offering wine to Ra-Hor-akhty behind whom stands a goddess.

The part of the northern wall of the Second Hypostyle Hall which is immediately to the west of the Chapel of Thot bore a scene showing Ramesses embracing a mummiform god. This cannot be Osiris as his hands are colored red.

The Chapel of Min.

The Chapel of Min is the central one in the row. The dedication text on the western side of its doorway says that Ramesses "made it as his monument for his father Min."

The Western Wall of the Chapel of Min.

At the southern end of the western wall, Ramesses offers incense before six sacred standards and the portable statue of a god. The standards seem to be regarded as incarnations of the gods to whom they are dedicated as we may see by their accompanying inscriptions. The first standard is of Wepwawat and is surmounted by a jackal standing upon a cobra. The God says, "I give to thee the lands in their full extent with all life and prosperity from me."

The second standard is that of Thot, but the ibis which should have surmounted it is destroyed. He says to Ramesses, "I reckon for thee millions of years of jubilees from me."

The third standard is of Horus, but again the top is missing. He says, "I give to thee all valor and victory from me."

The tops of the remaining standards, as well as the beginnings of the inscriptions are all destroyed, but they promise Ramesses "hundreds of thousands of years," also "all lands in satisfaction," and "all nomes, cities and deserts" (Fig. 24-2).

The Northern Wall of the Chapel of Min.

An offering bench stands at the base of the northern wall, and the scene above it depicts Ramesses anointing the God Min with perfumed ointment. Between the King and the God are two rows of an inscription in enigmatic writing. The signs, which are beautifully drawn and colored, are also larger than usual. Behind Min stands a goddess, but her name is lost.

The Eastern Wall of the Chapel of Min.

The southern part of the eastern wall had a large scene showing Ramesses burning incense and pouring a libation in front of the sacred boat of Min. The upper part of the boat is destroyed, but the prow-post terminates in a papyrus umbel. The boat has the usual crew of kingly statuettes (Fig. 24-3).

Behind the boat is

Fig. 24-2. Chapel of Min. Western wall. The name of the temple and good wishes to Ramesses. Left: "I give to thee all lands in satisfaction." Right" "I give to thee all nomes, cities, deserts." The Temple of Ramesses II.

the lower part of the figure of a goddess.

The scene on the northern part of the wall is almost completely destroyed, and no scenes remain on that part of the northern wall of the Second Hypostyle Hall that lies to the west of the

Chapel of Min.

The Chapel of Osiris.

This is the westernmost of the three chapels, and the dedication text in its doorway reads: "He made it as his monument for his father Osiris, the

Fig. 24-3. *The prow of the sacred boat of Min. The Chapel of Min. Eastern wall. The Temple of Ramesses II.*

Lord of Abydos, making for him a chapel for the Company of Gods who are in it (Abydos) that he may give him life."

The Western Wall of the Chapel of Osiris.

At the southern end of the western wall is a very well-preserved group showing Horus conducting Ramesses into the chapel. The colors in this scene are as brilliant as on the day that they were applied and give us a glimpse of the extraordinary splendor which these temples of the New Kingdom must have presented in their heyday (Fig. 24-4).

Ramesses wears a brilliant blue war helmet. The upper part of his body is clad in a short vest of very fine transparent linen dotted with small, white spots very similar to modern spotted Swiss voile! It is fastened by tieing its lower ends into a simple knot in front. Over this are two falcons with outspread wings apparently made of gold inlaid with turquoise and lapis lazuli. These are arranged so that their bodies lie against the King's sides, and their outspread wings cross each other over his chest and back.[1] Ramesses wears the military kilt (or is it priestly?), and an overdress of fine linen caught in at the hips by the usual royal belt and

[1] Similar ornaments to these with jointed, flexible wings were among the treasures of Tutankh-Amon and are now in the Cairo Museum.

its ornamental apron. He also wears a wide collar of gold, turquoise and lapis lazuli, and wide, golden bracelets. Altogether, a handsome young man in a handsome costume!

Horus walks ahead of the King but turns his head and upper body to face him. He holds a small Key of Life to the royal nose. The God wears the Double Crown and a turquoise colored tunic with a golden belt.

Next is a doorway leading into the northern Statue Hall after which is another scene of which only the lower part remains. It shows Ramesses as dead and identified with Osiris. A goddess stands behind him supporting his left elbow, and in front of him was an Iwn-mut-ef priest of whom only the

222

Fig. 24-4. *Northwestern Chapel of Osiris (western wall). Ramesses and Horus. Note the robes of Ramesses as he receives the Key of Life and is ushered into the chapel Holy Place (see text). Temple of Ramesses II.*

legs and one paw of his leopard skin remain.

offering bench shows Osiris in the form of a living god clad in a golden corselet and seated in a shrine. He holds a notched palm branch from which dangles the Heb-sed emblem. In his right hand are the symbols of Life, Endurance and Prosperity attached to short cords. Behind the King stands a goddess who is embracing him.

The Eastern Wall of the Chapel of Osiris.

At the southern end of the eastern wall is a large figure of Ramesses performing the Heb-sed sprint. He wears the crown of Lower Egypt and the Shendyt kilt. In his right hand are three golden libation vases joined together, and in his left hand are three similar vases, but the bases of these end in a clump of papyrus reeds. Behind the King are the objects traditionally associated with this ceremony.

The sculpture of the King's figure is of the same high standard displayed in all the reliefs in this temple, but the painting is appallingly bad! Not only are the brush marks clearly visible, but in many places the color has gone over the edge of the relief and onto the background. Compare this with the beautiful and careful work on the opposite wall, and you immediately feel that two different hands painted them.

The scene on the northern end of the wall

The Northern Wall of the Chapel of Osiris.

The scene above the

shows Osiris with Isis and Horus standing in a shrine. In front of Osiris is a large, golden lotus flower on which stand mummiform figures of the Four Sons of Horus. The lotus is supported by a statuette of the King. Next come some golden offering stands followed by a Mert goddess who raises her arms and cries, "Come and bring, come and bring, come and bring!" She is followed by two rows of geneii three to each row. Those above are almost completely destroyed, but the lower row are falcon-headed, and each clutches a large golden libation vase to his breast. These are the Souls of Pe and Nekhen.

The Western Wall of the Second Hypostyle Hall.

At the northern end of this wall is the lower part of a scene showing the King embraced by a goddess. After this are the lower parts of the jambs of the doorway of the first northern chapel which seems to have been dedicated to Amon-Ra.

The Chapel of Amon-Ra.

On the southern side of the doorway is a well-preserved figure of the God Thot. He carries his writing kit in his left hand and raises the right one as he addresses the King, promising to protect the palace, to cause his son to love him, and to banish his enemies.

In the southern inner jamb of the doorway is a headless figure of Ramesses. He was performing the rite of "removing the footprints" and carries a broom and a libation vase.

The Southern Wall.

Here is a scene showing Ramesses making offerings to a sacred boat, but unfortunately the top of the scene is destroyed though the colors on the remaining parts are well-preserved. Under the hind carrying-poles are three sacred standards of Isis, Ra-Hor-akhty and Wepwawat which promise the King "all life, prosperity and endurance, like Ra," and "all health, like Ra," and "all gladness of heart, like Ra."

The remainder of the wall was occupied by two registers of seated goddesses; three to each row, but the upper ones are almost totally destroyed. The first goddess in the lower register is Nut. She wears a golden Vulture crown which is topped by her name-signs. The toes are all that remain of the second figure while the third is totally destroyed.

The Western Wall.

At the base of the western wall is a well-preserved offering bench above which is a damaged scene showing Ramesses opening the door of a golden shrine in which is seated a god, almost certainly Amon-Ra. In front of him stood a goddess who wears a white robe over which is a network of red beads. Another god stands behind Amon-Ra, but all the figures are headless, and no inscriptions are preserved.

The Northern Wall.

The scenes here are practically the same as those on the southern wall. At the western end, the upper register of seated goddesses are nearly all destroyed, but the three in the lower register are well-preserved. They all wear golden Vulture crowns and carry scepters of Prosperity. The name of the first goddess is destroyed. She wears a red robe. The second is the Scorpion Goddess Serket who wears a turquoise colored robe, and she is followed by Hathor in a red robe (Fig. 24-5).

To the south of the doorway of the Chapel of Amon-Ra, the western wall of the Second Hypostyle Hall bears a damaged scene showing Ramesses conducted by two goddesses into the presence of Osiris. All the figures are headless, and no inscriptions are preserved.

Next comes the doorway of the Alabaster Sanctuary, but the sandstone jambs are badly damaged.

The Alabaster Sanctuary of Osiris.

This sanctuary measures nearly seven meters (23 feet) long and four and a quarter meters (14 feet) wide. In its original state, it must have been one of the most beautiful

Fig. 24-5. Chapel of Amon-Ra, northern wall. The Goddesses Serket and Hathor. Temple of Ramesses II.

sanctuaries in Egypt both by reason of the materials used in its construction, and the very distinguished, restrained taste displayed in its decoration. Incidently, it is accurately described in the building inscription on the southern exterior wall of the temple.

The base of the walls, to a height of one meter (3 feet), is of deep red quartzite sandstone. Above this, the remainder of the walls are of fine alabaster,

sculptured in incised relief and having the details picked out in dark blue and turquoise paint. The roof was of red granite, and at the time of writing, its broken blocks lie on the desert to the west of the temple, but very little effort is needed to restore it. The pavement, now destroyed, was of alabaster as is the threshold of the doorway.

The Southern Wall of the Alabaster Sanctuary.

Most of the upper part of this wall is destroyed; all that remains of its decorations is part of a horizontal inscription. Even this is hidden by a group of black granite statues wrongly placed here in recent times.

The Western Wall of the Alabaster Sanctuary.

The center of the western wall is occupied by a beautiful false-door of alabaster, sculptured with scenes in bas-relief, and incised inscriptions, the hieroglyphs are colored light and dark blue. The door's upper part is destroyed. This monument is supposed to represent a double-leaved door, but it is highly conventionalized. The two door-leaves bear scenes showing Ramesses embracing Osiris. The surface has a smooth, satiny finish. The inscriptions on the frame of the doorway seem to have described the chapel, but all that we can gather from the damaged condition is that something was made of lapis lazuli with a door of electrum.

An Unexpected Discovery.

The false-door stands upon a block of red granite, and at the time when the Antiquities Department first began to make some restorations to this temple, the granite block was tilted forward causing the false-door to fall face down into the sanctuary.

225

While digging to make a more secure foundation for the granite block, the body of a young girl was found only about 70 centimeters (28 inches) below the level of the floor of the sanctuary. The body, little more than a skeleton, lay in a crouching position and wore a string of small, carnelian beads around the neck. Perhaps there was a pre-dynastic cemetery in this site, and when Ramesses decided to erect his temple here they preferred to build right over it rather than disturb the burials. Reverence for the dead was an age-old tradition deeply rooted in the Egyptian's subconscious.

To the south of the false-door the western wall is entirely destroyed, but to the north is a scene of the Nile Gods of Upper and Lower Egypt tieing the lily and papyrus to the symbol of Union.

Below this is the commencement of a horizontal inscription which continues onto the northern wall where it is destroyed just at the part where it starts to become interesting!

The Northern Wall of the Sanctuary.

The eastern end of this wall is completely destroyed so far as the decoration is concerned. The central part bears a damaged representation of the standard of Abydos of which however, only its characteristic pedestal and the carrying-poles remain. To the west are

two registers of standing deities, those in the upper register being incomplete, but those in the lower register are much better preserved. The first from the east is Nepthys after whom comes a god with the head of a heron. His name is Keky, the God of the Primeval Darkness who was worshiped at Khemenu. The fourth god also has the head of a heron, and his name is Her-ef-em-khuu (Fig. 24-6).

At the western end of the wall, a damaged scene appears to have shown Ramesses dedicating a statue of himself to a goddess.

Below these scenes is the continuation of the horizontal inscription. Most of the remaining part consists of the titles and names of Ramesses. It then says, "He made it as his monument for his father Osiris, the Lord of Abydos, making for him a great chapel, its walls..." For our bad luck, the rest of it is destroyed!

The Roof of the Sanctuary.

The roof of the sanctuary was composed of four massive blocks of red granite, each measuring about 6.3 meters (21 feet) long and 1.8 meter (5.9 feet) wide. These were laid crosswise between the northern and southern walls, and oblique openings cut in their undersides admitted light and air. A single vertical line of inscription ran down the underside of the roof. After giving

the royal titles it reads: "He made it as his monument for his father Osiris, making for him a great chapel of pure alabaster; it is roofed with granite..." Here the inscription is destroyed.

Apparently this sanctuary was not completed until Ramesses was reigning alone because on the roof, as well as on the frame of the false-door, the King's prenomen has the simple form of User-maat-Ra, but in the horizontal inscription on the walls, the later form with Setep-en-Ra is used. Also the style of the reliefs on the walls are quite different from that of the rest of the temple. The figures are all tall and slender and are not so well done. They compare most unfavorably with the beautiful work on the false-door.

The Granite Statue Group.

This group of statues, all of which are life-sized, was found in fragments, scattered all over the temple, and many pieces are still missing. It was reassembled by the Antiquities Department as far as possible and placed in its present position against the southern wall of the Alabaster Sanctuary, but its original place was against the western wall of the Chapel of Sety I (see page 209). The group represents the Gods Osiris, Isis and Horus, with the deceased Sety and (of course!) the inevitable Ramesses. All are seated together on a long bench;

the high back of which
serves to support the figures and their crowns (Fig.
24-7).

Osiris occupies the
central position in the
group and to his right is
Horus; the upper part of
whose figure is totally
destroyed, but his name
is inscribed on the back
of the seat. To the right
of Horus is Ramesses, but
all that remains of him
are the left half of his
face and part of his Double
Crown. To the left of
Osiris sits Isis whose figure is better preserved.
She embraces Osiris with
her right arm. Her face
is perfectly preserved
except for some slight
damage to the nose, and
she wears a calm, thoughtful expression. Her fig-
ure is gracefully modelled
with round, firm breasts
and a slender waist, softly
rounded arms and graceful
shoulders. It is really
wonderful how the sculptor
had succeeded in imparting
life and giving the ef-
fect of soft living flesh
to the hard, unyielding
black granite. And let
us not forget that he had
only copper tools with
which to work! To the
left of Isis is King Sety
whose figure is the best
preserved in the group.
Except for the nose, his
face is undamaged, but it
is not quite a faithful
portrait of the handsome
King. The modelling of
the body and shoulders is
very good, but the face
is too round and plump.
It is clear that the sculptor had not given this figure the same reverent care

Fig. 24-6. *The northern wall of the Alabaster Sanctuary.*

that he had bestowed on
that of Isis.

On the western wall
of the Second Hypostyle
Hall, to the south of the
Alabaster Sanctuary, is
a scene similar to that
on the northern side, but
here it is two gods who
conduct Ramesses into the
presence of Osiris.

Next comes the door-
way of the southernmost
chapel in the row. It is
not certain to whom it
was dedicated as the in-
scriptions are damaged,
but from the speech of
Ramesses recorded on the
southern side of the door-

Fig. 24-7. *The black granite statue group seen from above.
Going from left to right, the profiles of Ramesses, Horus,
Osiris, Isis and Sety I. The Alabaster Sanctuary (Note
that Ramesses and Sety I are included as gods in this
group in the Holy Sanctuary.). Temple of Ramesses II.*

way, it may be the Chapel
of Horus. Here the King
is shown, censer in hand,
reciting the offering formula, which is inscribed
in front of him, on behalf
of Horus.

The Southern Wall of the
Chapel of Horus.

Very little remains
of this wall; in fact the
western end is destroyed
down to floor level.

The Western Wall.

Above the damaged of-
fering bench is the lower
part of a scene showing
Ramesses conducted by a
god (probably Horus) into
the presence of an enthroned
deity who seems to be Osiris-
Andjty. Behind the latter
was a goddess.

The Northern Wall.

The easternmost scene
on this wall seems to have
shown Ramesses making of-
ferings to a sacred boat
of which only the carrying-
poles remain. The scene at
the end of the wall is very
interesting. Here were
two registers of deities
three to each row, and all
of whom were seated. In
the upper register, the
name of the first god is
missing. The second fig-
ure is that of the Goddess
Hekat who is usually shown
in the form of a frog or a
frog-headed woman. But
here she appears as a dainty
little lady wearing the
Vulture crown on her human
head and clad in a white
robe bound by a red sash.
It is only her inscription

"Hekat, Mistress of Abydos"
that tells us that the
homely frog has become here
a beautiful queen.

The third god is also
in full human form. But
we are in for another surprise, for the inscription
tells us that he is "Anubis,
Lord of the Sacred Land."
So far as we know, this is
the only example of Anubis
with a human head; usually
he is shown as a jackal-
headed man or as a jackal.
Even here, the small hieroglyph determing his name
is that of a seated jackal-
headed man.

The scene on the
western wall of the Second
Hypostyle Hall to the
south of the Chapel of
Horus is like that at the
extreme northern end, and
showed Ramesses embracing
Osiris, but only the feet
and legs of the figures
remain.

The Southern Wall of the
Second Hypostyle Hall.

The southern wall of
the Second Hypostyle Hall
and also the chapels
which lead out of it are
very badly damaged.

At the extreme west-
ern end of the wall is the
doorway of a chapel, but
we cannot say to whom it
was dedicated as only the
lower parts of all the
scenes and inscriptions
remain. In its western
wall is a doorway leading
into the southern Statue
Hall.

To the east of this
chapel, the damaged scene
on the southern wall of
the Second Hypostyle Hall
shows only the feet of

Ramesses and a mummiform
god.

Next comes the door-
way of the central chapel
of the row which seems to
have been dedicated to
Osiris as the damaged scene
above the offering bench
on the southern wall showed
Ramesses offering to this
god behind whom stood Isis.

The Southern Chapel of
Osiris.

With the exception
of the scene on the southern wall just mentioned,
little is left of the
decoration of this chapel,
but the remnants of a
scene on the eastern wall
are interesting.

At the southern end
of the wall are the red
legs of a seated god;
Ramesses was standing in
front of him, and behind
the latter, part of a
horizontal text reads,
"...neck, real jewelry
from the things of the
equipment gathered from
the storehouse..." This
seems to refer to the ornaments placed upon the
statues of the gods in the
daily cult ceremonies.

The scene on the
southern wall of the hall
to the east of the Chapel
of Osiris also showed
Ramesses and a mummified
god.

The Clothing Room.

The last chapel in
the southern row had a
double identity, for the
dedication text on the
eastern side of its door-
way says that Ramesses
made it as "his monument

for his father Osiris Khenty-Amentiu, who dwells in the 'House of Ramesses Mery-Amon Who Enriches the Abydos Nome,' making for him a room for clothing, for veiling the limbs of the God."

This shows that the chamber was used in connection with the clothing of the divine statues in the daily cult ceremonies. Apparently the bulk of the clothing was stored in the still unexcavated magazines behind the temple, but the garments needed for the daily reclothing of the statues were brought here and laid out on the stone benches, that once stood at the foot of its southern and eastern walls, from whence they could be taken by the priests as required.

The Western Wall of the Clothing Room.

Here is the lower part of a scene which seems to have shown a number of priests bringing clothing and equipment. They are supervised by Ramesses who was, of course, drawn upon a much larger scale. A damaged inscription refers to some sistrums. In front of the legs of a group of priests is the injunction, "Take for thyself this thy beautiful clothing which is given by King User-maat-Ra."

In the next scene, Ramesses was presenting strips of red and yellow cloth to a god. The head and shoulders of the King are missing, and the figure of the god has entirely disappeared. In front of Ramesses is the lower part of an inscription which refers to a goddess called "Weaver of Clothing."

The Southern Wall.

The base of the southern wall is still occupied by a stone offering bench.

Above the offering bench is the lower part of a scene in which Ramesses offers strips of linen to Osiris and Isis while Horus stands behind him.

The Eastern Wall.

This wall is better preserved, and bears two scenes. At the southern end of the wall Ramesses offers strips of cloth to Amon-Ra. Between them are the ends of ten lines of inscription concerning the offering of clothing. Apparently the God is finally requested to grant to Ramesses "everything which he desires in this day of clothing Amon-Ra."

The scene on the northern end of the wall shows a large, well-preserved figure of the King who holds a libation vase and a jar of perfume. In front of him we see that the scene is divided into two registers; the upper one of which preserves only the small scale legs of a number of priests. Between the two registers is a horizontal inscription.

In the lower register four priests are carrying a golden chest that is shaped like a shrine. In addition to its carrying-poles, the chest is also mounted upon a sledge so that if necessary, it could be dragged along. The priests who are all dressed alike in white kilts and stoles walk in pairs before and behind the chest, and over their heads is the totally unnecessary inscription: "Holding the carrying-poles."

Underneath the chest is inscribed: "The procession of clothing to the Great Chapel."

Next come two more priests who carry menat necklaces to Thot who stands in front of them. The first priest cries, "Purify the Necropolis! The God comes protecting the land." To which his companion answers, "Thot! The God comes protecting the land!"

CHAPTER TWENTY-FIVE

THE TWO STATUE HALLS

The Northern Statue Hall.

As mentioned above (page 222) a door in the western wall of the northern Chapel of Osiris opens into the northern Statue Hall. This hall measure about 8.0 meters (26 feet) from south to north and about 7.0 meters (23 feet) from east to west. Its roof was supported by two rectangular pillars of sandstone; the upper parts of which bore the large representations of Osiris and the Djed Pillar. In each of the southern, western and northern walls are three niches in front of which is a broad stone shelf for offerings. All the decorations in this hall are in bas-relief, and much of their brilliant coloring is preserved.

The Eastern Wall of the Northern Statue Hall.

The eastern wall is divided into two halves by the entrance, but both halves bear large scenes showing Ramesses dedicating statues (of himself) and making an offering of perfume. In both scenes the statues are colored a grayish-green to denote that they were made of schist, and some of them stand on rectangular blocks of alabaster; the markings of which have been very cleverly imitated.

At the northern and southern ends of the scenes are guardian geneii holding large knives and seated on the floor. Some have the heads of baboons while others have the heads of lions or cats.

The Southern Wall of the Northern Statue Hall.

The niches for statues have an average measurement of 1.6 meter (5.3 feet) wide, 1.3 meter (4.3 feet) deep, and 1.7 meter (5.6 feet) high. The jambs of all of them bear two vertical lines of inscription in brightly colored signs giving the King's titles and names and claiming that he is beloved by certain deities. But these divine names do not always coincide with the gods to whom Ramesses is shown making offerings on all the walls of the niches.

For example, the deities mentioned on the jambs of the eastern niche are "Ptah-Soker who dwells in Shetyt" (a district of Memphis), also "Wepwawat, Lord of the Sacred Land," and "Horus, the son of Osiris." But on the eastern wall of the niche, Ramesses burns incense to Hathor. On the southern wall, he offers a tray laden with four small cups to Wepwawat, and on the western wall, only the lower part of the scene remains, but there is enough to show that he was offering to a goddess. The most interesting niches in this hall are the following:

The Western Niche of the Southern Wall.

The gods mentioned on the jambs are "Osiris, Lord of the Sacred Land," and "Horus, the son of Isis," and "Osiris, Lord of Eternity," and "Isis the Great."

On the southern wall of the niche, Ramesses offers perfume to Horus-Merhy who has the head of a bull.

The Western Wall of the Northern Statue Hall, the Southern Niche.

The jambs bear the names of Osiris, Wepwawat, Min and Isis. Min appears on the northern wall of the niche where he receives the adoration of Ramesses. The figures on the western and southern walls are damaged, but both deities were male.

The Central Niche.

On the western wall of the central niche in the western wall of the hall, Osiris is seen being anointed by Ramesses while the King offers wine to a goddess (incomplete) on the northern wall.

The Northern Wall of the Northern Statue Hall.

This wall is not at all well-preserved and the scenes in its niches are so badly damaged that the deities cannot be identified.

Fig. 25-1. *The southern Statue Hall (western wall of the southwestern niche). Ramesses anointing Osiris behind whom is a winged Djed Pillar. The Temple of Ramesses II.*

The Southern Statue Hall.

This Statue Hall is reached through a door in the western wall of the unidentified western chapel opening out of the southern wall of the Second Hypostyle Hall. It resembles the northern Statue Hall in every respect, but it is not so well-preserved.

The Eastern Wall of the Southern Statue Hall.

There is an offering bench along the base of this wall, but the scenes above it are too badly damaged to be identified. The most interesting niches are the following:

The Northern Wall of the Southern Statue Hall.

The inscriptions on the central niche are destroyed, and the scenes on its walls are badly damaged. Isis and Osiris are mentioned on the eastern jamb of the western niche, but again the scenes are very badly damaged.

The Western Wall of the Southern Statue Hall.

Isis may be the goddess to whom Ramesses offers perfume on the northern wall, but the interesting and well-preserved scene is on the western wall.

Here Ramesses is anointing Osiris with perfumed ointment. Behind the God stands a large Djed Pillar which has a pair of multi-colored wings. These droop forward in an attitude of protection for Osiris (Fig. 25-1).

The winged Djed Pillar may be seen in some of the highly decorated wooden coffins of the XXIst through XXIIIrd dynasties, but so far as we know, this representation is the earliest of its kind. There is however, a badly damaged example in the upper register of scenes on the western wall of the great Osiris Hall in the Temple of Sety.

The western niche in the southern wall of the hall is also worth notice. The gods mentioned on the jambs are Ptah, Tefnut, Mut and Monthu. Tefnut appears again with Ramesses on the western wall of the niche, and on the southern wall, Ptah receives a tray laden with four small cups from the King. The mummiform god on the eastern wall is badly damaged.

On the western wall of the central niche, we see Ramesses in the costume of an Iwn-mut-ef priest, and he seems to be offering perfume to Min.

Fig. 26-1. The Egyptian army. Note the fly-fringes on the horse's browbands. Western exterior wall. The Temple of Ramesses II.

CHAPTER TWENTY-SIX

BATTLES, MERCENARIES AND MERCY

The Exterior Walls of the Temple.

As we may expect, the exterior walls of the temple bore a version of the famous story of the Battle of Kadesh. The scenes and inscriptions of this campaign are on the northern and western walls, and it is very unfortunate that the ruin of these walls has destroyed the upper parts of all the scenes, as what remains are in a beautiful, incised relief, full of lively movement and interesting details. The remaining scenes are really a kind of dado in which are depicted the Egyptian troops, their enemies, and some of the incidents in the campaign.

Running along the entire length of both the western and northern walls is a band of zigzag lines. This represents the river Orontes on the banks of which most of the battle took place. Above this come rows of men, horses and chariots in various stages of action. In some places the massed line of galloping horses succeed in conveying an effect of rapid, forward movement which surpasses in effect the more perfect sculpture of the famous equestrian frieze of the Parthenon at Athens.

The racial characteristics of the Egyptians and their enemies are also well-defined. The Egyptian troops are invariably shown as handsome, well-groomed young men with stylish haircuts and trim uniforms. But all foreigners, even the Sharden mercenaries

Fig. 26-2. On the top: Beating the enemy's spies. On the bottom: Some of the Sharden mercenary guardsmen. The western exterior wall. The Temple of Ramesses II.

axes. They are met by more Egyptian chariots galloping southwards. After this comes a break in the wall of about three and a half meters (11 feet).

The next scene represented the temporary Egyptian camp, "on the northwest of Kadesh," where two spies in the Hittites' pay were captured and brought before Ramesses for interrogation, and where, after a good beating, they revealed the position of the enemy (Fig. 26-2).

Outside the camp (in the lower register) is the waiting chariot of Ramesses (Fig. 26-3). A unique feature is the sunshade with a gay, scalloped border which is fixed to the front rail of the chariot. With no seat, and innocent of springs, the Egyptian chariot cannot have been a very comfortable vehicle in which to make long journeys over uneven roads, and we must compliment Ramesses for making use of this small contribution to comfort. He could put up with the jolting, but he did not intend to get sunstroke!

Sharden Mercenaries.

The camp of Ramesses was guarded by Sharden mercenaries. They wear helmets not unlike the "tin hats" of modern warfare, but these are surmounted by round knobs and a pair of horns (Fig. 26-4). They are armed with long, double-edged swords, and carry round shields.

in Egypt's pay, are figures of fun though their racial types are faithfully rendered. The Hittites with their hair in pigtails, and their empty, stupid-looking faces, their Semitic allies, hook-nosed and bush bearded with heavy, clumsy garments, provoked the contempt and ridicule of the Egyptian artists, and these figures are, in a way, the ancestors of all modern political caricatures.

The Western Exterior Wall.

At the southern end of the western wall is a massed array of Egyptian troops, both chariotry and infantry, marching northwards (Fig. 26-1). The chariot horses all have fringes on their browbands to protect their eyes from the annoyance of flies. Next infantrymen carry large shields and are armed with spears, daggers, and curved battle-

Fig. 26-3. *The chariot of Ramesses. Note the sunshade fixed to the front rail! The western exterior wall. The Temple of Ramesses II.*

enjoying their job! The inscription accompanying the scene reads: "The arrival of the scout of Pharaoh (life, prosperity, health to him!). He is bringing the two spies of the Vanquished One (the King of the Hittites) into the presence of Pharaoh (life, prosperity, health to him), and they are beating them to make them tell where is the Chief of Kheta."[1]

The Hittite Chariots.

At the northern end of the wall are shown some incidents in the battle. A troop of Hittite chariotry charges into the fray. The chariots and the harness of the horses are similar to those of the Egyptian army, but each car carries three men, a charioteer, a shield-bearer, and a warrior (Fig. 26-5); whereas the Egyptian chariots carry only a charioteer and a warrior. As the long inscription says, every Hittite chariot carries a Hittite and members of their allies.

Their features look Irish, but they are believed to be Sardinians.

Some Spies are "Questioned."

The scene of the beating of the spies is somewhat damaged, but obviously the artist had relished working on it. The miserable spies kneel and cringe before some Egyptian soldiers who, armed with canes, beat them with impassive thoroughness. The artist has given free rein to his sense of humor in the contrast between the violent contortions and woebegone faces of the luckless spies, and the serene and cheerful expressions of the Egyptians, decorous in the presence of Pharaoh, but obviously

Hand-to-hand Combat.

There are also some fine, spirited groups of hand-to-hand combat in which, of course, the enemy is always the one who comes to grief! The southernmost group shows an Egyptian archer apparently caught unawares by the sudden attack upon the Egyptian

Fig. 26-4. *The Sharden mercenaries (detail). The western exterior wall. The Temple of Ramesses II.*

[1]"Kheta" is the Egyptian name for Hatti or Hittite.

camp. He had no time or perhaps no space to use his bow, and seizing a Hittite by the hair proceeds to bash his brains out with a club (Fig. 26-6).

Another Hittite meets his fate at the hands of a Sharden guard who stabs him with a dagger; another enemy meets the same fate at the hands of an Egyptian who is armed with a spear (Fig. 26-7).

The northernmost group shows a Sharden busily hacking off the hand of a dead enemy which he will turn in after the battle to be among those counted by the military scribes (Fig. 26-8). In this group the artist has cleverly contrasted the vigorous, active figure of the Sharden with the flaccid corpse of the enemy.

The Northern Exterior Wall.

Apparently the western end of the northern wall bore a large scene showing Ramesses in the thick of the battle, but the whole of the upper part of this scene is lost. All that remain are the dead and wounded enemies and their unfortunate horses who were hurled into the river by the superhuman force of the young King's charge. One of the enemy casualties is inscribed: "Tigannasa, the charioteer of the Fallen One of Kheta." By the looks of the man, the Hittite King had no choice but to get himself a new driver!

At the eastern end

Fig. 26-5. Chariots of the Hittites and their allies. The northern exterior wall. The Temple of Ramesses II.

of the scene some Hittite soldiers on the banks of the river are trying to rescue some of their comrades from the water (Fig. 26-9). One man tries feebly to swim ashore, and his friend on the bank puts his hand under his chin to support his head. Other Hittites are dragging out a man who is either dead or unconscious. The inscription tells us that he is "Sapathara, the brother of the Fallen One of Kheta."

Fig. 26-6. An Egyptian soldier kills an enemy in han-to-hand combat (left). Egyptian infantrymen armed with battle-axes and shields (right). The western exterior wall. The Temple of Ramesses II.

Fig. 26-7. *Hand-to-hand combat. Right: A Sharden stabs a Hittite. Center: An Egyptian spears a Hittite. The western exterior wall. The Temple of Ramesses II.*

The Unlucky King of Aleppo.

Behind the rescuers is a massed array of Hittite soldiers among whom a group of four have rescued the half-drowned King of Aleppo. They are giving him first aid by holding him upside-down in the hope that he will disgorge the water that he has swallowed (Fig. 26-10). The bedraggled figure of the luckless King whose closed eyes, gaping mouth and limp arms testify to his plight, is made still more undignified by his long, wet hair that

Fig. 26-8. *Scenes of hand-to-hand combat. Left: A Sharden cuts off the hand of a dead enemy. Right: An Egyptian spears a Hittite. The western exterior wall.*

hangs in dripping "rattails.

Ramesses Surrounded!

The next scene shows Ramesses and his charioteer Menna completely surrounded by the enemy who is described as "warriors of Thaperath, and chariots of the Fallen One of Kheta" (Fig. 26-11). The upper part of the group representing Ramesses and Menna is destroyed. Menna is driving the horses while Ramesse bends down to take his bow from a case hanging on the side of the chariot.

To the east of this scene is the Hittite camp situated on a tract of land lying between the Orontes and its tributary now known as the Brook El Mukadiye. This is shown in the relief by a division in the band of zigzag lines; the lower band continuing horizontall along the bottom of the wal while the brook branches of in an upward curve (Fig. 26-12).

The Hittite Camp.

In the space between the two bands of zigzag lines are massed the armies of the Hittites and their allies. In the center are the baggage wagons with closed sides and four wheel each wagon is drawn by a pair of oxen with high, humped shoulders like Indian cattle, and having short, downward curving horns (Fig. 26-13).

The final large scene shows the fruits of victory where Ramesses receives the spoils of war and presides over the counting of hands

of the slain enemies. The
King sits informally on
the front rail of his chariot with his back to the
horses. The latter are
held by grooms while four
stable-lads massage their
legs (Fig. 26-14). In front
of Ramesses an inscription
reads: "A list of these
Asiatic countries slain
by His Majesty, all of
which he took with his
hands as the victory of
his sword alone: Hands
cut off, horses from the
chariots of this miserable
land of Kheta, chiefs,
chariots, bows, swords,
all weapons of war of the
foreign countries, coming
with the Fallen One of
Kheta as living prisoners."

*Fig. 26-10. (Below) The
brother of the Hittite
King rescued from the river
Orontes by his comrades
(upper right). The half-
drowned King of Aleppo
driven into the river by
Ramesses receives first
aid from his soldiers
(center)! He is held up-
side-down (see top). The
northern exterior wall.*

*Fig. 26-9. Enemy casualities fall into the river Orontes.
The northern exterior wall. The Temple of Ramesses II.*

"These are the Prisoners
of my Own Capture."

Below the group of
Ramesses in his chariot
are some Egyptian soldiers
marching to the sound of
a trumpet. With them
are some high officials
and a fan-bearer. In
front of them is an in-
scription explaining the
scene: "Behold! Bringing
in all the prisoners in
front of His Majesty,
those which he brought
off in the victory of his
sword in this miserable
land of Kheta. His Maj-
esty caused it to be an-
nounced to his infantry
and his chariotry saying,
'Behold! These are the
prisoners of my own cap-
ture while I was sole
Lord there being no in-
fantry with me, no of-
ficers with me, no char-
iotry!'"

In front of Ramesses
the scene is divided into
registers in each of which
military scribes have the

unpleasant task of count-
ing the hands of the enemy-
dead which are piled in
two heaps before them.
A man takes a hand from
one heap and when his
companion, armed with pen
and papyrus, has checked
it, throws it down on
the second heap (Fig. 26-
15).

The remainder of the
registers show Egyptian
officers and high officials
leading long lines of prisoners, captured horses
and chariots (Fig. 26-16).
One procession is headed
by a royal prince; he may
be one of the brothers of
Ramesses as the latter was
too young at that time to
have had a grown-up son of
his own.

The prisoners who
are of various racial
types have their arms
bound and are linked to-
gether by a cord passing
around the neck of each

237

Fig. 26-11. *Surrounded by the enemy troops, Ramesses draws his bow from its case. The charioteer Menna stands beside the King. The northern exterior wall. The Temple of Ramesses II.*

man. The artist yielding to his irresistible Egyptian sense of humor has permitted himself to have some fun with this scene. Some of the prisoners are struggling violently to escape, and Egyptian of-

ficers rush up and shake their canes at them (Fig. 26-17). But not only are the human prisoners giving trouble, for at the end of the lower register a spirited stallion kicks furiously with both hind

Fig. 26-12. *The Hittite camp. Note the baggage wagons drawn by humped oxen. Above, an ass carrying provisions and water. The northern exterior wall. The Temple of Ramesses II.*

legs. A display of temper which causes no concern to the imperturable Egyptian who leads it (Fig. 26-18).

The Account of the Battle.

The remainder of the eastern wall bears the lower end of one hundred and two lines of vertical inscription which gives an account of the battle. This is a version of the so-called "Poem of Pentaur"[2] of which there are other copies and from which we are able to restore most of it. The account opens by enumerating all the peoples who had made a sort of confederate alliance with the Hittites who were entrenched at Kadesh (Tel Nebi Mend?) in order to attack Egypt. These included the Kheta, who were the ringleaders of the trouble,[3] Naharina, Irthu (Aroad), Pidasa, Kedi Keshkesh, Kadesh, Ikarath, Mushenth, Arwena, Luka, Dardeny.

The Egyptian army with Ramesses consisted of four divisions besides his personal bodyguard and the Sharden mercenaries. The Egyptian divisions were named after the Gods Amon, Ra, Ptah and Set. "His Majesty led the way, every foreign country trembled

....
[2] Preserved on the Sallier Papyrus No. 1.
[3] As the text of the Temple of Ramesses is so badly damaged, the reconstruction is mostly taken from the Sallier Papyrus; the passages still preserved here being between quotation marks.

before him. His Majesty
proceeded northward."

Apparently Ramesses was
taking it easy, and his army
was strung out behind him
with a good distance between
each division. The two
captured spies at first
said that the Hittite King
had fled in terror before
Ramesses and had taken ref-
uge at Aleppo, but a good
thrashing made them change
their minds; the enemy was
now near at hand!

Ramesses is Trapped.

Actually, the enemies
were hidden "behind the
city of Kadesh; they being
prepared for battle."
Ramesses promptly gathered
his officers and opened a
council of war. But while
they were arguing the pros
and cons, the wily enemy
sneaked out and began to
attack the Egyptian camp.
They had already struck
at the Division of Ra
which was still straggling
along in the rear. They
fled in all directions
but sent a messenger to
tell the King of their
plight. "Then came one to
tell of it to His Majesty."
But Ramesses had enough
troubles of his own. The
enemy was now actually
inside his camp pillaging
and slaying! However if
Ramesses was one of the
world's worst generals,
from a purely tactical and
military standpoint, he
was decidedly a brave and
determined warrior of quite
an indomitable spirit.
"Then His Majesty arose
like Monthu.[4] He seized
....
[4]The Thebian War God.

Fig. 26-13. Ox-drawn baggage wagon in the Hittite camp.
Northern exterior wall. The Temple of Ramesses II.

his arms like Baal[5] in his
hour (of might). The great
horses of His Majesty
named Nakht-em-Wast and
Mut-Hotep were from the
royal stables. Then did
His Majesty dash on; he
....
[5]Baal of Syria was at this
time recognized in Egypt
where he was identified
with Set and regarded as
a God of War.

entered into the midst of
the foes of the Fallen One
of Kheta. He was alone by
himself; no other was with
him."

Ramesses Realizes his Plight.

When His Majesty turned
and looked behind him, he
found around him two thousand five hundred chariots
in his outward way and "all

Fig. 26-14. Grooms massaging the legs of Ramesses' chariot horses after the battle. The northern exterior wall.
The Temple of Ramesses II.

Fig. 26-15. *Counting the hands cut off from enemies slain in battle. The northern exterior wall. The Temple of Ramesses II.*

the light troops of the vile Kheta with the multitudes who were with them from Arvad, from Mausu, from Pidasa, from Keshkesh, from Arwena. There were three men on each chariot; they were united. But there was not a chief with me. There was never a charioteer; there was never an officer of the troops, never a

horseman. I was abandoned by the infantry, the chariots fleeing away before them to flight along with me."

Ramesses Appeals to Amon-Ra.

Then said His Majesty, "What is in thy heart my father Amon? Does a father

Fig. 26-16. *The fruits of victory. Prisoners of war and captured horses brought before Ramesses. The northern exterior wall. The Temple of Ramesses II.*

ignore his son? I have made petitions and hast thou forgotten me? Lo, even in my goings I heeded thy words; I never broke thy commands. What is thy will concerning these Asiatics O Amon, the wretched ones who are ignorant of God? Did I never make great monuments for thee? I filled thy holy temples with my prisoners; I built for thee a Temple for Millions of Years. I have given to thee all my possessions as a deed of gift. I have not neglected anything relating to thee, building for thee pylons of stone, setting up their masts myself. Bringing thee obelisks from Elephantine. I cause eternal stones to be brought for thee and established ships upon the sea to bring thee the tribute of the foreign lands. Please order an evil fate to befall him who attacks thine excellent plans, and a good fate to him whom thou accountest just. Behold thou all that I have done has been with a loving heart. I call on thee my father Amon for I am in the midst of many nations whom I know not the whole of every land is against me. I am alone, no other is with me, I being deserted by my troops. My chariots never once look to me though I cry out to them. But I find that Amon is worth more than millions of troops, more than hundreds of thousands of chariots. Never the deeds of an abundance of people but that the excellence of Amon is more than they. I end this waiting on the decrees of thy mouth Amon!

"Amon came to me because I cried to him. He gave me his hand, and I rejoiced."

Amon's Answer.

"He cried out to me, 'My protection is with thee Ramesses beloved of Amon. I am with thee. I am thy father. I am more use to thee than hundreds of thousands of men for I am the Lord of Might. All that I have done has come to pass for I am like Monthu. I have captured. I have seized. I am like Baal in anger upon them!

"'I found two thousand five hundred chariots I being in the midst of them. They became terrified before my horses. Not one of them found his hand to fight; their hearts rotted in their bodies for fear. They were unable to shoot an arrow; they could not even shoulder their weapons. I caused them to fall into the water even as the crocodiles. None of them turned his face. Every fallen one among them did not lift himself up again.'"

The Cowardly King of the Hittites.

Behold the vile Chief, the Smitten One of the Kheta stood among his troops and chariots gazing upon the fight of His Majesty, for that His Majesty was alone by "himself, there being no infantry with him, no chariotry. He (the King of the Hittites) was standing

Fig. 26-17. Egyptian archers admonishing refractory prisoners of war. Temple of Ramesses II. Northern exterior wall.

and turning about for fear of His Majesty. Then he ordered many chiefs to come, and they were equipped with their weapons of war. The Chief of Awad and Chief of Masa, the Chief of Dardeny and Chief of Keshkesh, the Chief of Karkemish and the Chief of Karash being altogether two thousand five hundred chariots; I came up to them quicker than fire. I carried them off. I was like Monthu. I gave them a taste of my hand. In the passing of an instant I was slaying them where they stood."

The Enemy Panics.

Then one started

Fig. 26-18. A rebellious prisoner! A captured Hittite horse tries to kick his way to freedom (lower right). The northern exterior wall. The Temple of Ramesses II.

crying to another, "no man is this who is in our midst. It is Set, great of might. It is Baal in the flesh; never did a man do deeds like him! Come, let us flee from before him. Let us seek life and health.

"They never knew how to grasp the bow nor the spear 'likewise.' When he saw them come to the junction of the roads, His Majesty was upon them like a griffon slaying among them. They escaped him not.

"Then I shouted to my soldiers and charioteers saying, 'Steady yourselves! Steady your hearts my soldiers and my chariots! Behold ye, see there my mighty deeds. I am alone, and it is Amon who sustains me. His hand is towards me.'"

Menna Wants to "Call it a Day."

"When Menna my charioteer beheld that multitudes of chariots completely surrounded me, he became cowardly, and a very great terror was in his limbs. He said to His Majesty, 'My good Lord, you are in the midst of the enemy. Behold, they abandon us the soldiers and the chariots. O save us Ramesses loved of Amon my good Lord!' Then said His Majesty to his charioteer 'Steady, steady thy heart my charioteer! I am going in among them like the striking of a falcon. I shall slay them and throw them in the dust by Amon! They are extremely vile in ignoring God who shall

never shine his face upon millions of them. Then His Majesty led rapidly; he arose and penetrated the enemy. I was slaying among them none escaping from me."

Ramesses "Dresses Down" His Troops.

Then called His Majesty to his soldiers and his chariots likewise to his chiefs who had failed to fight. His Majesty said to them, "It is evil in your hearts O my charioteers. It is unworthiness that fills your hearts. There is not one among you but what has secured good fortune from my hand. If I had never risen as Lord you would have been in a bad case. I made you like chiefs every day. I allow the son to succeed to the goods of his father. If any pest comes to Egypt, I remit to you your taxes. I give to you your share of the plunder. Never a lord did for his soldiers what I have done for you. I allowed you to rest in your houses and in your towns, and each boasted of the deeds he would do. Behold, your first great deed was to desert me leaving me alone! You have made a miserable return all of you together. Not one of you gave his hand to me! I was fighting alone I swear by the Ka of Amon my father!"

Honorable Mention for the Chariot Horses.

Ramesses then goes on to say that the only mortals who aided him in the battle

were his charioteer Menna and his two brave horses, and he gave orders that the latter were to be fed and watered in his presence every day. Nobody can fail to understand the fierce disdain underlying this outburst of Ramesside anger.

We can imagine the discomfort of the runaway troops wriggling their toes in the dust and hanging their heads as Ramesses gave them a good "dressing down" ending by saying that he was glad that they had deserted him as now he knew that he did not need them. He was quite capable of fighting any future battles on his own!

It is rather difficult to believe that this account of the battle is literally true in every detail. One must allow for a certain amount of bragging on the part of Ramesses! In a big way he was actually quite that type of man! In a hand-to-hand fight with such an uncouth, merciless enemy like the Hittites, Ramesses alone could stand a very thin chance of escaping alive in a battle of such density and fierceness and against a notoriously well-trained army of born warriors.

The Southern Exterior Wall of the Temple.

It is very unfortunate that only the lower part of this wall is preserved as it bore a calendar of the holy feast days and lists of offerings to be presented on these occasions. The offerings seem to have been provided by a royal endowment. It is also mentioned to whom these offerings should be given. The great part of the offerings consisted of various kinds of grain measured in hekats (bushels) or parts of hekats, but bundles of vegetables, baskets of fruit, jars of honey and of course, beer and wine are mentioned.

After the recording of one hundred and forty-four entries, there comes a speech made by the Goddess Seshat in which she praises the generosity of Ramesses. This is followed by a damaged representation of the Goddess. The inscriptions are now interrupted by the jambs of a small doorway that once opened into the portico but was apparently blocked up in ancient times. Both jambs bear figures of Ramesses and the warning that everyone entering the temple should be purified four times!

After the doorway is the lower part of a large scene which originally showed Ramesses offering to Osiris, Isis and Horus. Next comes the second part of the calendar and offering lists which is less well-preserved than the first part. At the end of this list are the jambs of the southeastern doorway that gave access to the court. They resemble those of the southwestern doorway (Fig. 26-19).

Underneath both calendars and offering lists are two long, horizontal inscriptions. After an enumeration of the royal titles and names, the east-ern inscription reads: "Live the good God, the son of Osiris, glorious seed of the Lord of Eternity whom he begat as heir upon his throne. Since he came forth from the body, the reckoning of his sphere of influence extends to the limits of eternity. He spends all night awake seeking the welfare of his fathers the Lords of the Necropolis, rejoicing in love, making real offerings, deriving enjoyment for his limbs, placing offerings for the Lords of the Underworld, provisioning the Gods of the Underworld. The exact plummet of the balance for the common people; there is not his equal. His Majesty commanded that divine offerings be placed for his father Osiris Khenty-Amentiu, Isis the great, Mother of the God, Horus the avenger of his father, Wepwawat of the South, Guide of the Two Lands, the Leader of the Sacred Boat, protected by the King of Upper and Lower Egypt, User-maat-Ra Setep-en-Ra, are the gods and goddesses who are in the 'House of Ramesses Mery-Amon' by the permanent establishment of all divine offerings for the feasts belonging to Heaven, belonging to earth at the beginning of every season and every day that shall be."

Ramesses Describes His Temple.

The more interesting inscription is the western one which commences under the damaged figure of Seshat and reads: "Live Horus the Mighty Bull, beloved of Maat, dispatching his armies to conquest, returning with victory. Favorite of the two ladies, rich in years, great in might causing their enemy's chiefs to retreat, Ruler of the Nine Bows causing the overthrow of their thrones, King of Upper and Lower Egypt, User-maat-Ra Setep-en-Ra, the son of Ra, Ramesses Mery-Amon, beloved of Osiris Khenty-Amentiu, Horus the avenger of his father, Isis the great Mother of God, and the great Company of Gods who are in the Sacred Land.

"Lo, His Majesty (life, prosperity, health to him!) was as 'Son whom he loves,'[6] the avenger of his father, Wennefer, making for him a beautiful and august temple fashioned excellently for eternity of beautiful white limestone of Ayan, two pylon towers of excellent work, doorways of granite stone, door-leaves made of copper wrought with inlaid figures of real electrum, a sanctuary of pure alabaster roofed with granite stone his glorious seat of the Beginning, a resting place for his Company of Gods. His august father rests in its interior like Ra when he reaches Heaven. His divine form protects him who created it like Horus upon the throne of his father. He made en-

6.......................
[6]This is a priestly title, but Ramesses here is comparing himself with Horus the son of Osiris.

Fig. 26-19. The calendar of feasts and list of offerings on the southern exterior wall of the temple. The Temple of Ramesses II.

during the divine offerings; he established the permanent daily offerings for the first of the seasons' feasts at their dates. He filled it (the temple) with everything, overflowing with food and provisions, oxen, shorthorns, bulls, fowl, incense, wine and fruit. He filled it with serfs, doubled its cultivated lands, made abundant its herds of cattle, its granaries are filled to overflowing, the heaps of grain neared to Heaven. The slaves of the storehouse of the divine offerings are from the spoils of his victorious sword.[7] Its treasury[8] encloses every precious stone, silver

and gold in ingots. Its magazines are full of everything from the tribute of every land. He planted many gardens set with every kind of tree all sweet and fragrant plants, the plants belonging to Punt (incense trees). He made this for it (namely) the son of Ra, Lord of Diadems, Ramesses Mery-Amon, beloved of Osiris Khenty-

....

[7] There were no slaves. They were all prisoners of war. Slavery was not known in Egypt even in this time of intense building and construction of the XIXth dynasty.

[8] The treasury of the Temple of Ramesses remains to be discovered.

Amentiu, the great God, Lord of Abydos."

So far as the parts of the temple are still preserved, we can see that the description of it in the first part of the inscription is quite correct and not in any way exaggerated. The pylon of white limestone, the granite doorways, the sanctuary of "pure alabaster" with its granite roof are there for us to see and touch which is proof that Ramesses was not quite the great liar that some historians would have us believe. So let us be more charitable to this very likeable young man even if he was occasionally what the French might call "Charmant Blaguer."

CHAPTER TWENTY-SEVEN

ABYDOS UNDER THE SUCCESSORS OF RAMESSES II.

Mer-en-Ptah.

After a long and obviously happy reign of sixty-seven years, Ramesses died and was succeeded by Mer-en-Ptah, number thirteen of his many sons. The latter was already a mature old man at the time of his accession. Although he erected monuments at Karnak and elsewhere, his only contribution to Abydos was to plaster his titles and names all over his father's and grandfather's temples, and decorate the hitherto undecorated and mysterious Osirion. He was a modest and reasonable man who did not often claim to have built anything that did not belong to him. Instead of throwing some light on the real origin of the Osirion, his decoration of this extraordinary temple seems to have added to its perplexing mysteriousness.

After the death of Mer-en-Ptah, the XIXth dynasty seems to have ended in a family squabble over the succession, and so far as large royal monuments are concerned, Abydos was neglected.

However, it seems that the kings were still coming for pilgrimage to the Holy City to celebrate the great Feast of Osiris, and a stela of Amon-mes, one of the more aggressive royal squabblers, was found here. It bears a scene of a procession of priests accompanied by dancers.

Ramesses III.

Ramesses III of the XXth dynasty was the next king to build a large temple at Abydos. In the great Harris Papyrus which records the endowments and offerings made by Ramesses III for the gods, he says concerning Abydos, "I restored Abydos by benefactions in Ta-wer (the Abydos nome). I built my temple in the midst of his (Osiris) temple like Atum's great house in Heaven. I settled it with people bearing numerous offices, rich and poor of all that exists. I made for it divine offerings, the gifts for its altars, O my father Osiris, Lord of the Abydos Nome.

"I made for him a statue of the King (life, prosperity, health!) presenting monuments and table vessels likewise of gold and silver.

"I surrounded the Temple of Osiris and Horus the son of Isis with a great wall of gritstone, with ramps, and towers bearing battlements and having doorposts of stone and door-leaves of cedar wood.

"I hewed a great barge of Osiris like the Evening Boat which carries the sun."

List of people given to Abydos: To the "House of Ramesses Ruler of Heliopolis",682 heads; people whom he gave to the temple of his august father Osiris, 162 heads. Total heads equalled 844.

The temple referred to seems to have entirely disappeared, but "I built my temple in the midst of his temple" suggests that it was somewhere within the great enclosure of Kom el Sultan. A block of limestone bearing a relief of Ramesses III and Queen Thiy-mer-en-Isit was found there. Whether the Temple of Osiris and Horus, which he says he surrounded with walls, is the same building is not clear. There is a very suspicious-looking area in the desert immediately to the west of the modern market place. Looking down from the top of the mountain one can see a great rectangular structure thinly veiled by sand. One can see indications of brick walls running south to north. But it has never been excavated.

Ramesses IV.

Ramesses IV concerned himself with the Holy City, and we have already seen his outsized inscriptions in the Temple of Ramesses II and more modest ones in that of Sety I. But in spite of his short reign of not more than six years, Ramesses IV was active in erecting monuments in both Upper and Lower Egypt. He built a temple at Abydos at first apparently intending it to stand to the north of Kom el Sultan. Here the ground was cleared and levelled, and even foundation deposits were placed under what should have been the corners of the building. But that is as far as the project went.

However, Ramesses IV actually did erect a temple at Abydos at about five hundred meters (1600 feet) to the north of that of Ramesses II. Here lying on the surface of the ground are a few sections of polygonal columns of white limestone and some inscribed blocks. It has never been excavated, but taking a hoe and digging down beside one of the larger blocks, I found the side of a small doorway still in situ. On its eastern face was part of an Osiride statue, and beside it the cartouche of Ramesses IV. In the debris were many fragments of finely carved but rather flat bas-reliefs. Some of which were colored.

Royal Impertinence.

Mariette found a stela of Ramesses IV at Abydos dated to the fourth year of his reign. It is now in the Cairo Museum. The inscription on it shows the impudence which had no precedent in the long Egyptian history! The King adopts a bullying tone as he addresses Osiris: "Thou shall give me health, life, a long existence, a prolonged reign, endurance to my every member, sight to mine ears, pleasure to my heart daily. And thou shalt give me to drink until I am drunk. And thou shalt establish mine issue as kings in the land forever. And thou shalt grant me contentment every day, and thou shalt hear my voice whenever I speak to thee, and thou shalt grant what I ask with a loving heart, and thou shalt give me high and plenteous Niles in order to supply thy divine offerings and those of the other gods and goddesses, and to preserve alive the sacred bulls and the people and their lands and cattle.

For it is thou who hast made all, and thou canst not forsake them to carry out other plans. That is not right. And thou shalt be pleased with the land of Egypt, thy land, in my time, and thou shalt double for me the long duration, the prolonged reign of Ramesses II, the great God, for I have done more good things for thee and thy temple during these four years than Ramesses II did for thee in all his sixty-seven years. So thou shalt give me the long existence and prolonged reign which thou gavest to him as King. Give me the reward of the great deeds which I have done for thee even life prosperity and health, a long existence and a prolonged reign. And thou shalt give to me every land and country under my sandals that I may present their tribute to thy Ka and to thy name."

Apparently Ramesses IV and Osiris did not see eye-to-eye, and instead of the long reign he kept demanding, all that the King got was six years.

The remaining kings of the XXth dynasty were all named Ramesses. They submitted to and were increasingly dominated by the powerful High Priests of Amon-Ra of Thebes.

Although no more great temples were being built at Abydos, it continued to thrive. Pilgrims came every year, but the existing temples were maintained in a less lavish manner than before.

For some reason, Ramesses VIII was unable to make his pilgrimage to Abydos, so his scribe Hori was sent on his behalf. Hori erected a stela to commemorate the occasion on which he says to Osiris,[1] "I am a servant of thy city Busiris which is in the Delta. I am the son of a servant of thy temple, the scribe of Pharaoh (life prosperity, health!), the Protector of Abydos, Pekauti son of Seny thy servant. I have been brought from my city in the Delta to thy city Abydos being a messenger of Pharaoh, thy servant. I have come to worship before thee, and to beseech for him (Pharaoh) jubilees. Thou wilt hear his prayers according as he is profitable to thee, and thou wilt accept from me the hand of Pharaoh my Lord, and give me favor before him daily. Make thy designs; I will cherish them. It is said, 'Who can reverse thy plans?' Thou art the God of Heaven, Earth and the Underworld, and men do as thou sayest. O give me mortuary offerings of bread and beer and a sweet north wind for my father Pekauti and his son the scribe of Pharaoh, Hori the Justified."

At the end of the XXth dynasty the kings of the old royal line had become so feeble that the High Priests of Amon-Ra were the virtual rulers. Finally, the High Priest Heri-Hor ousted Ramesses XIII and proclaimed himself King and founded the XXIst dynasty (the Priest Kings.)

....
[1] This is now in the Berlin Museum, No. 2081.

SEKHER

FALL

PART III

SEKHER = THE FALL

CHAPTER TWENTY-EIGHT

HELAS ABYDOS...THY GLORY FADES

The Shadows Gather.

The successors of Heri-Hor were well-meaning, pious, but completely inefficient rulers, and so far as Egypt was concerned, they "paved Hell with their good intentions."

Heri-Hor does not seem to have paid any attention to Abydos, but his eldest son Paankh came here on pilgrimage and left a stela to record his visit. He should have succeeded Heri-Hor, but apparently he died before his father, so it was his son Pinedjem ("the Sweet") who reigned in his grandfather's place. This king was the one responsible for the re-wrapping and re-burying of the mummies of the great pharaohs of the New Kingdom whose tombs had been robbed at the end of the XXth dynasty. Pinedjem's contribution to the monuments of Abydos was a stone altar probably dedicated when he made his pilgrimage there.

Tomb Robbery at Abydos.

From the reign of Pinedjem II we have some disquieting news from Abydos. Apparently the guards policing the great necropolis had been lax in their duty. This frequently happened in ancient Egypt when the central government was weak and the guards did not receive their pay regularly. The tombs were being robbed, and among them was that of a young man of Libyan origin named Ni-maat. The family of Ni-maat had been settled in Egypt for many years and had acquired great wealth and influence. Ni-maat's father Sheshank[1] complained to King Pinedjem II about the robbery of his son's tomb. The King took a serious view of the matter and called in the oracle of Amon-Ra to decide who among the several persons arrested were the real culprits. The King made the petition in person "kissing the ground" before the statue of the God. He also prayed to Amon-Ra on behalf of Sheshank whom he referred to as the "Great Chief of Chiefs," and he also compensated him liberally for all the things stolen from Ni-maat's tomb. A statue of Osiris and an offering table were dedicated in Ni-maat's name in the Temple of Osiris, and the King gave to the tomb endowment two Syrian slaves costing 15 deben of silver,[2] and 20 deben of silver, 50 stat[3] of land valued at 5 deben of silver per stat, six slaves at 3 deben, one kidat[4] each, also a child

....
[1]This man was the grandfather of the future King Sheshank I the founder of the XXIInd dynasty.
[2]One deben equalled 91 grams of silver.
[3]One stat equalled $2/3$ of an acre.
[4]One kidat equalled 91 grains of silver.

slave at $4^3/4$ kidats of silver, a garden in the high ground of Abydos at ...22 deben of silver, a female slave at $5^2/3$ kidats of silver and a male slave at $3^2/3$ kidats of silver, as well as four measures of wine and incense which was to be issued daily from the treasury of the Temple of Osiris and many other gifts and endowments. These royal gifts were duly recorded in the temple archives and engraved on a red granite stela. The latter was actually found by Mariette to the south of the entrance to Kom el Sultan. He left it in situ, but it has since disappeared. The interesting point about this inscription is that it shows the great power which this Libyan family had acquired that made even the King so anxious to pacify the angry father. And it also shows the comparative values of slaves and land at that time.

King Sheshank I.

When King Sheshank I (the Sheshank of the Bible) founded the XXIIth dynasty, he had a "Middle Eastern" problem on his hands, and according to combined Biblical accounts[5] "Sheshank, King of Egypt, came up against Jerusalem with twelve thousand chariots and sixty thousand horsemen and the people without number that came with him out of Egypt. And he took the

....
[5]The Biblical accounts that tell of the King's problem are I Kings 14, and II Chronicles 12.

fenced cities of Judah and came to Jerusalem. And he took away the treasures of the House of Jehovah and the treasures of the King's house. He took away all, and he took away all the shields of gold that Solomon had made."

This is born out by contemporary evidence from Egypt and explains why Sheshank was too busy to do any sizeable building, and what he did do was mostly in Lower Egypt.

Sheshank I was succeeded by Usarkon I who also seems to have confined his building activities to the Delta. During his reign the annual pilgrimage to Abydos was still taking place. A stela dated to the twenty-sixth year of Usarkon I was dedicated by a priest of Amon-Ra named Pashed-Bast who claimed descent from Ramesses II. He relates that while he was walking in the desert of Abydos near the tomb of Osiris, he noticed a neglected stela which resembled those of the Memphite necropolis. "He fenced it and surrounded it with stelae and gave it land (as an endowment) and established for it daily offerings from the divine endowments, wine, incense and libations of water for the pleasure of its Lord, Osiris Khenty-Amentiu, Lord of Abydos, as an everlasting possession."

King Takalot I dedicated a green faience statuette of himself to Abydos. We do not find any more royal monuments here until the XXIVth dynasty, and the first of these is only a graffito of Shabaka.

The Enigmatic Cartouche.

About the year 1968, I was collecting copies of Greek graffiti in the Temple of Sety I when I noticed a roughly scratched cartouche (in hieroglyphs, of course) on the uninscribed edge of one of the doorways between the First and the Second Hypostyle Halls. It was the cartouche of Shabaka and seems to have been scratched with the point of a knife in the soft sandstone. But who made it? Ordinary layfolk were not allowed in the inner temple, so was this cartouche scratched by a loyal priest, or was it done by Shabaka himself? The kings of the XXIVth dynasty were known to have been called "the Puritans of Egypt," and certainly they did not neglect to make their pilgrimage to Abydos. Did Shabaka himself record his visit? If so, this is a unique example of a pharaoh's handwriting with no known parallel in Egyptian pharaonic history.

Disaster: The Assyrian Hordes.

Now unfortunately, it was time for Egypt to witness what the poet describes:

"The Assyrians came down Like wolves on a fold, Their cohorts were gleaming With purple and gold."

The last king of the XXIVth dynasty was Tanut-Amon, and when Ashurbanipal of Assyria invaded Egypt in

663 B.C., he fled to Upper Nubia leaving the enemy in possession.

Even before this great disaster, the shadows were gathering and dimming the glory of Egypt. The old, prosperous days of the Empire had gone forever, and weak, ineffectual kings had impoverished the land and its people. Pilgrims still continued to come to Abydos, but they were growing less in number. Fewer people were able to afford the journey. Poverty was beginning to show its unmistakable print.

It is possible that the great temples were now understaffed, and that their rich endowments had been nibbled away by lazy, careless or dishonest officials, and no new ones were being made, and all new construction had come to a standstill.

The Assyrians who constituted the XXVth dynasty wrought terrible havoc at Thebes by pillaging and destroying, but there is no evidence that they did the same at Abydos probably because the place had no political importance. During the years of their occupation, there were few pilgrims coming to the Holy City, and these few would have come from near-by nomes.

But the end was not yet. Just as the evening sky glows with light and an array of glorious colors, just before the sun sinks and plunges the world into darkness, so was there a brief burst of glory for Egypt and Abydos with the rise of the XXVIth dynasty.

CHAPTER TWENTY-NINE

THE SPLENDOR AT THE SUNSET

The Saitic Period.

The kings of the XXVIth dynasty ruled Egypt from Sais, their Delta capital. They were mostly wise and powerful, active at home and able to exert Egypt's power abroad.

The policy of the time was to look back with a strong yearning to the "good old days" of the Old Kingdom when Egypt was free, rich and powerful. This strong yearning to the past is more inexplicable when we realize that more than two thousand years separated the Old Kingdom from the Saitic Period. It must have been something stronger and deeper than a mere sentimental upheaval. The personal names, the titles, the art forms of the Old Kingdom were revived. The old necropoli were used again for burials, and the cult of the pyramid builders of the IVth dynasty became very popular.

Although most of their works were in Lower Egypt, the Saitic kings did not neglect Abydos. Psamtik I did some building or restoration here, and a lintel bearing his name and that of his daughter Neit-Ikeret (a good, Old Kingdom name!) was found by Mariette.

The Suez Canal Comes to Life.

Psamtik I was succeeded by his son Ne-kaw II (the Necho of the Bible). We do not find any of his monuments at Abydos, but he is famed for having dug (or re-dug) the Suez Canal. When this project was three-quarters completed, and oracle from the temple (at Sais?) commanded him to stop the work as such a canal would cause trouble to Egypt and permit the "People of the Sea" to flood the land. Being a wise man, Ne-kaw obeyed!

According to the Bible,[1] Ne-kaw invaded Syria as far as Karkemish. He was attacked by the Jewish King Josiah but defeated and slew him at Megiddo. Josiah was succeeded by Jeohaz, but Ne-kaw deposed him and put Jeohaz's brother Johakim in his place and demanded a tribute of one talent of gold which had to be raised from the private wealth of the Jews.

Psamtik II built some large monument in or near Abydos, but all that is so far known of this is a large block of quartzite sandstone. Apparently it is the lower part of a wall. It bore a frieze of Nile Gods and figures of the King himself. This block was discovered in the near-by town of Balyana where it was serving as the threshold to the entrance of an old mosque. It was rescued by one of the inspectors of the Antiquities Department who tactfully suggested that perhaps a nice, new reinforced concrete threshold would be more suitable. The mosque authorities quite agreed, and so now Psamtik's relief lies

....
[1]II Kings 23:29 and
 II Chronicles 35:20.

safely in the court of the Temple of Ramesses II.

Psamtik was succeeded by Wah-ib-Ra a great builder whose monuments are found from the northern Delta to Nubia.

Rebellion Ferments in Siwa.

At Abydos Wah-ib-Ra rebuilt the old Temple of Thotmes III at Kom el Sultan placing his foundations over the original ones of Thotmes. He also constructed a beautiful naos of red granite of very fine workmanship.

But Wah-ib-Ra was not popular with his subjects, and apparently he had a nasty temper. Hearing that a rebellion against him was being hatched up in Siwa Oasis, he sent one of his officers, a certain Ahmes (Amasis), to quell the uprising. However, when he arrived at Siwa, the rebels persuaded Ahmes to join their ranks, drill them and lead them to battle against the unpopular King. He agreed. Some months passed, and Wah-ib-Ra had no word from Ahmes, so he sent another messenger to find out what had happened and told him to bring back an answer from Ahmes. This man arrived at Siwa and found Ahmes mounted on a horse and drilling his army. He handed him the King's letter. Ahmes read it, but he continued to sit on his horse in silence. "Well" said the messenger, "what answer shall I take back to the King?" Ahmes leaned forward a little and broke wind loudly. "Take that answer back to Wah-ib-Ra!" he cried.[2] When the man delivered this message to the King, he was so furious that he ordered the unfortunate messenger to have his ears and nose cut off. But this unjust action turned his few remaining supporters against him. The rebellion was successful and Ahmes came to the throne as Ahmes II. He also was a great builder, and his monuments are found from the Delta to Nubia.

At Abydos, Ahmes II dedicated a splendid red granite naos containing an inner shrine of electrum, and he continued the rebuilding of the Temple of Osiris Khenty-Amentiu where he also dedicated an altar of granite.

Apparently much of this activity was due to the palace physician who rejoiced in the name of Pef-nef-di-Neit. This man visited Abydos, apparently on pilgrimage, but he did not like what he saw! He found the ancient monuments falling into ruin, the temple endowments confiscated, the offerings and incomes diverted.

The Age-old Caravan Route.

Since the time of the XVIIIth dynasty all products from the Great Oasis entering the Nile Valley had to

pay duty at Abydos which lay at the head of the caravan route.[3] The income from this duty was supposed to go towards the upkeep of the temples, but at the time of which we are now speaking, Abydos had the misfortune to be governed by a very unpleasant nomarch who was a firm believer in the custom of "feathering one's own nest." Apparently his misdeeds were a well-known local scandal. Anyhow, Dr. Pef-nef-de-Neit heard about them and duly reported all that he had seen and heard to the King. He tells us, "I transmitted all the affairs of Abydos to the palace that His Majesty might hear them. His Majesty commanded that I do the work in Abydos. I did greatly in improving Abydos. I put all its affairs in order seeking the God of Abydos. I besought favors from my Lord every day[4] in order that Abydos might be furnished. I built the Temple of Khenti-Amentiu in excellent eternal work as His Majesty commanded me. I surrounded it with walls of brick and the necropolis with granite and an august shrine of electrum. The ornaments

and divine adornments and amulets (for the God's statues) of gold, silver and every costly stone.

"I built Pega, I set up its altars, I dug its lake, planted with trees. I provisioned the Temple of Khenti-Amentiu increasing that which came into him as a daily offering. His magazines were settled with male and female slaves. I gave to him one hundred stat of land of the fields of the Abydos nome equipped with people and all small cattle. Its name was established as "Establishment of Osiris" in order that divine offerings might be furnished from it throughout eternity. I made him groves of date palms and vineyards with people to work them of foreign countries brought as living captives.

"I restored the archives which were ruined. I recorded the offerings of Osiris, and I put all his contracts in order.

"I hewed from cedar the sacred boat which I found made only of acacia wood.[5] I repelled the chief of the devastators from Abydos. I defended Abydos for its Lord. I protected all its people.[6]

[2] Needless to say, we owe this story to that old gossip Herodotus, but from what is also known of the character of Ahmes who was witty, wise, though somewhat vulgar. It is probably quite true!

[3] There are still some old people living in Abydos who remember taking the ancient desert road which ran between Abydos and the Oasis which was a good three weeks walk!
[4] No doubt that is why King Ahmes II sent him to "do the work in Abydos!"

[5] A cheap kind of native wood still largely used for the construction of Nile sailing boats.
[6] This may mean that he deputized for the King in the Mystery Play during the Great Feast of Osiris, or it may refer to a great row that he had with the dishonest Nomarch. Probably the

251

I gave to the temples the
things that came from the
Desert of Abydos (the Oasis)
which I found in the pos-
sessions of the Nomarch in
order that the people of
Abydos might be buried.[7]
I gave to the temple the
ferry boat of Abydos[8]
which I took from the Nomarch, for Osiris desired
that Abydos be equipped.
His Majesty praised me
for what I had done.

"May he (Osiris) grant
life to his son Ahmes.
May he grant favor for His
Majesty and honor before
the great God.

"O priests, praise
God for me. O everyone
coming here praise ye in
the temple, speak my name
Pef-nef-de-Neit born of
Ne-nes Bast."

This inscription is
engraved on a statue of
the worthy doctor which
was found at Abydos and
is now in the Louvre,
Paris (no. A.93).

Ahmes II actually did
build at Kom el Sultan,
and a block bearing his
cartouche, as well as his
foundation deposits, was
found there.

....
latter as in the next
sentence he starts tell-
ing us all about the Nom-
arch's dirty work!
[7] In order to provide tombs
for the poor?
[8] Evidently a free public
ferry boat plying be-
tween Abydos and the Nile
which had been comman-
deered by the Nomarch. Or
did Dr. Per-nef-di Neit
"highjack" one of the
Nomarch's own boats in
order to provide such
a ferry?

Fig. 29-1. Kom el Sultan. The bank of white limestone
chips. All that remains of the Temple of Nakht-neb-ef.

The Persian Invasion.

Ahmes II was succeeded
by his son Psamtik III,
but he hardly had begun to
reign when the Persians
attacked Egypt, and aided
by the treachery of Psamtik's
Greek mercenaries, they
overran the land founding
the XXVIIth or Persian
dynasty under the tyrannical
and apparently mad Cambyses
in 525 B.C.
We know nothing of
Abydos during this period
though the wise and kindly
Darius, who followed
Cambyses, built many mon-
uments in Egypt.
The Persian domination
ended in 405 B.C., and
there was a brief period
in which Egyptian kings
again ruled Egypt.

The Last Egyptian Dynasty.

Judging by the number
and wide distribution of
their monuments, the kings
of the XXXth dynasty must
have been influential and
the country fairly pros-
perous. Nakht-Hor-heb,
the first ruler of that
dynasty, built a temple
at Abydos. It now lies

unexcavated under the
houses of the village.
Its presence is betrayed
by a number of finely
sculptured and inscribed
fragments of limestone;
many of which have been
built into the walls of
the houses (including mine!)
An inscription in one
of the local quarries
(which is still in use)
is dated to the year five
of Nakht-Hor-heb and re-
cords the extraction of
stone for the building of
this temple.
Nakht-Hor-heb also
made an unusally fine naos
of red granite, but for
this he reused stone from
some XIXth dynasty gateway!
The last pharaoh of
this dynasty, Nakht-neb-ef,
built a new Temple of
Osiris at Kom el Sultan.
But this has been entirely
destroyed, and all that
remains of it is a great
bank of chips of white
limestone (Fig. 29-1).
By the end of the
XXXth dynasty, Abydos was
doomed. The end was as
inevitable and as imminent
as Fate itself. The death
of a town is always tragic;
so was the end of Abydos.

CHAPTER THIRTY

ICHABOD "THE GLORY HATH DEPARTED"

At the end of the reign of Nakht-neb-ef, the Persians again invaded Egypt and remained in control for eleven years when they were driven out by the forces of Alexander the Great.

We know little more of the fate of Abydos from then onwards. Certainly the great Temple of Sety was still open, but the magazines and the two painted corridors (page 38) were now used for the burial of sacred cattle and rams whose bodies, preserved with bitumen, were packed into them in hundreds. This exactly bears out what Herodotus relates about the burial of sacred cattle which he says were all interred in a sacred place. Judging by the number of Greek graffiti on its walls, columns and even the roof, the Temple of Sety was still being visited in Ptolemaic times, but whether some of the recorded names (most of them Greek) were those of pilgrims, worshipers or tourists, we cannot say.[1] The Egyptian name Wennefer,

....

[1]The Temple of Ramesses II was closed or perhaps partly buried by this time as the only Greek graffiti are in the court, and they are very few. Further proof that this temple was no longer in use is the fact that it escaped being burned by the Romans.

inscribed in Greek letters near the entrance to the Corridor of Kings, may have been written by an Egyptian priest who prided himself on his ability to write Greek.

Alas, the glory of the sunset had long been departed. Fewer people were able to make the pilgrimage, and no doubt most of the enterprising citizens of Abydos had moved away to the more thriving cities on the banks of the Nile. In the temples, the chants and prayers were dying away with the northern breeze. Then came the terrible day when Abydos received its deathblow. It is not difficult to imagine what happened, and it was certainly one of the awe-inspiring moments in Egyptian history.

After Egypt had refused to obey Rome's edict to close the temples, there must have been a period of restrained but tense waiting. Then came the Christian Emperor's orders to burn, pillage and slay. No doubt news on the "grapevine" telegraph flew ahead of the destroyers, and let us hope that the priests of Abydos had at least the presence of mind to remove all the precious things still remaining in the temples and hide them in the treasury or some secret and safe cache.

Then one day a boat-load of Roman soldiers landed at the quay in front of the Temple of Sety and marched up the stairs. We may suppose

that some of the resolute townsfolk tried to defend their temple, but what could an unarmed mob do against the might of Rome? The vandals battered down the great door of the pylon with unshaken ferocity and entered the court. Some made their way to the burial place of the sacred animals. They were seeking for possible plunder. The rest forced their way into the temple mercilessly killing the handful of priests who tried to defend the sanctity of the holy place. There are many more martyrs in history than those whose names are recorded in Christian and Islamic annals!

We hope that the Romans found the temple bare of treasures, but there were still many wooden offering tables and statues in the hypostyle halls, and these the angry soldiers set alight. Did they first strip off the precious metal from the great door-leaves, or did they let the fire melt it down into more portable lumps and ingots? The Romans were usually very thorough and systematic when it came to destruction!

Meanwhile they had set on fire the mummies of the sacred animals whose bitumen soaked bodies blazed fiercely and then died down into dense clouds of black smoke that blew into the temple further staining the walls and roofs. When night fell, the glow of the fire was visible for miles around, and from the surrounding city, the wailing of the women ascended to Heaven with the smoke of the great burning. Their grief must have been unfathomable, and who knows what horrors took place in the city itself.

Gradually the stars faded, and the first rays of the sun touched the western mountain. But for Abydos the Holy City, there was no new dawn. An immense black cloud still hung over the Holy City, the Jerusalem of the Ancients, a city known and revered by foreigners as well as by Egyptians for at least three thousand years or even more. No, there was no dawn over Abydos on that sinister day; Ichabod..."The glory hath departed!"

And so it is finished this story of Abydos. Dr. Hanny El Zeini's beautiful pictures taken with such care and feeling and our words have tried to portray the rise, glory and fall of the world's oldest known holy city. We have tried to portray the great and good men who adorned her, the vile men who robbed her, the pilgrims who left their homes and undertook long and difficult journeys to worship at her shrines, and the unknown martyrs who willingly died for her.

And for those who love her, Abydos still has a mysterious life. Other ears than mine have heard music at night in the hypostyle halls of Sety. The tinkle of sistrums, the beat of a tambourine and the wail of a reed pipe have been heard. I have seen the golden glow of a lamp in the Cult Chapel of Osiris when no lamp was lit; and I have stood alone at night in Pega the Gap, on the first night of the Great Feast of Osiris, listening to the howling of the jackals. But when midnight came, the cries of the jackals were hushed, a deep silence fell, and then suddenly I felt as though I were surrounded by a great multitude of people. I could see nothing but the starlit desert, but all around me I could hear the breathing of many people and the soft whisper of sandalled feet upon the sand. I walked in the midst of this unseen crowd right up to the walls of Kom el Sultan. Then it seemed as though all the people went through the gateway and vanished into the past, and I was left outside cold and lonely in the present.

Yes Abydos still retains a life of her own, but you have to live in or near it to understand what I mean. But even those tourists who are usually in a hurry to get back to the comfort of their floating hotels or anxious to continue their voyage in their cars frankly admit that there is something peculiar, something very special about Abydos that makes them unwilling to leave it.

SOME OF THE GODS REPRESENTED IN THE TEMPLES OF ABYDOS

In Abydos one can see the whole pantheon of the gods of ancient Egypt represented on the walls of the temples. Some of the more important deities to be found in the temples of Sety I and Ramesses II and the Osirion are here listed.

1. Amentet.

Amentet was a goddess personifying the West; here regarded as the home of the dead and the Kingdom of Osiris.[1] She is often referred to as "The Beautiful West With Her Beautiful Hair." She is represented as a lovely woman wearing on her head her name-sign of Amenty, a falcon perched on a half circle with an ostrich plume in front of it.

2. Amon-Ra.

Originally called simply Amon ("The Hidden One"), he was a form of the great Creator God as worshiped at Thebes. When Thebes became the capital of Egypt and later also the capital of the Empire, Amon was associated with Ra under the name of Amon-Ra and was called the "King of the Gods" and "Lord of the Thrones of the Two Lands." His priesthood became extremely rich and powerful. Amon-Ra is usually represented as a handsome man with his flesh colored blue (symbolical of mystery), he wears a flat-topped crown surmounted by two tall falcon's plumes and having a long red streamer hanging down behind. Sometimes Amon-Ra was represented as a ram-headed man or simply as a ram as in the famous Avenue of Rams at Karnak. Curiously enough, he is sometimes represented in the form of the God Min. The wife of Amon-Ra was the Goddess Mut and their son was Khonsu. The curly-horned ram and the goose were sacred to Amon-Ra.

3. Anubis.

Later legends claim that Anubis was the illegitimate son of the Goddess Nepthys by Osiris. He was the God of Embalmers and was said to have preserved the body of Osiris. Anubis is shown either as a jackal-headed man or as a jackal. A very unusual representation of him in the Temple of Ramesses II shows him in full human form.

4. Atum.

In the earliest texts, Atum is regarded as the "Creator" dwelling in the Primeval Ocean as a spirit. He brought himself into being by uttering his own name and then proceeded to create the Universe. The analogy between this theory of creation and the first chapter of Genesis, the first book of the Old Testament, is very striking. By masturbation, Atum produced the first pair of gods, male and female. These were Shu and Tefnut (Air and Moisture). Later, Atum was regarded as the Sun God of the Evening. He is usually represented as a kingly man wearing the Double Crown of Upper and Lower Egypt. The shrew mouse and ichneumon were sacred to him, and sometimes he is represented in the form of the latter animal crowned with a solar disk.

....

[1]The ancient Egyptians seem to have been the first people to refer to a dead person as having "gone west."

5. Dwa-mut-ef.

Dwa-mut-ef was one of the Four Sons of Horus. He was usually represented with the head of a jackal and as guardian of one of canopic jars, he protected the lungs of the deceased. He was also the God of the Eastern Cardinal Point. In the temples of Abydos, Dwa-mut-ef is always represented in full human form.

6. Geb.

Geb was the God of the Earth and the husband of Nut. He is sometimes represented as a man with a goose standing upon his head and sometimes reclining under the arched body of Nut. In this latter position, he sometimes has plants sprouting out of his body. In the Chapel of Soker-Osiris, in the Temple of Sety, Geb is shown as a bearded man wearing a skullcap.

7. Hapi.

Hapi, the God of the Nile, is usually shown as a rather fat man with the breasts of a woman showing his dual role as Father and Mother of Egypt. He usually carries vases of water and trays of food which are all gifts of the Nile while bunches of wheat-ears and lotus flowers hang from his arms (Fig. 1).

In many temples, including those of Abydos, a dado of standing or kneeling Nile Gods surround the lower part of the walls of hypostyle halls. Sometimes these figures wear on their heads clumps of lillies or papyrus which are emblems of Upper and Lower Egypt. Or they may wear the standards of the forty-two nomes (or administrative districts) through which the Nile flowed. A very unusual figure of Hapi occurs twice in the Temple of Sety I, and so far as we are aware in no other place.

8. Hapi.

Hapi was also the name of one of the Four Sons of Horus. He usually has the head of a baboon and as guardian of one of the canopic jars, his function was to protect the small intestines of the mummified deceased. He was also the God of the Northern Cardinal Point. At Abydos he appears in full human form.

9. Hathor.

The name of Hathor means "House of Horus," and she was the Goddess of Love and Beauty identified by the Greeks with Aphrodite and by the Syrians with Astarte. In Thebes she was also regarded as a Goddess of the Western Mountain, the necropolis. In the Temple of Sety I, Hathor is represented in the form of a beautiful woman crowned with either a disk and cow's horns or a disk and two tall plumes or even with the unusual headdress described in the text.

Elsewhere, Hathor may be represented as a woman with the ears of a cow as on a sistrum held in the hand of Isis on the western wall of the Inner Chapel of Osiris. Or she may appear as a woman with a cow's head or even as a cow (her sacred animal) as in the Temple of Ramesses II.

10. Hekat.

Hekat was the Goddess of Childbirth and had an important cult center in Abydos. She is usually represented in the form of a frog or as a woman with a frog's head. In the Temple of Ramesses II, she is uniquely represented in full human form.

11. Horus.

The original Horus was Horus the Elder, the brother of Osiris, Isis, Set and Nepthys and was represented as a falcon-headed man or as a falcon, his sacred bird. As Horus of Edfu (Hor-Behdty) he is shown as a winged solar disk, that beautiful emblem so often seen on the lintels of temple doorways. His wife was the Goddess Hathor.

Horus the son of Osiris and Isis sometimes called "Horus the Child," was depicted as a naked boy wearing the side-lock of youth and placing his finger in his mouth. He may also wear the Double Crown of Upper and Lower Egypt. In the course of time, the two Horus Gods seem to have become confused in the minds of the people and when shown as an adult, Horus the son of Osiris and Isis is also represented as a falcon-headed man wearing the Double crown or more rarely the Itef crown. Curiously enough, it is only the adult form of Horus the son of Osiris and Isis which appears in the temples of Abydos.

12. Imesti.

One of the Four Sons of Horus, Imesti is always shown in full human form. As guardian of a canopic jar, he protected the large intestine of the deceased. He was also the God of the Southern Cardinal Point.

13. In-hert.

Often called In-hert Shu, he was a Warrior God. His name means "He Who Brought the Far One," and he earned it in this manner: The Goddess Tefnut once became very angry, and changing herself into a, lioness fled away to the deserts of Nubia. All the gods tried in vain to induce her to return to Egypt. Finally, In-hert went to her and "sweet-talked" her into appeasement, so that she meekly followed him back to Egypt. In-hert is usually shown wearing a short, curly wig surmounted by two tall plumes. He often wears a long garment with horizontal stripes and carries a spear.

14. Isis.

The real name of this goddess is Iset, but Isis is the better known Greek form. She was the sister-wife of Osiris and the mother of Horus and was probably the most beloved of all the Egyptian goddesses. She was the perfect type of a loyal and devoted wife and a loving mother. She had many titles including "Mistress of Heaven," "Mother of God," "Great of Magic," and later at Alexandria, she was called "Star of the Sea" and became the patroness of all who go down to the sea in ships. During the Ptolemaic and earlier Roman Periods, the Cult of Isis spread to Greece and Rome and from thence to western Europe even as far as Germany and England. In the Cologne Cathedral there is an old Roman statue of Isis (placed in one of the side-chapels) which was anciently mistaken for that of the Virgin Mary.

15. Iwf.

Iwf, whose name means "Flesh," was considered during the New Kingdom to be the nighttime form of the Sun God who sailed through the Underworld during the hours of darkness. He is shown as a ram-headed man usually standing in the cabin of the Night Solar Boat.

16. Iusaas.

Iusaas was a Heliopolitan goddess the wife of Ra-Hor-akhty. Her cult goes back to the Old Kingdom, and she is mentioned in the Pyramid Texts. In the Temple of Sety, Iusaas is shown as a beautiful woman crowned with the solar disk and cow horns similar to Hathor.

17. Khepera.

Khepera was a form of the Sun God of the Early Morning. He is sometimes represented as a man wearing a scarab on his head or with a scarab replacing his human head or simply as a scarab.

18. Khnum.

Khnum was the Divine Potter who fashioned the bodies of mankind from clay. His chief cult was based at Elephantine and Philae. He was represented as a ram-headed man, and the ram was his sacred animal.

19. Khonsu.

Khonsu was the son of Amon-Ra and Mut and was a Moon God. He is sometimes represented as a man crowned with the full and crescent moons as a falcon-headed man or as a human mummy wearing the side-lock of youth. In both these latter forms, he also wears on his head the full and crescent moons (Fig. 2). His statues were considered to have the power of casting out demons.

20. Maat.

Superficially, Maat was the Goddess of Truth and Justice and was called "Daughter of Ra," but she had also a much deeper significance. She represented the unalterable, fundamental Law of Nature that governs the Universe and that cannot be broken. Maat is represented as a woman wearing an ostrich feather upon her head. The ostrich feather being her symbol or emblem. Another symbol of Maat is an elongated rectangle with a wedge-shaped end. This is frequently seen under the thrones or the feet of gods, and it signifies that their authority is based on Maat.

21. Merhy.

Sometimes called Horus-Merhy, he was an ancient Memphite god about whom very little is known. He is represented as a man with the head of a bull like the Minotaur of Crete.

22. Min.

Min was the God of Generative Energy that gave all living things the power to reproduce themselves. He is represented as an ithyphallic man wearing a flat-topped crown similar to that of Amon-Ra. His body is closely wrapped, only one arm and the erect phallus being uncovered. The upper arm is raised at shoulder level, the elbow and forearm being bent upwards. A flail is balanced over the raised, open hand but is never, as one would expect, held in the hand. The worship of Min goes back to pre-dynastic times.

23. Monthu.

Monthu (or Montu) was a Thebian War God and was depicted as a falcon-headed man crowned with a solar disk and two tall plumes. His chief cult center was at a place near Thebes called Per-Monthu corrupted by the Greeks into Hermonthis, and now in

Arabic Arment. A bull named Men-wer (Mnevis of the Greeks) was sacred to Monthu.

24. Mut.

The Goddess Mut, whose name means "Mother," was the wife of Amon-Ra and the mother of Khonsu. She is usually represented as a handsome woman wearing the Double Crown of Upper and Lower Egypt.

25. Nefer-tem.

Nefer-tem was the son of Ptah and Sekhmet and the third person of the Memphite Triad. He is usually represented as a man wearing a lotus flower upon his head from which spring two tall plumes. Sometimes he is shown standing on the back of a lion. In his chapel in the Temple of Sety are some very unusual representations of Nefer-tem showing him as a lion-headed man and as a lion-headed mummy. In the Pyramid Texts, Nefer-tem is called "the Lotus Flower at the Nose of Ra."

26. Nepthys.

Nepthys is the familiar Greek form of the Egyptian name Nebet-het which means "Mistress of the Palace" (or temple). This Goddess was the sister of Osiris, Isis and Set and wife of the latter. After the murder of Osiris, Nepthys left her husband and became the loving companion of Isis. Nepthys is usually shown in the form of a woman who wears on her head the symbol of her name, a basket (Nebet) and a house (Het).

27. Nun.

Nun was the God of the Primeval Ocean out of which all life emerged. He is usually represented in human form and wears a headdress consisting of a pair of horizontal ram's horns surmounted by two high plumes. Nun and his female counterpart Nunet were members of the eight gods worshiped at Khemenu "The Eight City" which was called Hermopolis by the Greeks and is now known as Ashmunein. Nun is often called the "Father of the Gods."

28. Nut.

Nut was the Goddess of the Sky, daughter of Shu and Tefnut, and mother of Osiris, Isis, Set, Nepthys and Horus the Elder. For this reason she is often called, "The Mother of the Gods." Nut is sometimes represented as a woman wearing her name-sign, a round jar on her head. Sometimes she is shown as a naked woman, her star-spangled body arching over the reclining figure of Geb the Earth God. She is balanced on her hands and the tips of her toes, and sometimes her body is supported on the upraised arms of Shu as God of the Air and Atmosphere. Nut may also be represented as the Celestial Cow whose four legs are the four Cardinal Points. But this form of the Goddess is not found in the temples of Abydos. In the Chapel of Soker-Osiris in the Temple of Sety, Nut appears as a pregnant hippopotamus squatting on its haunches which is a form usually associated with the Goddess Ta-wert.

29. Osiris.

Osiris was one of the children of Geb and Nut. He became King of Egypt and brought civilization to his people who had previously been primitive, semi-nomadic hunters. Osiris taught them the arts of agriculture, gave them a settled existence, and introduced the hieroglyphic script which had been invented by the God Thot. In all his work, Osiris was helped by his sister-wife Isis, and the royal pair was greatly

honored and beloved by their subjects. But the God Set, their evil brother, was
jealous of the esteem in which Osiris was held, and he wished to have a share in the
government of Egypt. Knowing the evil nature of his brother, Osiris refused this
request, and in anger, Set murdered him and seized the throne. This original account
has been repeatedly modified. According to the earliest version which occurs in the
Pyramid Texts (Vth dynasty), Set murdered Osiris at Abydos and left his body lying
on the banks of the canal. Here it was found by Isis and Nepthys who with the help
of Anubis emblamed and buried it. But with the rise in importance of the Cult of
Osiris, this simple and natural story was elaborated, and it was later said that Set
found the embalmed body of Osiris[2] and tore it into fourteen pieces which he scattered
up and down the whole length of Egypt. On hearing of this fresh outrage, Isis set out
to search for the scattered fragments of the body of Osiris, and wherever she found
one, she buried it and built a shrine to mark the spot. According to this version of
the story, the head was buried at Abydos. Later the story of Osiris was still further

Fig. 1. Temple of Sety I. Hapi, the God of the Nile. Second Hypostyle Hall.

[2]The body of Osiris was the first corpse to be embalmed in Egyptian history. About
its actual burial place, several locations have been suggested.

elaborated, and the classical author Plutarch tells that under the guise of friendship, Set tricked Osiris into entering a beautiful decorated chest which was then fastened shut and thrown into the Nile. The river carried the chest out to sea, and it was finally washed up on the beach at Byblos in Lebanon where overnight an acacia tree sprang up and enclosed it. The King of Byblos had the tree cut down and made into a pillar for his palace? Meanwhile, Isis, by supernatural means, learned the whereabouts of the body of her husband and, disguising herself as a poor widow, obtained a post as nurse to the ailing, only son of the King of Byblos. As in the ancient Greek story of Demeter (Ceres), Isis cured the child by laying him each night in the fire. The child recovered from in his sickness, and Isis claimed as her reward the pillar which contained the body of Osiris. To the astonishment of the King and Queen of Byblos, Isis opened the pillar and revealed the chest containing the body of the God with which she returned to Egypt leaving the empty pillar to be preserved as a sacred relic in the temple at Byblos. This element of the story is probably based on the annual religious ceremony of "Setting Up the Djed Pillar" which symbolized the resurrection of Osiris. Both the early and later accounts tell how Isis, fearing the wrath of Set, fled to the marshes of the Delta where her son Horus was born and reared. When he had reached manhood, Isis inspired Horus to avenge the murder of Osiris and claim the throne of Egypt as his rightful inheritance. After many military and legal battles, Horus finally vanquished Set and regained the throne of Egypt ruling in the high traditions of Osiris and becoming the perfect type of pharaoh for all future kings to imitate. Because of his virtuous life on earth, Osiris was resurrected to rule as King and Judge of the Dead in the Other World. In his great Hall of Justice, the heart (the seat of the conscience) was weighed in a balance against the ostrich feather of Maat. This element is also found in the early and late versions of the story and is the earliest written evidence ever known of the belief in man's responsibility for his actions on earth and shows the high ethical character of the Egyptian religion attained at such an early stage in man's attempt to build his moral and ethical principles. The story of Osiris is no longer dismissed as a pagan myth, and many modern historians see in him an enlightened ruler of early times (perhaps during the Ist dynasty), his murder by the usurper of the throne Set, and the final victory of Horus as actual historical facts shrouded in the romantic but attractive mist of legend; a legend so popular that it had inspired parallels in other lands of the Ancient World. Osiris is usually shown as a mummified man, his flesh colored green. He wears the crown of Upper Egypt often flanked by two ostrich plumes and holds the crook and flail. Or he may be shown as a living god also colored green and wearing a pair of curved wire-like ornaments on his head. This is a form which probably originated in his northern cult center Busiris.

30. Ptah.

Ptah was the creator God of Memphis. He was the maker of all visible forms, and as such he was the patron of artists and artisans. Ptah is represented as a mummiform man wearing a skull cap and a square-ended false-beard instead of the usual plaited beard with a turned up end (Fig. 3). By the process of Synectrism for which the Egyptians were noted, Ptah became assimilated with Soker and Osiris and was sometimes called Ptah-Soker-Osiris.

31. Qebh-sennu-ef.

Qebh-sennu-ef was another of the Four Sons of Horus. As god of a canopic jar, he guarded the liver and gall bladder of the deceased. He was also the God of the Western Cardinal Point. He is usually represented as a falcon-headed man.

32. Ra.

Ra was the great Sun God of Heliopolis with whom so many other deities were later assimilated. In the royal inscriptions, the title "Son of Ra" precedes the personal name of the king since the time of the Vth dynasty; the first four rulers of which were supposed to be the physical sons of the Sun God. Ra is usually represented as a falcon-headed man crowned with a solar disk.

33. Ra-Hor-akhty.

This god was originally called Hor-akhty meaning "Horus the Horizon Dweller." He was another form of Horus the Elder and a solar god. During the New Kingdom, Hor-akhty became assimilated to the great Sun God of Heliopolis and his wife was the Goddess Iusaas. Ra-Hor-akhty is usually shown as a falcon-headed man crowned with a large solar disk. But in the Temple of Sety, he also appears with the head of a ram with twisted, horizontal horns and also crowned with a solar disk.

34. Renpet.

Renpet was the Goddess of the Year; but very little is known about her. In the Temple of Sety, she is represented as a very attractive woman wearing on her head the hieroglyph of her name which means "year."

35. Sekhmet.

The Goddess Sekhmet was the wife of Ptah and the mother of Nefer-tem. She was the Goddess of War, Fire and Pestilence, and she is represented as a woman with the head of a lioness and crowned with a solar disk (Fig. 3). In the "Legend of the Destruction of Mankind," Sekhmet is chosen by the Great God to exterminate mankind. After she had slaughtered millions, the Great God relented and tried to recall her, but she refused to leave her destructive work. Finally, the wise God Thot got her drunk on beer so that she returned to her place singing and waving her knife, and she did not recognize men when she saw them!

36. Seshat.

Later called Sefekh-abui, Seshat had a three-fold role. She was called "Lady of Books" and "Lady of Building" and was also the Goddess of History. As Goddess of Architecture, she assists the king in the foundation ceremonies of the temple. As Goddess of History and Writing, she assists or replaces Thot in writing and recording the deeds of the king. Seshat is represented as a woman wearing on her head a six-pointed star or flower and clad in a leopard skin tunic.

37. Serket.

Serket, the Scorpion Goddess, was called the "Daughter of Ra." She is usually represented as a woman wearing a scorpion on her head or as a scorpion with a woman's head crowned with a disk and cow horns. In the Temple of Ramesses II, she appears in full human form.

38. Shentayet.

Shentayet was the Goddess of Weaving, and she is said to have woven the mummy-wrappings of Osiris. In the Temple of Sety she is represented in the form of a cow.

262

. 2. *The Second Hypostyle, niche. The*
Khonsu, the third person of the Thebian
ad. He is represented as a mummified
and wears the side-lock of youth and is
wned with the full and crescent moons.

Fig. 4. *(Above), "Sarcophagus Chamber."*
Roof, western side. The God Shu support-
ing the Goddess Nut.

. 3. *(Right), Western Corridor,*
thern wall. Ptah (right), and
hmet (details). Temple of Sety

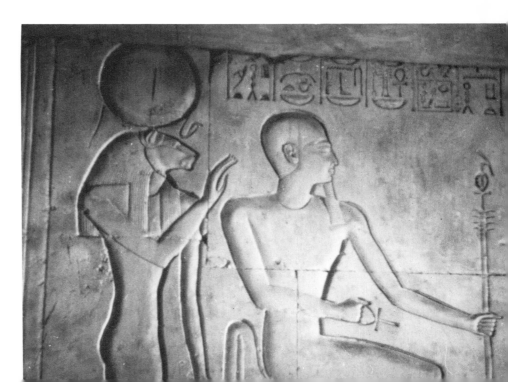

39. Shu.

Shu was the son of Atum, husband of his sister Tefnut, and father of Geb and Nut. He was the God of Air and Atmosphere. Shu is usually depicted in human form wearing an ostrich feather on his head (Fig. 4).

40. Soker.

Soker was the Memphite God of the Dead, and his name still survives at Sakkara, that wonderful field of monuments that was once the Memphite necropolis. Soker was early identified with Osiris and Ptah as Ptah-Soker-Osiris. His normal form is that of a falcon-headed man, but he is also shown as a mummified falcon. He may be bare-headed or wear the crown of Osiris, that of Upper Egypt, flanked by two ostrich feathers. The sacred emblem of Soker was the Henu boat which was a curious vessel with many oars and mystic symbols.

41. Ta-Tanen.

Ta-Tanen, sometimes assimilated to Ptah, was an ancient Earth God of Memphis. He is usually represented in human form and wears the divine headdress of two high plumes springing from a pair of horizontal ram's horns.

42. Tefnut.

Tefnut was the sister-wife of Shu. Her name means "The Spitter" and she was the Goddess of Rain, Dew and moisture in general. The legend of her angry flight from Egypt probably echoes a period of serious drought. Tefnut is usually represented as a woman with the head of a lioness.

43. Thot.

Thot was the God of Wisdom and Learning-the Divine Intelligence. As a Moon God, he was also the Measurer of Time. Thot is said to have invented the hieroglyphic script as well as the Egyptian language, and for this reason, he is called the "Lord of the Sacred Words." He was also the Scribe of the Gods and is often represented writing an inscription or noting down the kinds and quantities of offerings. Thot is usually represented as a man with the head of an ibis or as a baboon, or as Anubis, the latter creatures being sacred to him. The chief cult center of Thot was at Ashmunein (Khemenu),[3] But he was honored all over Egypt. Ramesses II dedicated a special chapel to him in his temple at Abydos.

44. Wepwawat.

The name Wepwawat means "Opener of the Ways," and one of the functions of this God was to guide the souls of the dead to the Other World. It is a known fact that persons lost in the desert can find their way to water by following the tracks of a jackal, the sacred animal of Wepwawat. This God was also the Protector of Tombs and the Necropolis, and he had an important cult center at Abydos where he was called "Lord of the Sacred Land." In keeping with the meaning of his name, Wepwawat, incarnate in his sacred standard, surmounted by the figure of a jackal, led all royal and religious processions. Wepwawat was depicted either as a jackal-headed man or as a jackal, and unless his name is inscribed, it is sometimes difficult to distinguish him from Anubis.

....
[3]Excavations in the neighborhood have revealed tunnels several miles long literally stuffed with countless numbers of mummified ibis.

APPENDIX II

COLORS USED BY THE ANCIENT EGYPTIAN ARTISTS

The colors used by the ancient Egyptians at all periods are basically the same: brick red, yellow, dark blue, light blue, green, white, and black. Is it by mere chance that these are the colors of the only precious and semiprecious stones known to them? The ornamental stones used mostly for jewelry were carnelian (red), yellow agate, lapis lazuli (azure blue), turquoise, root-of-emerald, white agate, and obsidian (black), all corresponding to the above mentioned colors in the same order. Variant shades of these basic colors were obtained by mixing them in varying porportions. As none of these colors clash with each other, even an unskilled artist could not go wrong in using them; and in the hands of highly skilled artists, such as those who decorated the monuments of Sety I, the effect is a glowing richness, even at the present day.

The materials of which these paints were made are known. Red and yellow were ochers, still found plentifully at Aswan. These are the most permanent colors. Blue and green are frits derived from oxide of copper,[1] but a certain very bright blue (much favored by Ramesses II) seems to have been cobalt. These colors are not so enduring as the reds and yellows, and tend to flake off the surface of the stone. White was lime and black was merely soot, and both often disappeared, being easy to rub off.

All these materials were ground to a fine powder; but what we do not know for certain is the medium with which they were mixed, and so transformed into paint. Some authorities say they were mixed with oil, while others say it was white of an egg. Individual artists probably had their own favorite medium or trick of the trade. Certainly in the Temple of Sety, the texture of the surface of the colors vary. In some places the colors, especially the reds and yellows, have a high hard gloss like porcelain and are completely waterproof.

There were certain rigid conventions for the use of colors. The flesh of all male figures, except the Gods Amon-Ra, Osiris, and sometimes Ptah, was colored brick red; Amon Ra was colored blue, Osiris green, and Ptah sometimes yellow. The flesh of women was colored yellow, sometimes pink in the New Kingdom and later. Blue was often used as a substitute for black, and in the temples of Abydos was used for the hair and beards of all male gods and for the hair of goddesses. Solar disks were colored red, but lunar disks were yellow as were all golden objects.

Certain hieroglyphs also have fixed colors, but bird and animal signs were colored according to the fancy of the artist, and we often find falcons, eagles, and vultures as brightly colored as parrots and having no relationship at all to their natural colors.

Recent researchers in the Egyptian Department of Antiquities have revealed some very interesting facts about the method used in the preparation of the ancient colors. It seems that the ancient Egyptian chemists used to prepare the paint by mixing appropriate amounts of silica with some natural ores to give a compound silicate paint of a determined color after fusion of the mixture at a very high temperature. Afterwards the fused mass was pulverized and the powder sifted before being mixed with the proper medium, such as oil, egg white, gum, etc., before use.

The fact that such colors have preserved their original brilliance in most temples, after such a long lapse of time is a definite support for this new theory. We must also mention that the amazing resistance of these paints to water is demonstrated by the fact that some open parts in some of the temples of Luxor and Abydos still retain their color in spite of sporadic and torrential rains.

....
[1]There is a particularly beautiful shade of bluish-green that is much used in the temples of Sety and Ramesses II at Abydos. It is quite impossible to imitate this shade exactly with modern water colors.

APPENDIX III

A NOTE ON THE RESTORATION OF THE MONUMENTS OF ABYDOS

The Temple of Sety I.

When first discovered by Mariette in the middle of the last century, the main part of the Temple of Sety I was in fairly good condition as far as the actual shape of the building was concerned. Some of the roofing-slabs had been removed, others were badly cracked, and the upper courses of some of the walls were missing. Most of the damage lay in parts of the western and southern ends of the building. Some columns had fallen, others were leaning. But the pylon and the walls and pavement were almost entirely destroyed, and the courts were occupied by houses of the modern village then known as Araba el Madfouna.

But the most serious damage to the temple was caused by the sinking of the foundations. This was due to faulty judgement on the part of King Sety's architect who built the side walls of the temple on virgin ground and the central part on the filling of the ancient conduction channel that had connected the Nif-wer Canal with the site of the Osirion. With the passing of the years, the bed of the Nile rose, and with it the subsoil water. Every year the inundation of the Nile increased the flow of the subsoil water which seeped through the filling of the channel and washed out the sand and debris from under the foundaitons of the temple. The result was that the whole of the center of the building sank causing the blocks of the walls to override each other, cracks to appear in the walls, roof and columns, and the back wall of the temple to lean out dangerously to the west.

The first architect appointed by the Antiquities Department to attempt restoration of the temple was Mr. Alexander Barsanti. His first concern was to prevent the dangerously cracked roof from falling. He placed heavy iron girders on the roof, drilled holes right through the damaged slabs and bolted them to the girders. He also straightened some of the leaning columns.

The French architect M.V.M. Baraize worked on the temple from 1923 to 1939. He roofed the three colored chapels leading out of the Osiris Hall and also the western end of the Second Hypostyle Hall. He used rather flimsy material interspersed with large skylights of reinforced glass. This was excellent from the point of view of visitors as it allowed in plenty of light so that the beautiful reliefs could be clearly seen and appreciated. Unfortunately, it also generated a great amount of heat in summer causing the surface of the walls to begin to flake off. It was also quite contradictory to the original appearance of the temple. Mr. Baraize also filled up unsightly holes in the walls, but he did nothing about the foundations.

The work of restoration was taken over by Mr. Abdel Solom Hussein until his untimely death in 1948. During these years he commenced rebuilding the upper parts of the walls using limestone from the quarries which had supplied the original stone for the temple. This work was continued by Mr. Mustafa Sobhy from 1950 to 1951.

By now, the movement of the foundations had become a serious problem, and the collapse of the western wall was imminent. In 1952 Mr. Abdel Moneim Akyf took over the work. To save the western wall, he sank huge pillars of steel and concrete between the foundations of the endangered wall and the Osirion and filled the spaces between with concrete. To support the upper parts of the wall, he gave it a thick coating of masonry on the outside.

For a while, the problem of the foundations seemed to have been solved, and when Mr. Mohammed Ahmed Loutfy took over in 1952, he devoted his attention to replacing the missing parts of the roof with steel and concrete. He also removed some of the paving blocks in the Osiris Hall to examine the foundations of some columns which had started to move. Under the columns were great holes and a few small blocks from an ancient building. These holes were filled in with concrete and the paving blocks

266

replaced. Dated strips of plaster and paper stuck over cracks in walls and columns showed that no further movements had taken place.

Mr. Yousef Khalil replaced Mr. Loutfy in 1962 and repaired the floor where the original paving blocks were missing, and in 1963 Mr. Helmy Basha restored the entrance staircase completely.

The whole of the temple was by now roofed, and the foundations seemed at last to be secure. Then came the completion of the High Dam at Aswan, and the trouble started all over again. The Nif-wer Canal overflowed its banks sometimes twice in a month. The subsoil water rose to such a height that the Osirion was permanently flooded, and the foundations of the temple started to move again. To this was added a new humidity. Old cracks in walls and columns widened and new ones are appearing. The spring of the vault in the roof of the Cult Chapel of Ptah has begun to crumble, and it is no longer safe to be visited. The base of the wall in the Chapel of Ptah-Soker is crumbling rapidly, and an old crack at the bottom of the last eastern column in the south end of the Osiris Hall has widened and spread, and a large triangular piece of the shaft threatens to break away.

The Antiquities Department has many similar problems and a reduced budget. But unless something is done, and done soon, the world is in danger of losing a masterpiece of architecture and sculpture that can never be replaced. Only those who have visited and admired Abydos can understand the real magnitude of such an appalling loss.

The Osirion.

The first restoration of the Osirion was made by Sety I, as can be proved by dovetail cramps inserted between some blocks to keep them from springing apart.

In recent years, Mr. Baraize restored the upper part of the walls of the Entrance Passage (used as a quarry in Roman times) and roofing it with a thin roof and glass skylights. The latter have all been smashed and never replaced. An attempt was made to restore the fallen roof of the western Transverse Chamber and the Great Hall. Visits by careless school children have erased much of the painted decoration in the Entrance Passage while the rise in the water level, humidity and the presence of salt in the stone has resulted in the new almost total destruction of the walls of the vaulted passage. In 1974 an attempt was made to cleanse the outer walls of the building, but it was discontinued after one season's work.

The Temple of Ramesses II.

Very little restoration has been done to the badly damaged Temple of Ramesses II. The walls have been built up to almost their original height, and some of the chapels have been re-roofed. As the area surrounding the temple has never been excavated, it would be unwise to make further restorations as there is a chance that future clearance here may reveal some of the ancient blocks which could then be replaced.

A large alabaster stela and a statue group in black granite, both found in fragments, have been restored, and the fallen false-door in the Alabaster Sanctuary has been set up in its original place.

This temple is in no immediate danger, and further restoration should not be attempted until its surroundings have been thoroughly examined.

****

To conclude, we believe it is our duty to emphasize the following:

a) The level of subsoil water in the whole area of Abydos must be carefully scrutinized to see its effects on the foundations of both Sety's Temple and the Osirion. Correctional work is needed.

b) The full restoration of one or two of the most important Archaic tombs would be very worthwhile.

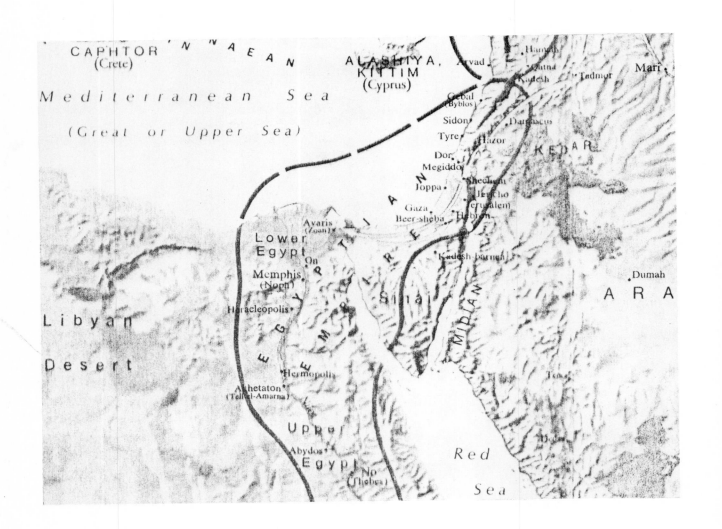